Focus On SDL

Ernest Pazera

Publisher: Stacy L. Hiquet

Marketing Manager: Heather Buzzingham

Managing Editor: Heather Talbot

Acquisitions Editor: Emi Smith

Project Editor/Copy Editor: Cathleen Snyder

Technical Reviewer: André LaMothe

Interior Layout: Shawn Morningstar

Cover Design: Mike Tanamachi

Indexer: Sharon Shock

Proofreader: Jenny Davidson

ISBN: 1-59200-030-4

Library of Congress Catalog Card Number: 2002111223

Printed in the United States of America

03 04 05 06 07 BH 10 9 8 7 6 5 4 3 2 1

Premier Press, a division of Course Technology
2645 Erie Avenue, Suite 41
Cincinnati, Ohio 45208

For Teri, Mark, Laura B., Laura W., Chris B., Nick, Sara A., Jeff B., Jaco, Jason H., Jason P., Tony, Reggie, Will, Martin, Joey, Amy, Kenton, Denise, Ruthie, Rain, Peggy, Sarah (with an H), Mike G., Mike C., Little Miss Dani, Dani R., Sharon, Rex, Jill, Rick, Paul T., Paul E., Bobbi, Tim, Jessica, Ramon, Terri, Ann, Nathan, Jeremy, Nate ("Ref"), the folks at Frank's Diner not already mentioned, the folks at Common Grounds not already mentioned, and the folks at Paddy O's not already mentioned. Yes, even Rent-A-Bob.

Acknowledgements

I would like to thank André LaMothe, all of the folks at Premier Press, all the folks at GameDev.net, and all of the people who have worked on developing SDL and related libraries, as well as all of the people who developed the games on the CD-ROM.

About the Author

Ernest Pazera was a programmer living his life in the Midwest when suddenly people started asking him to write books. Once he was allowed to do so, he kind of got addicted to it, so this is his fourth book. We are trying to get Mr. Pazera some professional help for his illness. We apologize for yet another book by Mr. Pazera showing up on the bookshelf, but please buy it anyway. We will continue to monitor his medication, and hopefully, in time, he will make a full recovery.

Contents

Part Three SDL Game Application Framework in C++ 217

Letter from the Series Editor

If you're going to write games on the PC, there's only one choice for high-performance graphics—DirectX, right? Wrong! In fact, amazingly enough, there is another API not written by Microsoft that is simpler than DirectX and is supported on a number of platforms, including Windows and Linux. The name of the API/SDK is the Simple DirectMedia Layer, or SDL for short. The cool thing about SDL is that if you use standard ANSI C/C++ along with it, you can port your games and applications to other platforms in a matter of hours or a day at most. This is the real power of SDL—portability. *Focus On SDL* will get you up and running with the SDL system almost immediately. This book will bring you up to speed with this elegant and clear API in no time. Ernest Pazera takes you through each important SDL core module, from graphics and sounds to networking. Once you have the basic SDL system under your belt, he proceeds to create a high-level wrapper class around the system to give you more flexibility. Of course, it's up to you whether you want to use it or just stick to the basics.

In conclusion, I highly recommend this book if you are a graphics or media programmer on any platform and you want an API that allows you to port quickly from platform to platform. In fact, I think this may be the only book on the subject that focuses 100% on SDL, rather than on SDL as just another API in a larger context.

Sincerely,

André LaMothe

Series Editor for the Premier Game Development Series

Introduction

I am a programmer who, after programming for about 13 years, suddenly had opportunity to write books. The one you are holding in your hands is the fourth book I have written. Moreover, I tend to be the author who picks the "odd little topics." My other books include *Isometric Game Programming with DirectX 7.0* (Premier Press, Inc. 0-7615-3089-4, 2001), the *Game Developer's Guide to the Cybiko* (Wordware Publishing, 2001), and *Focus On 2D in Direct3D* (Premier Press, Inc., 2002).

After writing four books, I think I've learned my "style" of writing and how I approach various topics. I don't make lots of very game-like demos when I'm talking about whatever API I happen to be writing about that month. Instead, I write very simple code that demonstrates a particular aspect of the API, so that the code for the new topic is easily isolated and understood by the readers.

I am also a very object-oriented programmer. When I write real code in C++, I use the three pillars of encapsulation, inheritance, and polymorphism. Much of the code in this book is, as I call it, "book code." Book code is a bit watered down and simplified to make it more understandable to readers with varying levels of experience. If I were to write code for a book the way I *really* write code, even I would have a hard time following it.

Who You Are

You are the primary reason I write books. You are the reader. You and you alone determine whether or not I have done my job sufficiently. You looked at this book on a bookshelf or at some online bookstore and said, "SDL? What is that?" Or maybe you already knew about SDL and you wanted something to help you on your path besides the SDL documentation, which is quality documentation but still rather dry when you really think about it.

Maybe you are tired of DirectX. I hear you. Perhaps you want to use OpenGL, but you want to use a nice cross-platform API for "the other stuff" that OpenGL doesn't do, such as sound and input. In any case, you have decided that learning what SDL is all about can't really hurt, and you might even enjoy it. I certainly hope so.

What You Should Already Know

This is a small book, folks. Books on game programming no longer cover every single aspect like they once did. That task is impossible because the subject matter has become too vast.

Also, this book does not teach computer programming in general. You should already be rather comfortable with programming and C++. By no means do you have to be at an expert level, but you should know the basics.

Why You Are Here

You are here to explore the API known as SDL (*Simple DirectMedia Layer*), a cross-platform multimedia API. SDL is an open source library that takes care of most of the tasks that typically belong to the domain of DirectX. The added bonus is that with SDL, you can compile the same code for Windows or Linux and it works the same way. SDL also removes the need for all of the code that typically exists in a Windows program, such as code for setting up window classes, creating windows, and creating window procedures. SDL hides all of that for you so you don't have to worry about it.

In other words, I am here to make your job shorter and easier. With SDL, you can be up and running with a small program in less than 20 lines, whereas a regular program for Windows would be five or six times that long. That's pretty cool, I think.

So let's get started.

PART ONE

The Core of SDL

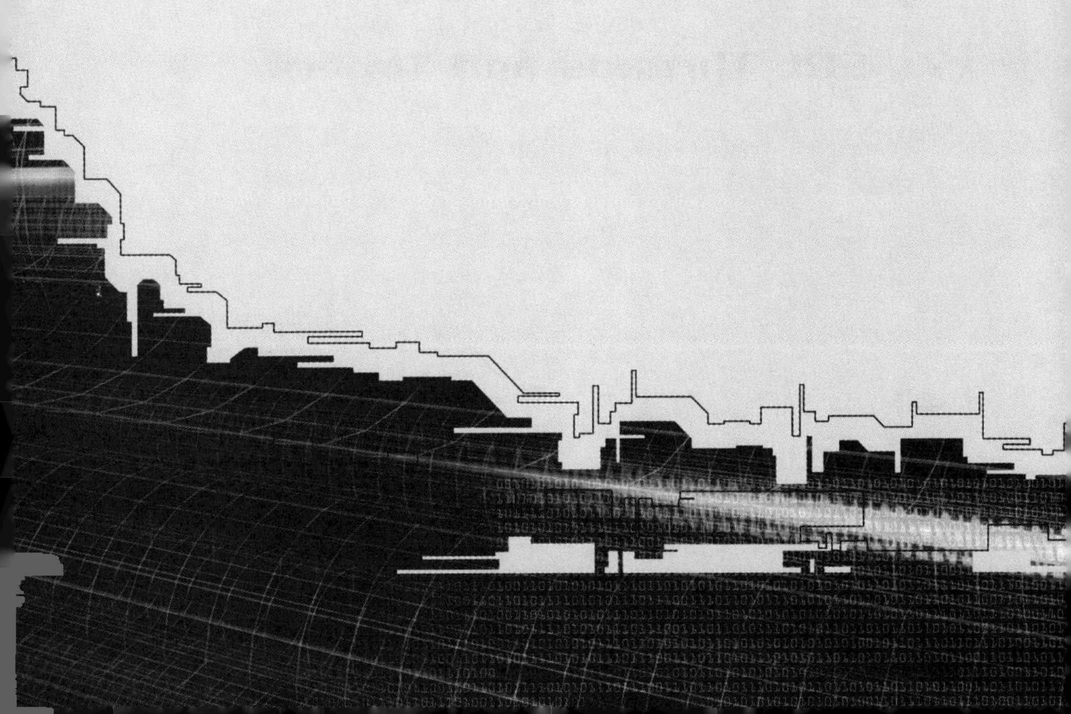

CHAPTER 1

Setting Up Your System for SDL

You will be up and running and using SDL before the end of the chapter. The application that you will create will hardly be impressive, but it will use SDL, and then you'll be on your way to creating platform-independent games with the wonderful library that is SDL.

Just so you and I are both on the same page (no pun intended), although this book is about SDL, it is not geared specifically toward cross-platform programmers. It is geared primarily to the Windows programmer, and the compiler used throughout the book is Visual C++—either VC++ 6.0 or VC++.NET will suffice. This is not to say that the book is completely unusable for programmers for other platforms (indeed, code in SDL should compile on almost anything), nor is it to say that users of other development tools are completely out of luck. The SDL developer distributions come with instructions for setting up SDL on almost any platform and development environment you can imagine. This book is intended for mainstream hobbyist game developers, and the vast market share points to Windows and Visual C++. I do not intend to slight anyone's personal preference of platform and compiler, but if I were to include all of the specifics for all platforms and compilers, it would take me years to write the book, which would be three times as long and expensive, not to mention confusing as all heck.

So that's where I am coming from. Let's begin!

Installing the Libraries on Your System

Naturally, before you can make use of the SDL libraries, you must first have them somewhere in storage so that your development environment can see them. Under normal circumstances, this would require a trip to the SDL Web site at http://www.libsdl.org. Since this book contains a CD-ROM, it would be irresponsible for me not to include the libraries on it. You will find a file named SDL-devel-1.2.3-VC6.zip in the LIBS directory of the CD. Copy it to your hard drive and use WinZip (or your favorite archive utility) to extract the files to somewhere convenient and easy to remember. For the purposes of this discussion, I will assume that you are going to place the files into C:\SDLDEV\SDL-1.2.3\. Later you can store other libraries and/or future versions in C:\SDLDEV, and everything will be nice and organized so you won't have to hunt around on your hard drive to find where you put something!

After you have extracted the files, take a look at the contents of the folder—always a good thing to do when you're getting to know a new library or API (see Figure 1.1).

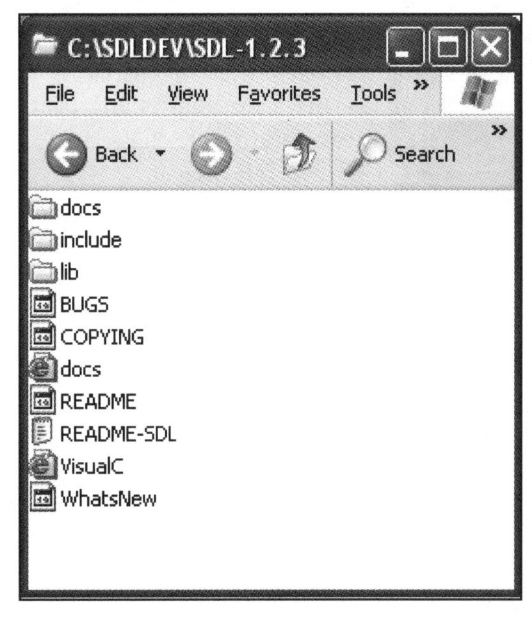

Figure 1.1 *Contents of C:\SDLDEV\SDL-1.2.3*

There are three subfolders—docs, include, and lib—and a number of files. You should take some time to explore most of these files and get familiar with them, especially the ones with the term "README" in the title. They are called README for a reason!

In the docs folder, as one might expect, you can find documentation on the various SDL functions. It is pretty well organized and detailed, and is an excellent resource when you need to look up the parameters for a particular function. I virtually never write anything using SDL without having the documentation open somewhere on my desktop.

> **NOTE**
>
> If you have read the README files that accompany SDL (like I said you should), then you have undoubtedly come across the term *GNU LGPL*. As a Windows programmer, you have probably seen similar notices before—more likely the GNU GPL, since the LGPL is rarely used. Both of these are licenses that deal with free software. Now, don't misinterpret the word "free" here. The free of which we are speaking is the same sort of free that we mean when we say "free speech," not "free lunch." As we all know, there ain't no such thing as a free lunch!

Always have your references handy!

In the include folder, to no one's surprise, you can find the header files for SDL. There are a number of them and, as luck would have it, knowing what any particular one does for you is not terribly important. When you start creating SDL-based projects, there is only one header file that you need to `#include`, and that is SDL.h!

Finally, in the lib folder, you can find the actual SDL binaries. There are three files—SDL.lib, SDLmain.lib, and SDL.dll. The .lib files are static libraries to which you will link your application, and SDL.dll is a dynamic link library that you must place in the same directory as your application (or into a system directory somewhere). I'll talk more about that a little later in the chapter, when you create a project.

Setting Up the VC++ Environment

Okay, you have the SDL binaries, include files, and documentation on your machine somewhere, so now what?

Now it is time to set up the VC++ environment so that you can use SDL. The first thing you need to do is let VC++ know where it can find the .lib and .h files for SDL. If you already have experience in doing that sort of thing, go ahead and skip the next few pages. If not, read on.

First, start VC++. With no project loaded, select Tools, Options, as shown in Figure 1.2.

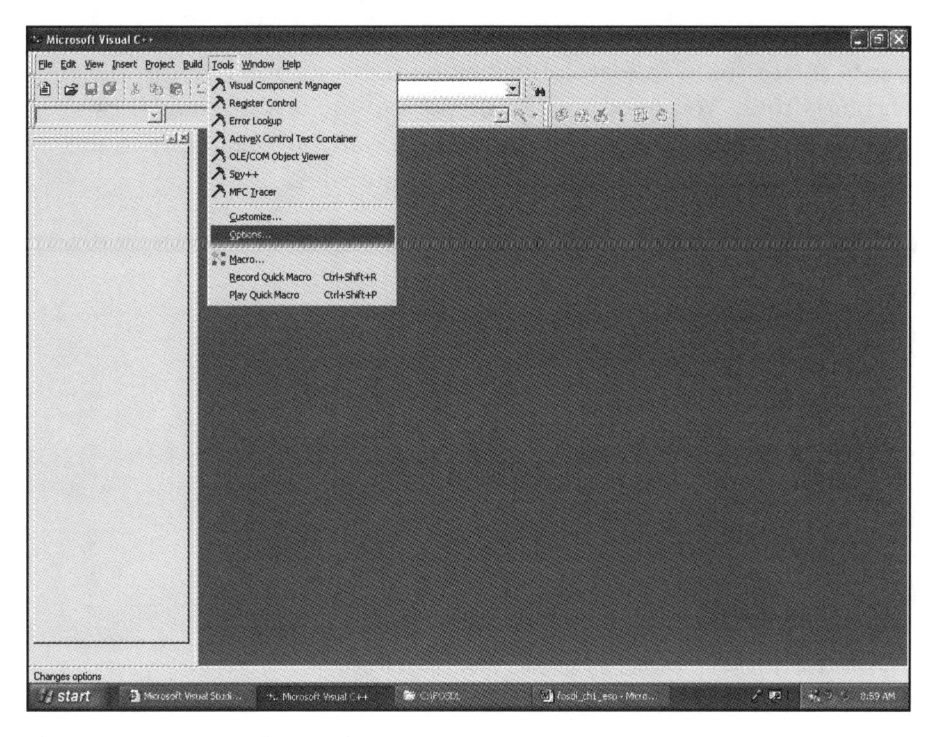

Figure 1.2 *Selecting Options from the Tools menu*

The Options dialog box will appear. Select the Directories tab, as shown in Figure 1.3.

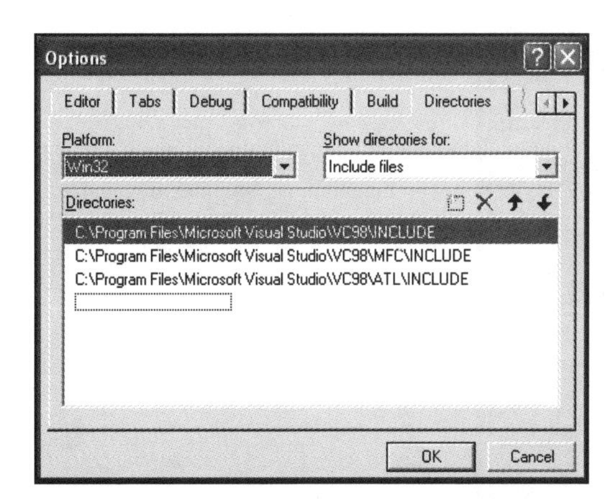

Figure 1.3 *The Options dialog box for VC++, with the Directories tab selected*

In Figure 1.3, the Options dialog box is set up for adding new directories to the list used to search for include files—in other words, files ending with .h. You need to add the path to the SDL include files to this list. To do so, simply click on the first available blank line in the list, and you should see something like Figure 1.4.

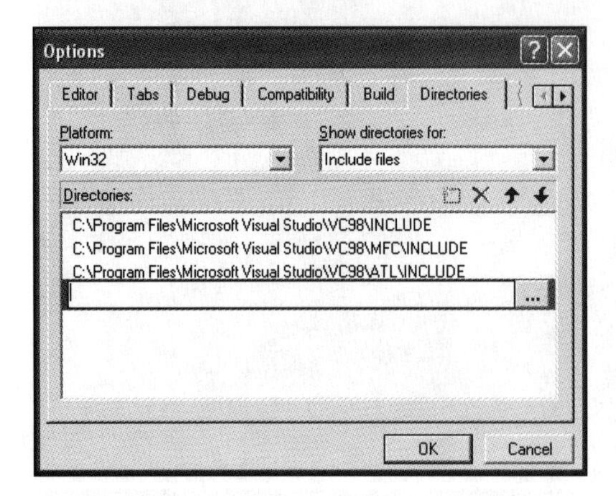

Figure 1.4 *Adding a new entry to the list of directories*

Here you can either type in the directory or click on the button with the ellipsis to browse for it. Whichever method you choose, get the directory containing all of the SDL include files into the text box, as shown in Figure 1.5.

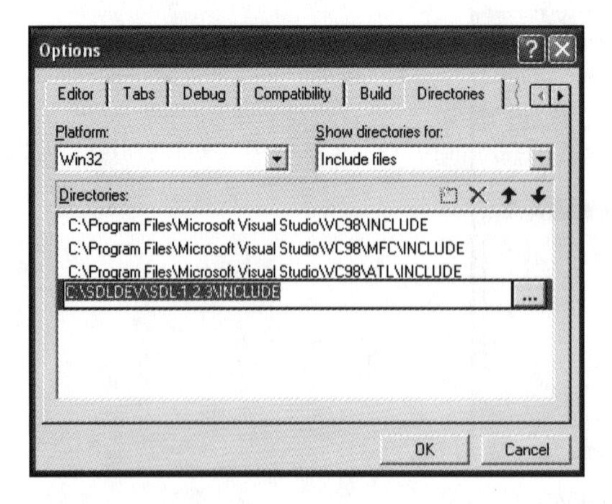

Figure 1.5 *A new path*

This next part is strictly optional, but I like to do it anyway. I always prefer to have the SDL include files first in the list. Click anywhere else on the list of directories so that the text box and the ellipsis button are no longer shown. Then click on the Up arrow until the SDL directory is the first in the list, as shown in Figure 1.6.

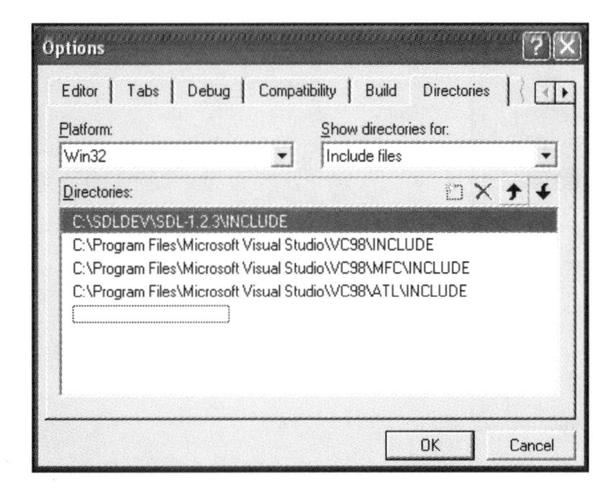

Figure 1.6 *SDL include files are first.*

Now that you have done this, you must do the same thing for the .lib files. Select Library Files from the Show Directories For drop-down list (see Figure 1.7).

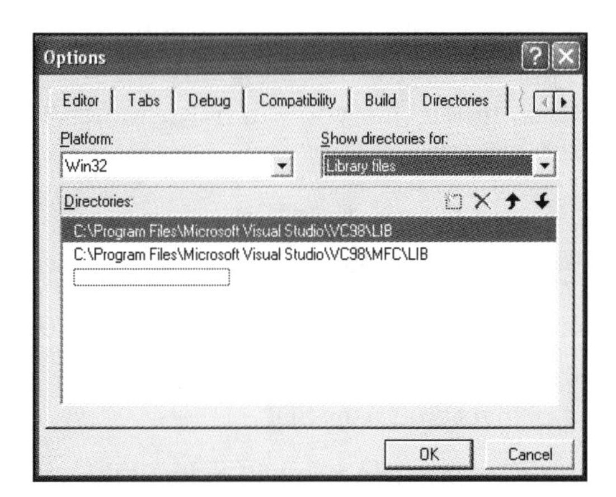

Figure 1.7 *Selecting library directories*

From here, the process is exactly the same as adding a directory to the list of include files. Get the path that has the SDL.lib and SDLmain.lib directories onto this list to set up the development environment. When you are finished, your list should look something like Figure 1.8.

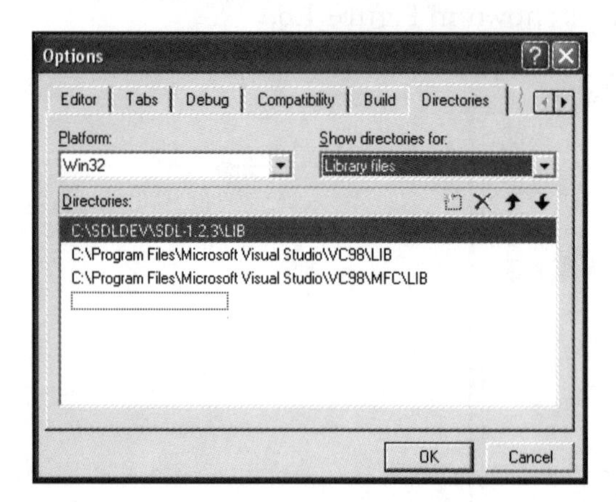

Figure 1.8 *Paths for library files are set up.*

In Chapters 8 through 11, you will add additional libraries and include files to the list. The process is the same for all of these. When you get to that point, I will refer you back to this chapter for the procedure.

You only have to set up your environment one time. The only reason why you would have to do it over again would be if you reinstalled VC++ or got rid of the paths you just added to the dialog box. Of course, you are going to love SDL so much that you will never want to use anything else!

Creating an SDL Project

The environment is set up, so it is time to create an SDL project. I'm going to take you through the procedure that you will need to repeat each and every time you create a project that uses SDL.

1. The first thing to do, naturally, is create a project. Select File, New; choose WIN32 Application; and name it FOSDL1_1, as shown in Figure 1.9. After you click OK, you will be prompted for what type of WIN32 project you would like to create. Select Empty Project, and then click Finish.

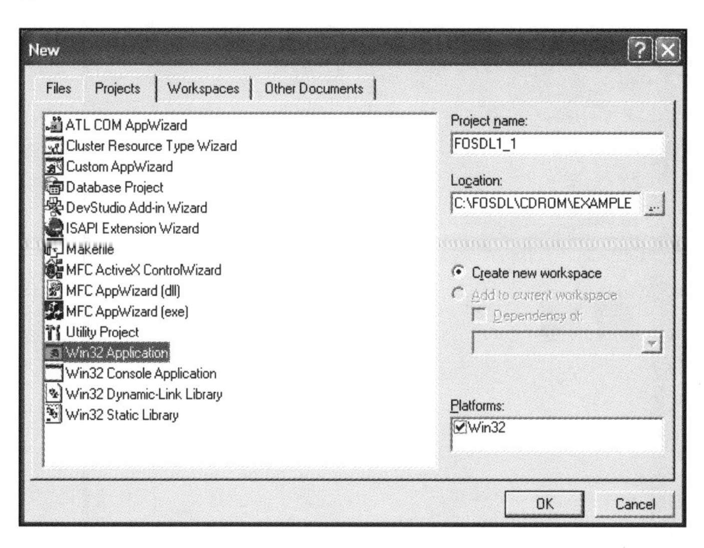

Figure 1.9 *Creating your first SDL-based application*

2. Next, you need to copy SDL.dll from the SDL libs directory to your project's current directory. Alternatively, you can put SDL.dll in a system directory somewhere, but I prefer not to mess with that if I can avoid it. After you have done this, your project folder should look like Figure 1.10.
3. Now select Project, Settings and select the Link tab in the dialog box that appears, as shown in Figure 1.11.
4. In the Object/Library Modules text box, type **sdl.lib** and **sdlmain.lib**. Make sure you use spaces to separate each item in the text box. I typically add these files at the beginning of the list, but it really doesn't matter. When you have finished, the dialog box should look like Figure 1.12.
5. Next, select the C/C++ tab. From the Category drop-down menu, select the Code Generation option (see Figure 1.13).
6. From the Use Run-Time Library drop-down menu, select Multithreaded DLL, as shown in Figure 1.14.
7. Finally, click on the OK button. You are all set to go! This might seem like a lot of hassle just to get a project started, but in time it will become second nature to you, and you'll find yourself getting through it rather quickly.

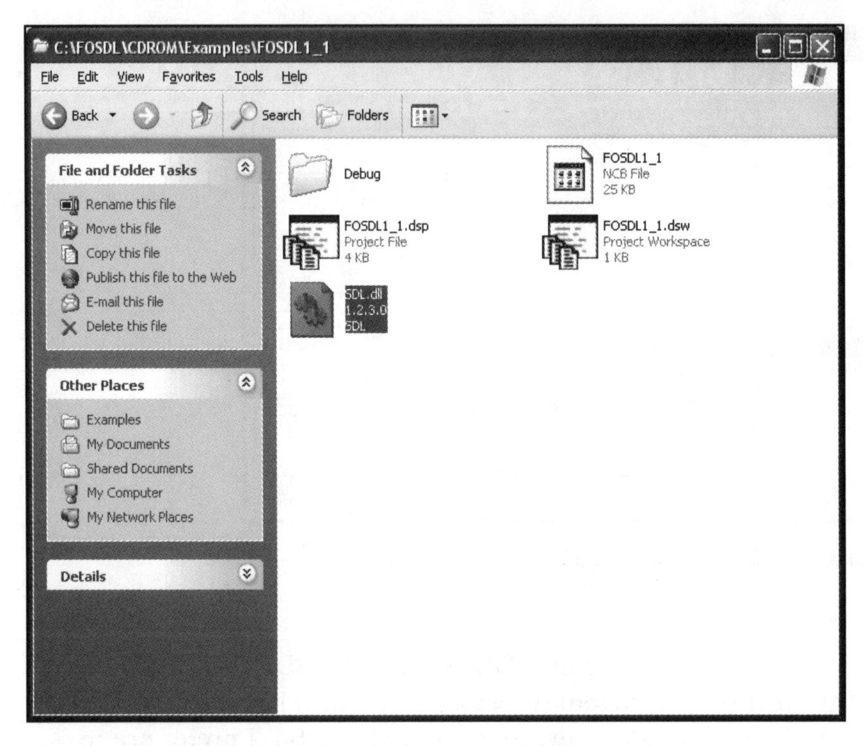

Figure 1.10 *Your project folder, after copying SDL.dll into it*

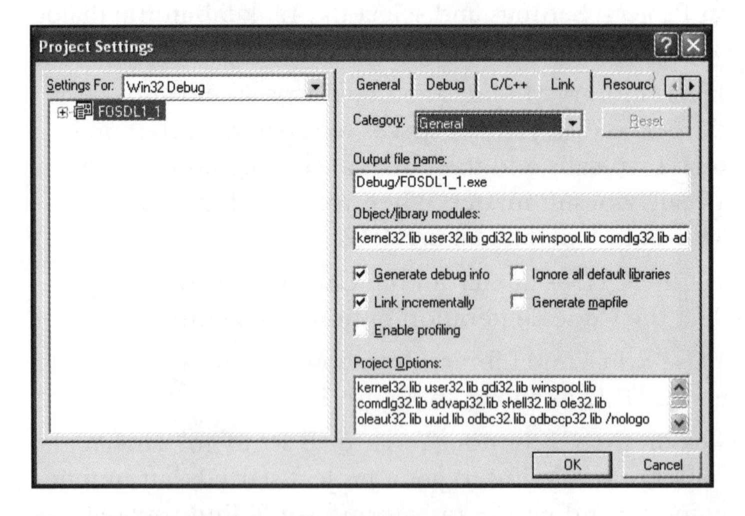

Figure 1.11 *The Project Settings dialog box*

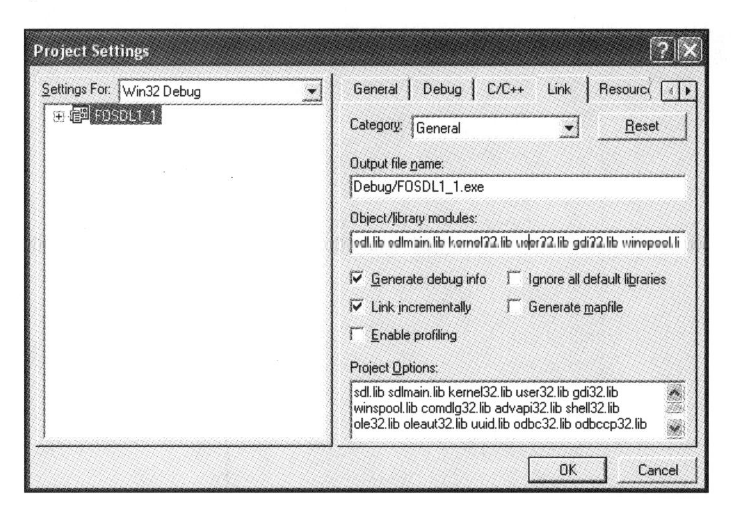

Figure 1.12 *Adding the SDL lib files*

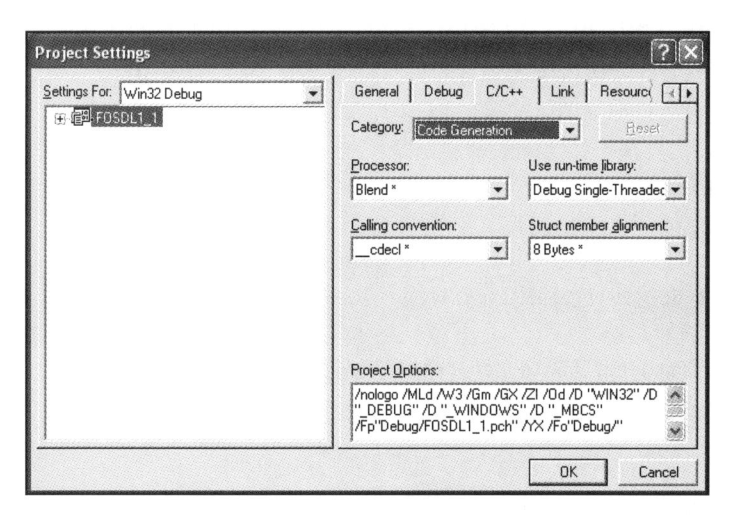

Figure 1.13 *The C/C++ tab, Code Generation category*

Testing the Environment

So, you've got the environment and a project set up. The only thing left to do is create a small application to test it all out. Create a new .cpp file, name it something clever like fosdl1_1.cpp, and make sure it is added to your project in the Source Files directory in File view of the IDE. (Just right-click and select Add Files to Folder.)

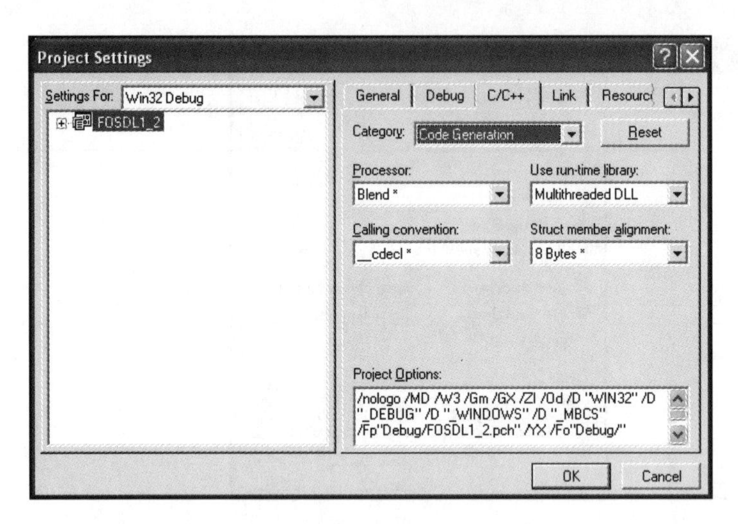

Figure 1.14 *Using the Multithreaded DLL run-time*

Place the following code into the source file. If you aren't interested in typing all of it, you can find the code on the CD-ROM in the Examples directory.

```
#include "sdl.h"
#include <stdio.h>
int main(int argc, char* argv[])
{
	if (SDL_Init(SDL_INIT_VIDEO)==-1)
	{
		fprintf(stderr,"Could not initialize SDL!\n");
	}
	else
	{
		fprintf(stdout,"SDL initialized properly!\n");
		SDL_Quit();
	}
	return(0);
}
```

For the sake of brevity, I deliberately removed all of the comments from this file. Although you are not even at square one as far as SDL is concerned, most of this code should be relatively obvious. In this short program, you attempt to initialize SDL. Depending on whether or not you are successful, you report either to `stdout` or `stderr`. (SDL automatically maps these to files entitled stdout.txt and stderr.txt, respectively.)

Now the only thing to do is compile and run the code. If all has gone well, it should compile just fine. If it doesn't, make sure that you've followed all of the steps for setting up the environment and the project. Once you run the project, you will get a file called either stdout.txt or stderr.txt. If you get stderr.txt, your system isn't properly set up to run SDL, and you should scour the SDL mailing list archives to find out what the problem is and how you can fix it.

While this example program does absolutely nothing to thrill or amaze, it performs the important task of checking to see whether or not you are properly set up to develop with SDL.

A Simple SDL Application

For your next endeavor, you will write a small SDL-based application. Like the first program, this one won't do much, but at least something will be visible. I'm not going to go over the functions involved just yet. Each function will be discussed in its own appropriate chapter.

This example is entitled FOSDL1_2, and you can find it on the CD-ROM if you don't feel like typing in the code. To save space, I have removed all blank lines and comments. The copy of this program on the CD-ROM contains the full commenting and is formatted better.

```
#include "sdl.h"
#include <stdio.h>
#include <stdlib.h>
SDL_Surface* g_pMainSurface = NULL;
SDL_Event g_Event;
int main(int argc, char* argv[])
{
	if (SDL_Init(SDL_INIT_VIDEO)==-1)
	{
		fprintf(stderr,"Could not initialize SDL!\n");
		exit(1);
	}
	else
	{
```

```
        fprintf(stdout,"SDL initialized properly!\n");
        atexit(SDL_Quit);
    }
    g_pMainSurface = SDL_SetVideoMode(640,480,0,SDL_ANYFORMAT);
    if(!g_pMainSurface)
    {
        fprintf(stderr,"Could not create main surface!\n");
        exit(1);
    }
    for(;;)
    {
        if(SDL_WaitEvent(&g_Event)==0)
        {
            fprintf(stderr,"Error while waiting for an event!\n");
            exit(1);
        }

        //check the type of event
        if(g_Event.type==SDL_QUIT)
        {
            fprintf(stdout,"Quit event has occurred.\n");
            break;
        }
    }
    fprintf(stdout,"Terminating program normally.\n");
    return(0);
}
```

Compile and run this program, and you will see something that looks like Figure 1.15. In addition, there will be some text in stdout.txt that tells you what happened (via all of the `fprintf` calls).

Now you have a simple shell program with which you can start working to make bigger and better things. In the next few chapters, I will explain all of the functions you used in this example. Actually, all of the functions' names accurately describe what they do, so you should have a halfway decent grasp of what is going on just by looking at the code. This is why I'm starting out simply. First I give you one or two functions to look at, and then I slowly add more. Before you know it, you'll know all of the SDL functions…or you'll at least be familiar with them.

Figure 1.15 *The output of FOSDL1_2*

> **NOTE**
>
> **You might be asking, "Where's `WinMain`?" A valid question. There isn't one; you aren't making a Windows application. You have probably also noticed that there are no calls to functions like `CreateWindowEx`. This is not to say that these functions aren't being used somewhere deep inside of the WIN32 SDL implementation, but they are not exposed to you as a programmer. This is a good thing because it frees you from having to know anything dependent on the operating system in order to program using SDL.**

Summary

As you can see, I'm not messing around here. You are already up and running, creating SDL-based applications. It isn't a difficult API to use. The rest of the book will give you the information you need to get the most out of all of what SDL has to offer, which is a considerable amount.

CHAPTER 2

SDL: The Big Picture

In Chapter 1, you got your feet wet and dug right into creating SDL applications. In this chapter, you will take a look at the capabilities of SDL on a conceptual level. When you are comfortable developing with SDL, you'll get as much mileage out of it as you need. More important, it's completely cross platform, so you can write your SDL application in Windows and compile it for Linux and it'll work—usually with very few snags.

SDL Subsystems at a Glance

Just like DirectX has subsystems such as DirectDraw, Direct3D, DirectSound, DirectMusic, DirectInput, and DirectPlay, SDL has its own subsystems for handling various aspects of a multimedia application. Table 2.1 briefly describes the seven subsystems of SDL. It also contains a column describing the DirectX equivalent of each subsystem.

As you can see, SDL does everything that DirectDraw, DirectInput, and DirectSound do, plus some extra stuff for playing music from a CD-ROM, threading, and timing. Figure 2.1 shows the basic layout of both SDL and DirectX side by side, as well as the obvious similarities between the two APIs.

But what about the other components of DirectX, namely Direct3D, DirectPlay, and DirectMusic? Well, SDL can tie into OpenGL if you want 3D rendering. For the same sort of functionality as DirectPlay, you can use SDL_net (detailed in Chapter 10). DirectMusic doesn't have an exact SDL equivalent, but you can do some interesting things with SDL_mixer (detailed in Chapter 11).

Now I will speak more in depth about each of these subsystems and how they can be of use to you.

Table 2.1 SDL Subsystems

Subsystem	Description	DirectX Equivalent
Video	Encapsulates the video display	DirectDraw
Event Handling	Encapsulates event handling	DirectInput
Joystick	Encapsulates using joysticks	DirectInput
Audio	Encapsulates working with audio hardware	DirectSound
CD-ROM	Streams music from a normal CD	N/A
Threads	Multi-threading helper functions	N/A
Timers	Timing helper functions	N/A

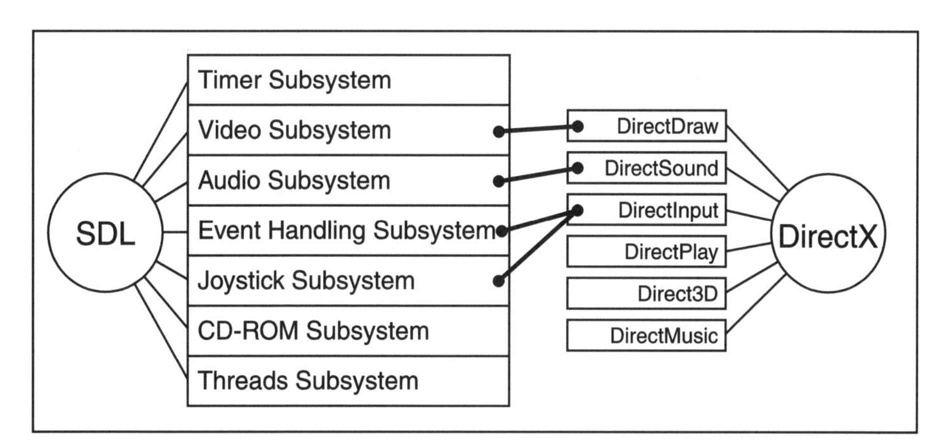

Figure 2.1 *SDL and DirectX side by side*

Video

In every SDL application, you will use the video and event handling subsystems at the very least. Without something to look at and a way to send it input, you really don't have much of an application, right?

DirectDraw is the DirectX equivalent for the video subsystem; in fact, the implementation for WIN32 uses a version of DirectDraw underneath the hood. If you actually dig through the source code for SDL (which is available for download at http://www.libsdl.org or can be found on the CD-ROM), you can really see how the video subsystem was put together. I'm not going to do any major analysis of this; I'm just telling you in case you are interested in those kinds of things.

Like DirectDraw, SDL's video subsystem deals primarily with surfaces but also has structures for rectangles, colors, palettes, and overlays (which are useful if you want to stream video data). It has support for transparent color keys, alpha blending, and run-length encoding. There are also a few functions for creating mouse cursors—nothing too fancy, but they do the job. Additionally, the video subsystem can be used in either a windowed mode or full-screen mode, and the difference is just a simple function call.

You will take a much closer look at the video subsystem in Chapter 3, "SDL Video."

Event Handling

In my opinion, the most important subsystem of SDL is the event-handling subsystem. Without it, you might as well be watching television because the program will have exactly the same amount of interactivity.

The event-handling subsystem is roughly the equivalent of DirectInput, but it is also the equivalent of a standard WIN32 message pump. With the event-handling subsystem, you can check for events and deal with them as they occur, as well as read the current state of the keyboard or mouse.

The event-handling subsystem of SDL is, in my opinion, much easier to use than a WIN32 message pump/window procedure. For one thing, there isn't any typecasting, which seems to happen all too frequently when you are dealing with WIN32 messages.

You will take a good look at the event-handling subsystem when you get to Chapter 4, "SDL Event Handling and the Window Manager."

Joystick

I suppose that, in theory, the joystick subsystem should be a part of the input-handling subsystem, since joysticks are input devices. (The SDL meaning of "joystick" is essentially any input device that is not a keyboard or a pointing device such as a mouse.)

However, in the case of keyboards and pointing devices, you are normally hard-pressed to find a system that doesn't have one of each. The more popular operating systems practically require both to be attached to the system, so dealing with input from them has become the standard.

This is not the case in the world of joysticks. Each joystick has a different number of buttons, axes, point-of-view hats, dials, levers, switches, and pretty much anything else you can imagine. Hence, SDL devotes an entire subsystem to these odd input devices. However, the input they generate is handled through the event-handling subsystem. Go figure. I'll talk in more detail about the joystick subsystem in Chapter 6, "SDL Joysticks."

Audio

Of all of the SDL subsystems, I am least pleased with the audio subsystem. It is simply not sophisticated enough for most needs. The DirectX equivalent, DirectSound, is much better equipped.

However, all is not lost. There is an add-on library called SDL_Mixer, which—at least in my opinion—is what SDL's audio subsystem should have been in the first place. I understand why the subsystem is the way it is, though. SDL is meant to be simple, and mixing sounds is just not all that simple. Ergo, the audio subsystem is perhaps a bit sub-par. I'll talk more about the audio subsystem in Chapter 5, "SDL Audio and CD-ROM."

CD-ROM

The CD-ROM subsystem is just a cool thing to have. You won't find one of these in DirectX. With SDL, you can play around with the CD-ROM drive. You can open it, close it, and make it play songs. You can even get information about the CD in the drive. This is very cool and quite useful if you are creating a game that has a data section and a music section that is meant to be played in the background. I'll talk more about this subsystem in Chapter 5.

Threads

The idea of multi-threading is hardly new, but it is often dismissed as unimportant in books like this. The SDL threading subsystem is a cross-platform way of programming multi-threaded applications.

A small warning here, however. While the code will work on whatever platform you compile it for, not all operating systems treat threads the same way, so you might want to do some testing on other operating systems before you go hog-wild with the threads.

The SDL threads subsystem can also handle mutexes, semaphores, and condition variables. I'll discuss this subsystem at greater length in Chapter 7, "SDL Threads and Timers."

Timers

As you know, precise timing is important to any high-performance application, such as a game. Certainly not all games are this way, but as a general rule, timing is important. To that end, SDL has a subsystem specifically for dealing with time and timers. It can count clock ticks for you, and you can even set it up to call a certain function periodically.

Like the threads, timers can have issues when they are ported to other operating systems, so be careful if cross-platform programming is important to you. I'll discuss this subsystem at greater length in Chapter 7.

SDL Initialization

In a way, you could call initialization another subsystem of SDL. It would be best described as one subsystem to rule them all. Without proper initialization of SDL, none of the other subsystems will work. I already partially introduced you to the initialization functions back in Chapter 1, but I did not say much about them; now I will take the time to introduce you to them.

There are six functions that you should know about before you begin any sort of real work with SDL. These functions are listed in Table 2.2, along with a brief description of what each one does.

Table 2.2 SDL Initialization Functions

Function	Description
SDL_Init	Initializes one or more SDL subsystems.
SDL_InitSubSystem	Initializes particular SDL subsystems. (This can only be used after SDL_Init.)
SDL_Quit	Shuts down all SDL subsystems.
SDL_QuitSubSystem	Shuts down particular subsystems without shutting down SDL totally.
SDL_WasInit	Checks to see what subsystems are currently initialized.
SDL_GetError	Retrieves the last internal error reported by SDL.

The next few sections describe each of these functions.

SDL_Init and SDL_InitSubSystem

To start with, take a look at the initialization functions—SDL_Init and SDL_InitSubSystem. Here is what the prototypes look like.

```
int SDL_Init(Uint32 flags);
int SDL_InitSubSystem(Uint32 flags);
```

Both functions look pretty much the same, don't they? Each returns an int, and each takes a single Uint32 parameter called flags.

The SDL_Init function should be the very first function that is called. If this function is not called, no other SDL function will operate. When you call this function, you specify which of the SDL subsystems you intend to use in the application. Table 2.3 shows the identifiers for each of the subsystems.

NOTE

What the heck is a Uint32? Well, since SDL is a cross-platform library, they had to come up with a way to represent data types in a platform-independent manner. In C and C++, an int is whatever size a machine word is. That is, an int is whatever size the computer handles most easily. In many cases this is 32 bits, but other sizes are possible. In SDL, you deal with a number of types that begin with either an S or a U. The S represents a signed value (either positive or negative numbers can be represented), and the U represents an unsigned value (only non-negative numbers can be represented). The S or U is followed by int, and is then followed by the size of the type in bits—8, 16, 32, or 64. This sort of convention actually makes reading code a lot easier because you can tell from the data type exactly how big the type is and whether it is signed in a compact manner.

Table 2.3 Subsystem Identifiers

Identifier	Subsystem
SDL_INIT_TIMER	The timer subsystem will be initialized.
SDL_INIT_AUDIO	The audio subsystem will be initialized.
SDL_INIT_VIDEO	The video subsystem will be initialized.
SDL_INIT_CDROM	The CD-ROM subsystem will be initialized.
SDL_INIT_JOYSTICK	The joystick subsystem will be initialized.
SDL_INIT_EVERYTHING	All subsystems will be initialized.

But what about the event-handling system and the thread system? Well, those don't need to be initialized. Technically, event handling is initialized when you initialize the video subsystem.

You might be tempted to always use SDL_INIT_EVERYTHING. You can do that, or you can simply add extra systems later using SDL_InitSubSystem. In many applications, you might have no need for joysticks or the CD-ROM portions of SDL.

Here's a quick snippet of code that initializes the video and audio SDL subsystems.

```
SDL_Init(SDL_INIT_VIDEO | SDL_INIT_AUDIO);
```

To initialize more than one system, you simply use the bitwise or operator, as shown in the preceding line of code. The return value of SDL_Init will be 0 if everything went smoothly and -1 if there was an error. *Always check your return values!* Yes, there will be times when I will show you code that does not check the return values, but that is to make the code easier to look at and read. It is just easier to teach things that way. In reality, the preceding snippet of code should look like this.

```
//initialize audio and video
if(SDL_Init(SDL_INIT_VIDEO | SDL_INIT_AUDIO)==-1)
{
    //an error occurred, so do something about it
}
```

I think you'll agree that the second time around, it's not as easy to read.

After you have done your initial call to SDL_Init, you can initialize other subsytems using SDL_InitSubSystem. Suppose you determine a bit later in the program that you really need to initialize the joystick subsystem. You can do this with a simple call to SDL_InitSubSystem.

```
//initialize joystick subsystem
if(SDL_InitSubSystem(SDL_INIT_JOYSTICK)==-1)
{
    //error!
}
```

As you might expect, SDL_InitSubSystem works in exactly the same manner as SDL_Init does, as far as its parameter and return value are concerned.

SDL_Quit and SDL_QuitSubSystem

Since you now know how to initialize SDL subsystems, it is time to take a look at how to shut them down. This is done using the SDL_Quit and SDL_QuitSubSystem functions. Here are the prototypes.

```
void SDL_Quit(void);
void SDL_QuitSubSystem(Uint32 flags);
```

The first function, SDL_Quit, is extremely easy to use. It takes no parameter and returns no value. It simply shuts down all SDL subsystems. As such, it is typically the last thing you call in your program, as in the following code.

```
//initialize SDL
SDL_Init(SDL_INIT_EVERYTHING);
//rest of program goes here
//shut down SDL
SDL_Quit();
```

This is a valid way to go about things, but it is typically not done this way with SDL. Normally, this is what the code would look like:

```
//initialize SDL
SDL_Init(SDL_INIT_EVERYTHING);
//set up to shut down SDL at exit
atexit(SDL_Quit);
//rest of program goes here
```

If you have never used the atexit function before, it is pretty neat. It adds a function (any old function, provided that it takes no parameters and returns no value). When the program terminates (either normally or by calling the exit function), it will call each of the functions added to the list of functions sent by atexit in the reverse order of how they were sent. The benefit of doing things this way is that if you detect an error somewhere, you can use the exit function and not worry about cleaning up after SDL—the program will do that for you.

The SDL_QuitSubSystem function, on the other hand, has more in common with SDL_InitSubSystem. It will only shut down the subsystems that you specify; it doesn't completely shut down SDL itself. If, for example, you wanted to shut down only the CD-ROM subsystem at some point in your program, you would use the following code.

```
SDL_QuitSubSystem(SDL_INIT_CDROM);
```

This function has no return value, so you don't have to worry about checking anything. If you really want to ensure that the subsystem was shut down, you can use SDL_WasInit to determine its state.

SDL_WasInit and SDL_GetError

Speaking of SDL_WasInit, it is the function you can use to determine whether or not a given subsystem or subsystems are initialized. Here's what the prototype looks like:

```
Uint32 SDL_WasInit(Uint32 flags);
```

This function takes a single parameter, a Uint32 called flags, and returns a Uint32. It takes a Uint32 that represents all of the initialized subsystems (each of the SDL_INIT_* values is a bit flag), performs a bitwise or with the value passed as the flags parameter, and returns the new value to the caller. If you are looking for a particular subsystem—for example, video—you pass SDL_INIT_VIDEO. The return value will either be SDL_INIT_VIDEO (video is initialized) or 0 (video is not initialized). If you pass SDL_INIT_VIDEO | SDL_INIT_AUDIO, the return value will be 0 (neither), SDL_INIT_VIDEO (video was initialized, but not audio), SDL_INIT_AUDIO (audio was initialized, but not video), or SDL_INIT_VIDEO | SDL_INIT_AUDIO (both were initialized). Typically, when you are looking at which subsystems are initialized, you call this function one time with SDL_INIT_EVERYTHING as the flags parameter, and then do bitwise checks with each of the other SDL_INIT_* values on the value returned.

The final function I will cover in this chapter is SDL_GetError. If something Very Bad happens (and Very Bad things can and do happen), an SDL function call will fail. For example, if SDL_Init fails, it returns a -1. I don't know about you, but a -1 just isn't very descriptive to me. I would like to know not only that the initialization failed, but also why it failed. That's where SDL_GetError comes in. When something fails, it puts a string into an internal buffer somewhere, which you can access using SDL_GetError. Here is the prototype.

```
char *SDL_GetError(void);
```

A simple enough function, it takes no parameters and returns a char*. Normally, you will want to write this string to a file log somewhere, as shown in the following code snippet.

```
fprintf(stderr,"%s\n",SDL_GetError()); //report the error
```

And that's all there is to it.

Summary

You now have a good general overview of what SDL has to offer. You can initialize any or all of SDL's subsystems, shut them down, check to see whether they were initialized, and retrieve an error message should something fail. While most of this information is rather simple and, for the most part, common sense, it is a solid foundation upon which you will build bigger, better, and more robust SDL applications.

Are you looking at the initialization functions and saying to yourself, "Gosh, these are really simple. Are all SDL functions this simple?" The answer is yes. SDL was built to be simple. If you are used to DirectX, then you are used to going through cartwheels and back flips to get everything initialized. With SDL, it's just a single function call.

CHAPTER 3

SDL Video

Welcome to SDL's video subsystem. For a typical human being, 70% of input is gathered from sight, so the SDL video subsystem is the most important one to know. This subsystem is used to create 2D graphics, just like DirectDraw, GDI, and other similar libraries. If you want to create 3D graphics, the SDL video subsystem ties in nicely with OpenGL.

The Video Subsystem at a Glance

In GDI, you have RECT, COLORREF, HDC, HBITMAP, and so on. In DirectDraw, you have IDirectDraw, IDirectDrawSurface, IDirectDrawClipper, and so on. In SDL, it is no different. There are seven different structures in SDL for dealing with the display. Each has its own well-defined purpose, and each is easy enough to work with in general. All of these objects are logically organized. You'll take a look at them on a conceptual level now, and in more depth later in the chapter.

SDL_Rect

With very few exceptions, games and other applications run on a full screen or in a rectangular viewport, so pretty much any method of creating computer graphics on a raster display involves rectangles in some way. Therefore, every API and library used to create graphics has some sort of structure for containing a rectangular area. This is exactly what SDL_Rect does. It stores the upper-left coordinate (in pixels) and the width and height (also in pixels) of a rectangle.

Now for the downside. Although SDL_Rect is a fundamental type used quite heavily in SDL's video subsystem, there are no functions for working with it. That is, unlike the WIN32 RECT type, which has a number of functions such as IntersectRect and UnionRect, SDL_Rect has none. I assume that this is because SDL is a multimedia library, and the users of said library should be smart enough to write their own rectangle functions if they so desire.

The equivalent in WIN32 is, as I stated earlier, the RECT structure.

SDL_Color

SDL_Color is another "helper" structure, much like SDL_Rect. It is useful for storing color information in a format-independent manner. SDL_Color's primary use is in palette management, but a creative user of SDL typically finds other uses for this structure as well.

In WIN32, there are several equivalents of SDL_Color, including COLORREF, PALETTEENTRY, RGBTRIPLE, and RGBQUAD.

SDL_Palette

You will primarily be concerned with 16-bit or higher graphics, so you won't often give a second thought to the 8-bit graphics days and color indirection using palettes. However, there are times when a palettized display is the way to go, so you will take a closer look at SDL_Palette later on in this chapter, in the "Palettes" section.

The WIN32 equivalent to SDL_Palette is the HPALETTE GDI object; in DirectDraw, the equivalent is IDirectDrawPalette.

SDL_PixelFormat

Since video cards vary so widely, there is a strong need for a structure that can represent exactly how the display hardware is currently representing colors. Information stored in an SDL_PixelFormat includes bits per pixel, bits for each channel, and whether the display is in an RGB mode or is using color indirection through palettes. SDL_PixelFormat describes exactly what sort of pixel data is stored in an SDL_Surface.

The DirectDraw equivalent to SDL_PixelFormat is DDPIXELFORMAT, as you might expect.

SDL_Surface

Naturally, the stock and trade of SDL's video subsystem is SDL_Surface. This structure abstracts a rectangular block of pixels. Of course, there is only one SDL_Surface that represents the actual display area. All of the other surfaces are buffers for storing pixel data that will eventually be shown on the main display. It is a very ephemeral thing.

The DirectDraw equivalent to SDL_Surface is IDirectDrawSurface.

SDL_VideoInfo

In theory, the ideal way to make a video game would be to tell the computer to set up the best video mode possible and have the display hardware scale all of your graphics to fit properly. Unfortunately, while doing this is possible, it isn't very efficient. In a few years, it might be a completely different story. A structure such as `SDL_VideoInfo` exists so you can examine the capabilities of a given display mode. It comes in useful; trust me.

The closest approximation of a DirectDraw equivalent for `SDL_VideoInfo` is getting the video capabilities using `IDirectDraw7::GetCaps`.

SDL_Overlay

Conceptually, `SDL_Overlay` is a structure very similar to `SDL_Surface`. Only the type of data taken is different. Overlays are used for streaming video data (such as from an .mpg or a similar video file). You can use this for effects such as cut-scenes, opening cinematics, and so on. In DirectDraw, an overlay is really just a different type of surface, and it is handled much the same as other surfaces.

Core Structures

As you can see, SDL's video subsystem is not overly complicated. There are only seven different types of "objects," each with a well-defined role. About half of them aren't even used that frequently.

Now that you're up to speed with what objects exist, it is time to take a closer look at each of them, starting with the most fundamental ones—`SDL_Rect` and `SDL_Color`.

SDL_Rect

The SDL video subsystem, being 2D in nature, deals primarily with copying rectangular blocks of pixels from one `SDL_Surface` to another. This has been the way of dealing with raster displays since their inception. It is The Way Things are Done.

Naturally, every API or library for dealing with 2D graphics needs to have a structure that can contain a rectangular area. The term "rectangular area" has a special meaning when you are dealing with raster displays. In this case, you are talking about rectangles whose sides consist of horizontal and vertical segments. In other words, a side of the rectangle mimics the orientation of the screen. In SDL, this structure is SDL_Rect, and it looks like this:

```
typedef struct{
  Sint16 x, y;
  Uint16 w, h;
} SDL_Rect;
```

Since the rectangle is aligned so that each of the edges are parallel to either the top or left edge of the screen, you need only two points to define it. Within the SDL_Rect structure, these points are defined as (x,y) and (x+w,y+h). The other two points are (x+w,y) and (x,y+h). Check out Figure 3.1 to see examples of what SDL_Rect can and cannot represent as far as rectangles are concerned.

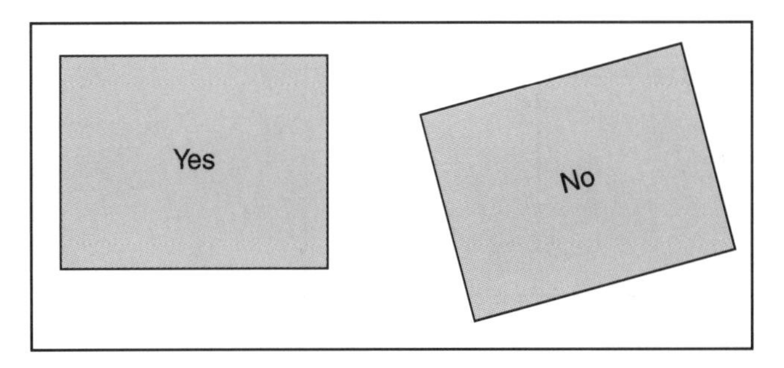

Figure 3.1 *Rectangles that can and cannot be represented by* SDL_Rect

The x and y members of SDL_Rect are Sint16 values, so they can range anywhere from -32,768 to +32,767. This is (at least in the conceivable future) more than enough to represent any resolution display mode.

The w and h members are Uint16 values, so they can be anywhere in the range of 0 to 65,535. Again, more than you should ever need to represent rectangular areas on surfaces.

Storing the width and height (in w and h) is a good thing, because you can easily move the SDL_Rect around in 2D space simply by changing the x and y values. In some APIs, such as WIN32 GDI, the structure for representing a rectangle stores both the left and right edges, which means that to move the rectangle horizontally while maintaining the same size, you need to change both values.

Now a few words about the SDL coordinate system. If you have worked with other raster display APIs in the past, you know that they almost always have the pixel location (0,0) in the upper-left corner of the screen. SDL is no different. The x value starts at the left edge with 0 and increases to the right, and the y value starts at the top edge with 0 and increases downward. This is upside down from the Cartesian coordinate system that you were taught in algebra class. For a graphical explanation of this difference, see Figure 3.2.

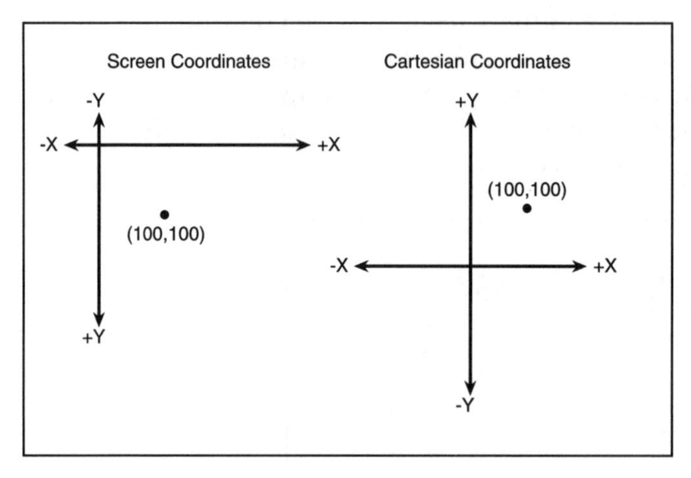

Figure 3.2 *The difference between screen coordinates and standard Cartesian coordinates*

Personally, I've been working with raster displays for so long that I simply gave up a number of years ago and started doing all of my math upside down. While I'm not actually suggesting that you start doing this, it has been helpful to me. Being able to think in both systems will help you immensely.

The more common questions to ask about a rectangular area such as SDL_Rect are, "What points are inside this rectangle?" and, "What points are outside?" As a result of both of these questions, "Is Point A inside or outside?"

Suppose for a moment that you have a structure that represents a single 2D point, like this:

```
typedef struct {
Sint16 x, y;
} Point;
```

Suppose you have a Point named A and an SDL_Rect named R, like this:

```
Point A;
SDL_Rect R;
```

Somewhere in your code, both A and R are given values (in other words, they have all of their members filled in with values). At some point later in the code, you find yourself needing to determine whether A is inside or outside of R.

Since `R.x` and `R.y` represent the upper-left corner of the rectangle R, you know that if `A.x` is less than `R.x` or `A.y` is less than `R.y`, then A must be outside of R. If `A.x` is greater than or equal to `R.x` and `A.y` is greater than or equal to `R.y`, then A might be in R, but you still have to perform further tests.

Because of the way that `SDL_Rect` is structured, the right edge (`R.x` + `R.w`) and the bottom edge (`R.y` + `R.h`) are *not* inside the rectangle. There is an actual explanation for this. You can look at the horizontal and vertical lines of pixels on a display in one of two ways. You can look at them as though positions 0, 1, 2, 3, and so on are lines passing through the very center of a column or row of pixels (see Figure 3.3).

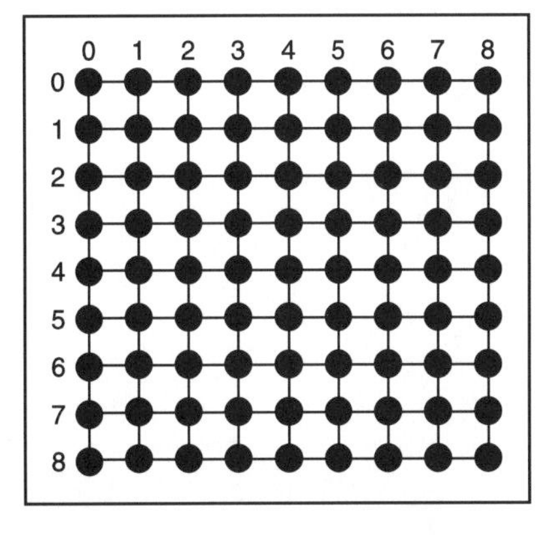

Figure 3.3 *Lines passing through the center of rows and columns of pixels*

You can also look at them as though the lines pass through the space between the pixels (see Figure 3.4). In this case, we are choosing the second method to represent the coordinate system as far as the rectangles are concerned, and the first method as far as the points are concerned.

So in order for A to be in R, it must pass the first two tests, and then the second two tests. `A.x` has to be less than `R.x + R.w`, and `A.y` has to be less than `R.y + R.h`. In code form, you can test whether A is inside R using the following snippet.

```
if ( A.x >= R.x && A.y >= R.y && A.x < (R.x + R.w ) && A.y < ( R.y +
R.h ) )
{
      //point A is inside R
}
else
{
      //point A is not inside R
}
```

One final note about `SDL_Rect` before I move on. If a rectangle has `w` and `h` both equal to 0, then it is empty. By empty I mean that there is not a single pixel within the rectangle, ergo there is no inside. By convention, empty rectangles will also have `x` and `y` values of 0.

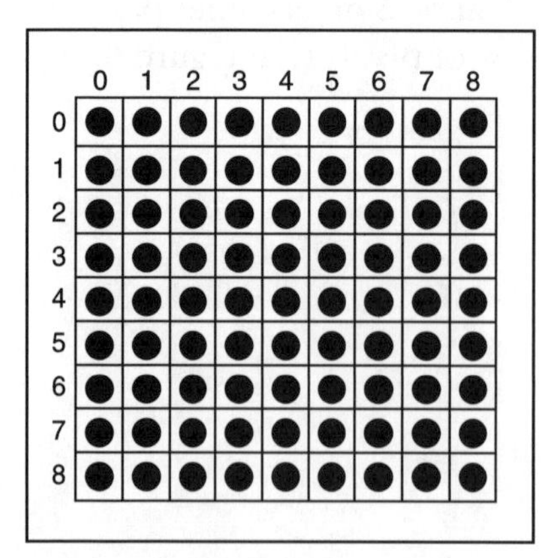

Figure 3.4 *Lines passing between rows and columns of pixels*

SDL_Color

Another fundamental object in SDL's video subsystem is SDL_Color. Here's what it looks like:

```
typedef struct{
  Uint8 r;
  Uint8 g;
  Uint8 b;
  Uint8 unused;
} SDL_Color;
```

The r, g, and b members represent the red, green, and blue intensity of a particular color, respectively. The range for these values is 0 through 255, with 0 meaning a lack of intensity on that channel and 255 meaning the maximum intensity for that channel. The unused member does not represent a color at all; it also ranges from 0 to 255. If you want, you can use it to store alpha information or something else.

Other than in palettes, SDL_Color is not used directly by SDL's video subsystem. There are places where you might use an SDL_Color, but it is not required.

Although you are likely entirely comfortable working with the RGB color space, it would be remiss of me not to at least take a little bit of time to talk about it, since it is fundamental to the way SDL represents color.

The RGB color space is three-dimensional. The dimensions are red (R), green (G), and blue (B). Each dimension is clamped so that only values between 0.0 and 1.0 are represented along each axis. As far as SDL_Color is concerned, 0.0 is represented by 0 and 1.0 is represented by 255, giving you 254 values in between these extremes and a total of 256 different values. Since there are three color axes, there are 256×256×256 different values that can be represented by an SDL_Color, for a grand total of 16,777,216 different and distinct colors. That's a lot of colors.

Naturally, not all video modes have a format that allows all of these colors to be represented. The number of bits per pixel might be 8, 16, 24, or 32. In the 24- or 32-bit modes, all of the colors in the RGB color space can be represented. In 16-bit modes, each of the color axes are truncated somewhat, typically down to 5 bits for red, 5 or 6 bits for green, and 5 bits for blue. In this case, the lowest few bits of the axis are insignificant and ignored.

In 8-bit modes, it gets even weirder. Since there are only 256 possible colors, truncating bits from each axis does little good because no matter how you slice it, the picture will be rather poor quality. Instead, we come up with 256 values that represent full `SDL_Colors` and map each value of the pixel to one of these 256 24-bit colors. This is called *color indirection* and it uses a palette, also known as a *color look-up table* (CLUT). With color indirection, you can get some interesting effects that are not possible with normal RGB modes. I'll talk more about palettized modes a bit later in this chapter.

Retrieving Information about the Video Subsystem

This section would be better titled "SDL_VideoInfo and How to Use It." Also, I know you are tired of me blabbing theory at you for countless pages, so you're finally going to do another example program. Yay!

To start with, take a look at the `SDL_VideoInfo` structure.

```
typedef struct{
  Uint32 hw_available:1;
  Uint32 wm_available:1;
  Uint32 blit_hw:1;
  Uint32 blit_hw_CC:1;
  Uint32 blit_hw_A:1;
  Uint32 blit_sw:1;
  Uint32 blit_sw_CC:1;
  Uint32 blit_sw_A:1;
  Uint32 blit_fill:1;
  Uint32 video_mem;
  SDL_PixelFormat *vfmt;
} SDL_VideoInfo;
```

As you can see, most of the members of `SDL_VideoInfo` are bit flags. They will either be 0 or 1, and they act much like a Boolean variable, with 0 meaning not present and 1 meaning present. There are nine of these bit fields and the names are somewhat cryptic, so take a look at Table 3.1, which attempts to explain each of them.

Table 3.1 Bit Flag Members of SDL_VideoInfo

Member	Meaning (if ==1)
hw_available	It is possible to create surfaces in hardware.
wm_available	A window manager is available.
blit_hw	Blits from hardware surfaces to hardware surfaces are accelerated.
blit_hw_CC	Blits from hardware surfaces to hardware surfaces using color keys are accelerated.
blit_hw_A	Blits from hardware surfaces to hardware surfaces using alpha information are accelerated.
blit_sw	Blits from software surfaces to hardware surfaces are accelerated.
blit_sw_CC	Blits from software surfaces to hardware surfaces with color keys are accelerated.
blit_sw_A	Blits from software surfaces to hardware surfaces with alpha information are accelerated.
blit_fill	Color fills are accelerated.

As you can see, the bit flags aren't really all that cryptically named, they're just abbreviated. The terms `hw` and `sw` simply mean hardware and software, `CC` and `A` stand for color keys and alpha, and so on. Having longer, more descriptive names really wouldn't be too helpful and would simply give you more to type.

The other two members of `SDL_VideoInfo` are `video_mem` and `vfmt`. The `video_mem` member is, as you might imagine, the amount of video memory available. Keep in mind that this is the *total* amount available measured in kilobytes, not how much is left.

SDL_PixelFormat

The `vfmt` member is a pointer to an `SDL_PixelFormat`. Now is as good a time as any to talk about this structure. You'll be using it later to set and get pixel values. Here's what it looks like:

```
typedef struct{
  SDL_Palette *palette;
  Uint8  BitsPerPixel;
  Uint8  BytesPerPixel;
  Uint32 Rmask, Gmask, Bmask, Amask;
  Uint8  Rshift, Gshift, Bshift, Ashift;
  Uint8  Rloss, Gloss, Bloss, Aloss;
  Uint32 colorkey;
  Uint8  alpha;
} SDL_PixelFormat;
```

There are many members here and believe it or not, nearly all of them are useful (unlike a number of the values in DirectDraw's `DDPIXELFORMAT` structure, which to this day boggle my mind).

I am not going to discuss the `palette` member of `SDL_PixelFormat` at this moment. I want to put the entire discussion of palettes in one place, and that place is a little later on in the chapter.

Next you have `BitsPerPixel` and `BytesPerPixel`. These are pretty well-named members; they tell you how many bits and bytes it takes to represent a single pixel in this pixel format. Typical values for `BitsPerPixel` are 8, 16, 24, and 32, and typical values for `BytesPerPixel` are 1, 2, 3, and 4. If the `BitsPerPixel` member is 8, there will be a palette. Otherwise, the various other members starting with R, G, and B will have values other than zero (in other words, it is an RGB mode instead of a color indirection mode).

The next 12 members are various masks and shift values. These are meant to work together for RGB modes to convert either to or from a 24-bit pixel value (in other words, an `SDL_Color` value). There are three types of values represented here—a mask (`Rmask`, `Gmask`, `Bmask`, or `Amask`), a shift value (`Rshift`, `Gshift`, `Bshift`, or `Ashift`), and a loss value (`Rloss`, `Gloss`, `Bloss`, or `Aloss`). Naturally, `R` stands for red, `G` stands for green, and `B` stands for blue. `A` stands for alpha. I'll talk a bit about alpha later, but keep in mind that when I'm talking about the other color components, the same idea applies for alpha.

So `Rmask`, `Rshift`, and `Rloss` work together somehow. (The same applies for the `G` and `B` members, but I'll only talk about red and you can extrapolate from there.) For just a moment, take a look at how a typical 16-bit pixel format is put together (see Figure 3.5).

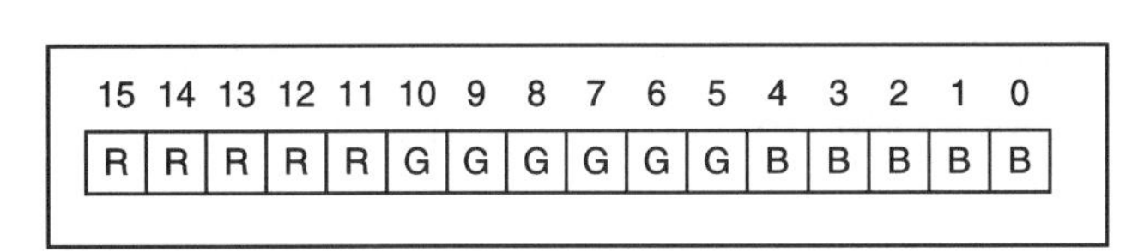

Figure 3.5 *A 16-bit RGB color format*

In Figure 3.5, you see that the top five bits (bits 11 through 15) are the red bits, the bottom five bits (bits 0 through 4) are the blue bits, and the six bits in the middle (bits 5 through 10) are the green bits. If you made a binary number with a 1 in each red bit and a 0 in all non-red bits, you would get a red mask, like this:

```
1111 1000 0000 0000 b
```

Since binary numbers are a little hard to work with, change the representation to hexadecimal (which your compiler can work with), like this:

```
F800
```

This is the value you would get from `Rmask` if the pixel format you were looking at were the same as the one I showed you in Figure 3.5. The value of `Rmask` represents the value at which a pixel is 100% red and 0% green and blue (still ignoring alpha for the moment). In other words, if you had an `SDL_Color` with an `r` value of 255 and `g` and `b` values of 0, it would map to the value stored in `Rmask`.

To determine `Rshift`, take the `Rmask` and keep shifting it right by one bit until there is a 1 in bit 0. In the example you are working with, you would have to shift right 11 times, so `Rshift` would be 11.

Finally, `Rloss` is the difference between the 8-bit representation of a color channel and the actual representation of the color in the format. In this case only 5 bits of red exist, so you have "lost" 3 bits; thus `Rloss` would be 3.

How you have arrived at these values, however, is academic. SDL figures it all out for you, so you don't even have to know how the color is represented to convert from an `SDL_Color` value into the native pixel format. Neat, huh? I'll be showing you just how to do this when you take a look at setting and getting individual pixels.

Finally, there are two additional members of `SDL_PixelFormat`—color key and alpha. The color key is the native pixel format representation of the color that is transparent. I will speak more about color keys later on in the chapter, along with alpha, the last member of SDL_PixelFormat.

Grabbing Information

Now that you have been formally introduced to SDL_VideoInfo and SDL_PixelFormat, it's time to actually take a look at the information they contain. To do that, you need to look at the SDL_GetVideoInfo function.

```
SDL_VideoInfo *SDL_GetVideoInfo(void);
```

This function takes no parameters and returns a pointer to an SDL_VideoInfo. The pointer returned by this function does not need to be freed, deleted, or otherwise deallocated. The information you access with this pointer is read-only.

It's time for a new example. You can find the code for this example in FOSDL3_1 in the Examples folder of the CD-ROM. The code is as follows (minus comments, error checking, and blank lines that do exist in the code on the CD).

```
#include "sdl.h"
#include <stdlib.h>
const SDL_VideoInfo* g_pVideoInfo = NULL;
int main(int argc, char* argv[])
{
     SDL_Init(SDL_INIT_VIDEO);
     atexit(SDL_Quit);
     g_pVideoInfo = SDL_GetVideoInfo();
     fprintf(stdout, "\nVideo Information:\n");
     fprintf(stdout, "hw_available? %d\n", g_pVideoInfo->hw_available);
     fprintf(stdout, "wm_available? %d\n", g_pVideoInfo->wm_available);
     fprintf(stdout, "blit_hw? %d\n", g_pVideoInfo->blit_hw);
     fprintf(stdout, "blit_hw_CC? %d\n", g_pVideoInfo->blit_hw_CC);
     fprintf(stdout, "blit_hw_A? %d\n", g_pVideoInfo->blit_hw_A);
     fprintf(stdout, "blit_sw? %d\n", g_pVideoInfo->blit_sw);
     fprintf(stdout, "blit_sw_CC? %d\n", g_pVideoInfo->blit_sw_CC);
     fprintf(stdout, "blit_sw_A? %d\n", g_pVideoInfo->blit_sw_A);
     fprintf(stdout, "blit_fill? %d\n", g_pVideoInfo->blit_fill);
     fprintf(stdout, "video memory(in K)? %d\n", g_pVideoInfo-
>video_mem);
```

```
    fprintf(stdout, "bits per pixel? %d\n", g_pVideoInfo->vfmt-
>BitsPerPixel);
    return(0);
}
```

As you can see, it is a rather simple program. You simply initialize SDL, grab the `SDL_VideoInfo` pointer, and then start printing the results to `stdout`. On my machine, the following information is sent to stdout.txt.

```
Video Information:
hw_available? 1
wm_available? 1
blit_hw? 1
blit_hw_CC? 1
blit_hw_A? 0
blit_sw? 1
blit_sw_CC? 1
blit_sw_A? 0
blit_fill? 1
video memory(in K)? 36864
bits per pixel? 16
```

NOTE

Just a little note regarding whatever you happen to get back as the bits per pixel in your own stdout.txt file. It might not match the actual bits per pixel at which your screen is currently set. When you call SDL_GetVideoInfo prior to setting the display mode (which you haven't quite gotten to yet), SDL will report the "best" mode's information (translation—the mode with the most capabilities, at least in theory). If you get a result other than the mode at which your video display is currently set, that's why.

My system has pretty good support for hardware-accelerated blitting (no alpha acceleration, but that's expected). I could have gone whole hog and reported every single member of `SDL_PixelFormat` along with this other information, but generally the bits per pixel is enough. That is more important to me than the actual representation of the pixel on the screen.

Creating and Destroying SDL Surfaces

So far you've been working with SDL's video subsystem, but you haven't actually *seen* anything yet. It's about time you do, don't you think?

You are now going to start using SDL_Surface, the basic building block of any SDL application that uses graphics. Here's what the structure looks like:

```
typedef struct SDL_Surface {
        Uint32 flags;
        SDL_PixelFormat *format;
        int w, h;
        Uint16 pitch;
        void *pixels;
        SDL_Rect clip_rect;
        int refcount;
} SDL_Surface;
```

To be completely honest, there are more members than what I've shown here. However, these are the only ones that you will need to use SDL_Surface. If SDL had been written for C++ instead of for both C and C++, the members shown would be public and the rest would be private.

When you get to creating surfaces, you will more fully explore the flags member. It has to do with whether the surface was created in hardware or software, whether or not to make a double buffer, and so on.

The format member is a pointer to an SDL_PixelFormat that describes, to no one's surprise, the manner in which the surface's pixels are formatted.

The w and h members are the surface's width and height. Don't ask me why they are ints instead of Uint16 or something. It's not like a surface with a negative width or height is even possible.

The pitch member has something to do with the width and the bytes per pixel of the surface, but it also deals with how video cards allocate memory for surfaces. Suppose for a moment that you create a 640×480 surface that has 16 bits per pixel, or 2 bytes per pixel. In an ideal world, each row of pixels would take up 2×640, or 1280 bytes, and from the first location in the pixel array (index 0) to the location in the pixel array that represents the pixel directly below it, the offset would be 1280 bytes. However, because of the way video cards work, this might not be so. If you based your calculations on width and bytes per pixel, you'd have a screwed-up image in no time. For instance, the number of bytes between the first location and the one below it might be something like 1,536. Why? Ask the video card manufacturers and designers. I'm just a programmer. And so I introduce the idea of pitch. From the first pixel location in a row, it is pitch bytes to get to the pixel location directly below it.

The `pixels` member is a pointer to the array of pixels that makes up this surface. The reason it is a `void*` is that there is no standard way to represent pixel data. On an 8-bit surface, you cast this to a `Uint8*`. On a 16-bit surface, you cast to a `Uint16*`, and so on.

The `clip_rect` member is an `SDL_Rect`. The values stored here limit the area on the `SDL_Surface` on which you can blit. SDL supports only rectangular clipping areas and only one rectangle at a time.

Finally you have `refcount`, which is a little odd to explain, but if you have worked with DirectX and/or COM in the past, then you already know what it does. Suffice it to say that when a surface is created, `refcount` becomes 1. When you later free a surface, it becomes 0 (in other words, it is reduced by one). Only when `refcount` is 0 is the memory allocated to the surface actually freed. If for some reason you have a number of things that depend on a particular `SDL_Surface` existing, you might want to increase `refcount` when you create an object that needs that particular surface, and then free the surface when you destroy that object. That way, you ensure that the surface exists as long as it is needed by other objects that depend on it.

Other than `pixels` and `refcount`, the members of `SDL_Surface` are read-only. You manipulate the data pointed to by pixels in order to create pixel-by-pixel graphics (such as lines or circles), and you manipulate `refcount` as described in the preceding paragraph. Other than that, `SDL_Surface` is just an informational structure.

Setting the Display Mode

The first surface you need to create in any SDL application is the display surface. This is the only surface that the user of your application will actually see. To set up the display surface, you call `SDL_SetVideoMode`.

```
SDL_Surface *SDL_SetVideoMode(int width, int height, int bpp, Uint32
flags);
```

This function takes three parameters and returns a pointer to an SDL_Surface. The return value represents the display surface. If you get a NULL, then the function failed.

The parameters are self-explanatory for the most part. The width and height parameters, for instance, specify how wide and how tall you want the screen or window to be, respectively. The bpp parameter tells SDL how many bits per pixel you want the surface to have.

This leaves the flags parameter, which you'll notice is also a member of SDL_Surface if you look back a bit. Coincidence? I think not. The flags parameter is a number of bit flags ored together that tell SDL exactly how you want your surface created. Table 3.2 contains the various flags and brief descriptions of them.

Table 3.2 Bit Flags for the Flags Parameter

Bit Flag	Meaning
SDL_SWSURFACE	The surface is to be created in the main memory.
SDL_HWSURFACE	The surface is to be created in the video memory.
SDL_ASYNCBLIT	You want to use asynchronous blitting.
SDL_ANYFORMAT	You want to use the pixel format of the actual display surface.
SDL_HWPALETTE	You want to use all 256 colors of the palette.
SDL_DOUBLEBUF	You want to use a double buffer.
SDL_FULLSCREEN	You want the application to be full-screen.
SDL_OPENGL	You are using SDL with OpenGL.
SDL_OPENGLBLIT	You are using SDL with OpenGL but would like to render with SDL.
SDL_RESIZABLE	You want a resizable window.
SDL_NOFRAME	If windowed, you do not want to have the standard window decoration around the display surface. In full-screen, this is the default.

As you can see, these flags give you a lot of options, but don't be fooled into thinking that just because you specified certain flags, you are going to get the surface you requested. SDL will try damned hard to give you what you ask for; failing that, it'll try its best to emulate what you requested. If you ask for a 100 pixel by 100 pixel full-screen surface, you will wind up with a larger resolution full-screen surface, but you will find that you can only write to the middle 100×100-pixel area. SDL aims to please.

After you call SDL_SetVideoMode, you can check the flags member of the returned surface to see which flags SDL was able to accomplish. So you can go ahead and ask for what you want, and then find out later what you actually got. This is unlike DirectDraw in that with DirectDraw, you have to first determine whether a particular configuration is allowed, and then make it happen.

Window or Full Screen?

Depending on the game that you are designing, you have a number of choices to make about how it presents information to the player. One of these choices is about whether or not to make the application take up the entire screen or simply occupy a window on the desktop. One option is to allow the player to choose the version with which he is most comfortable.

In SDL, creating a windowed environment is just as easy as creating a full-screen environment; both use a single call to SDL_SetVideoMode. In the case of a window, you use 0 for the bpp parameter and SDL_ANYFORMAT (as well as any other flags you might desire) in the flags parameter. If, for example, you wanted to make a 640×480 window, this is the call you would make.

```
SDL_SetVideoMode(640,480,0,SDL_ANYFORMAT);
```

If you wanted to make the application run full-screen in 640×480 mode at 16 bits per pixel, the call would look like this:

```
SDL_SetVideoMode(640,480,16,SDL_FULLSCREEN);
```

That is really the only difference between the two, as far as SDL is concerned. As a programmer, you don't really have to worry about anything. SDL sets up the environment for you, and you can just go ahead and render.

TIP

Typically, in full-screen mode you will also want to specify the SDL_DOUBLEBUF **flag, so that you can use double buffering and page flipping.**

But what about the other flags listed in Table 3.2? At this point, they aren't very important. Simply knowing that they exist will suffice. You can experiment with them a little later. Right now, you're just getting up and running.

If you want to play around with SDL_SetVideoMode for a while, I put together a quick example program on the CD-ROM that you can use. Simply change the parameters to SDL_SetVideoMode.

A final item: You don't have to do anything to clean up the surface that is created with SDL_SetVideoMode. When SDL_Quit is called, it does all of the cleanup for you.

FOSDL3_2 is the example that sets up the main display surface in windowed format. Be sure to check it out, because this small program forms the foundation for all other example programs throughout the book.

TIP

If for whatever reason you are in a piece of code that does not know what variable points to the main display surface, you can use the SDL_GetVideoSurface() **function to retrieve the pointer to the main display surface.**

RGB Surfaces

Naturally, you are going to need more than one surface for any sort of application that actually does something. For one thing, you need a place to store all of the graphical data that your game needs, such as tiles, sprites, and buttons.

In SDL, you can use one of two functions to create an off-screen surface. You can use either SDL_CreateRGBSurface or SDL_CreateRGBSurfaceFrom. These are the most flexible ways to create surfaces. Here are the prototypes.

```
SDL_Surface *SDL_CreateRGBSurface(Uint32 flags, int width, int height,
int depth, Uint32 Rmask, Uint32 Gmask, Uint32 Bmask, Uint32 Amask);
```

```
SDL_Surface *SDL_CreateRGBSurfaceFrom(void *pixels, int width, int
height, int depth, int pitch, Uint32 Rmask, Uint32 Gmask, Uint32 Bmask,
Uint32 Amask);
```

As you can see, these two functions are rather similar. First, take a look at SDL_CreateRGBSurface, and then I'll explain SDL_CreateRGBSurfaceFrom.

SDL_CreateRGBSurface has many parameters in common with SDL_SetVideoMode, such as flags, width, height, and depth (a.k.a. bpp). For the flags parameter, there is only a limited subset allowed—SDL_SWSURFACE, SDL_HWSURFACE, SDL_SRCCOLORKEY, and SDL_ALPHA. You have not learned about SDL_SRCCOLORKEY or SDL_ALPHA yet, but you will before the end of the chapter.

The Rmask, Gmask, Bmask, and Amask should look familiar; they deal with the pixel format. You can pretty much make up any old format you like, and SDL will try its hardest to accommodate you.

Suppose you wanted to make a 16-bit surface with 5 bits of red, 6 bits of green, and 5 bits of blue. Suppose you wanted this surface to be 100 pixels by 100 pixels. Finally, suppose you wanted this surface to be in video memory (so SDL_HWSURFACE would be indicated in the flags parameter). This is what the line of code would look like.

```
SDL_Surface pSurface = SDL_CreateRGBSurface(SDL_HWSURFACE, 100, 100, 16,
0xF800, 0x07E, 0x1F);
```

If there is a problem the function will return NULL, and you can use SDL_GetError to enlighten you about why it failed.

Whenever you are finished with the surface, you must call SDL_FreeSurface. Here's the prototype.

```
void SDL_FreeSurface(SDL_Surface *surface);
```

NOTE

Any SDL function that creates a surface must be called after you call SDL_SetVideoMode.

This function returns no value and takes as its single parameter a pointer to the surface for which you want to free the resources. The resources are actually only freed if the reference count of the surface drops to 0.

Now take a look at SDL_CreateRGBSurfaceFrom. Here again is the prototype.

```
SDL_Surface *SDL_CreateRGBSurfaceFrom(void *pixels, int width, int
height, int depth, int pitch, Uint32 Rmask, Uint32 Gmask, Uint32 Bmask,
Uint32 Amask);
```

For the most part, the parameters here are the same as for SDL_CreateRGBSurface. The notable differences are the lack of a flags parameter (a surface created with this function is always in the main memory) and the addition of the pixels and pitch parameters. Other than these differences, the usage of the parameters is the same.

The pixels parameter is a pointer to the pixel data that you want to use for the surface. You are responsible for allocating and freeing this memory. It will not be deallocated when SDL_FreeSurface is called. Naturally, the data pointed to by pixels should be large enough for the entire size of the surface and should use the pixel format specified by Rmask, Gmask, Bmask, and Amask. It should also follow the pitch specified in the appropriate parameter.

In other words, SDL_CreateRGBSurfaceFrom is the super hard-core surface creation function. You probably won't use it much, but it's good to know that it's there.

Loading Bitmaps

Typically, you won't need to use SDL_CreateRGBSurface or SDL_CreateRGBSurfaceFrom very often. You will have bitmapped graphics saved to a file somewhere, and for the game you simply want to load them in and go. SDL has supplied a function just for this occasion called SDL_LoadBMP. It is somewhat limited in its use because it will only load .bmp files, but it's better than nothing. For the ability to load other types of images, such as JPGs, you can use SDL_image, which I will talk about in Chapter 8. For now, just stick to .bmp files.

Here is the prototype for SDL_LoadBMP.

```
SDL_Surface *SDL_LoadBMP(const char *file);
```

This function takes a single parameter named file, which is a string that specifies which file you want to load. The value returned by this function is a pointer to a new surface that contains the loaded bitmap file. If this function fails, the return value is NULL.

Converting Surfaces

There will be times when you have one surface in some format and you want to copy a portion of it over to another surface with a different format. That is the basis of all 2D graphics on raster displays, after all...copying little rectangular blocks of pixels hither and thither.

However, when the surfaces have two different formats, it means that the pixel data needs to be converted from one format to another. While this conversion is not particularly difficult, it does take some time; if this conversion is happening most of the time, the application can slow down rather quickly.

So how can you minimize or eliminate this problem? The answer is to keep as much of the pixel data as possible in the same format (typically the same format as the display surface).

Here's a scenario: You have two surface pointers, `pSurf1` and `pSurf2`. You intend to copy data from `pSurf2` onto `pSurf1`. This will occur rather frequently and you want it to be as fast as possible, so you'd like to ensure that `pSurf2` is the same format as `pSurf1`. To do this, you use `SDL_ConvertSurface`. Here's the prototype.

```
SDL_Surface *SDL_ConvertSurface(SDL_Surface *src, SDL_PixelFormat *fmt,
Uint32 flags);
```

This function takes three parameters and returns a pointer to a newly created surface (if it's successful) or `NULL` (if it fails). The `src` parameter is the surface that you want to convert to another format (in this scenario, `pSurf2`). The `fmt` parameter is the pixel format into which you want to convert the surface (in other words, `pSurf1->format`). Finally, the `flags` parameter here has the same meaning as it did in `SDL_CreateRGBSurface`.

The result of this conversion is a new surface that allows data to be quickly transferred to the destination surface without any conversion. Good stuff.

Another conversion function does much the same thing and uses `SDL_ConvertSurface` internally. It is called `SDL_DisplayFormat` and, as you might imagine, it converts a surface into the same format as the display surface. Because the display surface tends to be the final destination of graphics, it's a format in which you will want most (if not all) of your surfaces.

```
SDL_Surface *SDL_DisplayFormat(SDL_Surface *surface);
```

This function takes a single parameter (a pointer to a surface) and returns a pointer to a new surface that has the same format as the display surface. You can then free the original surface because you don't need it any more.

Working with SDL Surfaces

Knowing how to create surfaces is all well and good, but what good is creating them if you don't know how to do anything with them? I don't know about you, but I don't find blank screens particularly interesting. Therefore, you are going to start filling them up with data in the form of pixels. There are primarily three ways to change pixel data on a surface—by using color fills, setting individual pixels, or blitting.

Color fills, which are detailed in the "Filled Rectangles" section that follows, are typically only used to clear the screen or a large rectangular portion of the screen. They are still important, nonetheless.

If you want to get hard core, you can set individual pixels. If you can set a single pixel, you can do anything graphics-wise, such as drawing lines, circles, ellipses, polygons, and whatever else you can imagine. SDL has no functions for drawing these primitives, so if you want them you have to implement them yourself. The ability to retrieve the value of individual pixels goes hand-in-hand with setting them. Both topics are detailed in the "Setting and Getting Pixels" section.

Finally, there is blitting, which is more heavily used than either of the other two methods. The basis of blitting is quite simple: You transfer a rectangular block of pixels from one surface to another. Heck, you can even do it yourself once you know how to set and get pixel data. Of course, because blitting is typically hardware-accelerated, you won't want to do it yourself. This topic is covered in detail in the "Blitting" section.

Filled Rectangles

The first thing that you're going to learn is how to render color-filled rectangles using SDL_FillRect.

```
int SDL_FillRect(SDL_Surface *dst, SDL_Rect *dstrect, Uint32 color);
```

This function returns an int. If successful, the value returned will be 0. If it fails, the return value will be -1.

There are three parameters. The first (dst) is a pointer to an SDL_Surface on which you are drawing the filled rectangle. The second (dstrect) is a pointer to an SDL_Rect that describes the rectangular area that you want to fill. The third (color) is a Uint32 that represents the color with which you want to fill the rectangle. The only problem is, that color has to be in the native pixel format for the surface (which is why this function doesn't take an SDL_Color).

Fortunately, there is a handy little function for taking an SDL_Color (or at least all of the components of it) and converting it into the native pixel format for the surface. This function is called SDL_MapRGB.

```
Uint32 SDL_MapRGB(SDL_PixelFormat *fmt, Uint8 r, Uint8 g, Uint8 b);
```

This function takes four parameters. fmt is a pointer to an SDL_PixelFormat for the surface to which you are mapping a color. The r, g, and b parameters are (naturally) the red, green, and blue components of that color. The value returned by this function is the closest approximation of the color specified in that particular pixel format.

So I guess it's time for another example. This is going to be nice and simple, but at least you're going to actually see something. You can find this example on the CD as FOSDL3_3. As usual, the version you see here has been stripped of comments and error checking to save space. The version on the CD is complete.

```
#include "sdl.h"
#include <stdlib.h>
const int SCREEN_WIDTH=640;
const int SCREEN_HEIGHT=480;
SDL_Surface* g_pDisplaySurface = NULL;
SDL_Event g_Event;
SDL_Rect g_Rect;
Uint8 g_Red, g_Green, g_Blue;
Uint32 g_Color;
int main(int argc, char* argv[])
{
	SDL_Init(SDL_INIT_VIDEO);
	atexit(SDL_Quit);
	g_pDisplaySurface =
SDL_SetVideoMode(SCREEN_WIDTH,SCREEN_HEIGHT,0,SDL_ANYFORMAT);
```

```
    for(;;)
    {
        if(SDL_PollEvent(&g_Event)==0)
        {
            g_Red=rand()%256;
            g_Green=rand()%256;
            g_Blue=rand()%256;
            g_Color=SDL_MapRGB(g_pDisplaySurface-
>format,g_Red,g_Green,g_Blue);
            g_Rect.x=rand()%SCREEN_WIDTH;
            g_Rect.y=rand()%SCREEN_HEIGHT;
            g_Rect.w=rand()%(SCREEN_WIDTH-g_Rect.x);
            g_Rect.h=rand()%(SCREEN_HEIGHT-g_Rect.y);
            SDL_FillRect(g_pDisplaySurface,&g_Rect,g_Color);
            SDL_UpdateRect(g_pDisplaySurface,0,0,0,0);
        }
        else
        {
            if(g_Event.type==SDL_QUIT) break;
        }
    }
    return(0);
}
```

This program will randomly draw filled rectangles of random colors to a window. Figure 3.6 shows the output of this example.

There are a couple of functions used in this example that I have not covered yet. One of these is `SDL_PollEvent`, which is covered in Chapter 4, "SDL Event Handling and the Window Manager." The other is `SDL_UpdateRect`, which is explained later in the chapter. This function is necessary to update the display surface; otherwise, it remains the same. If you are interested in doing an experiment, comment that line out and recompile the example. You will see that you simply get a black window. The rectangles are still being drawn, but you don't see them.

Setting and Getting Pixels

In theory, you can set an individual pixel using `SDL_FillRect`, simply by specifying a rectangle with a `width` and `height` of 1. This, however, is not a great idea. If you have a need to set individual pixels, the better way

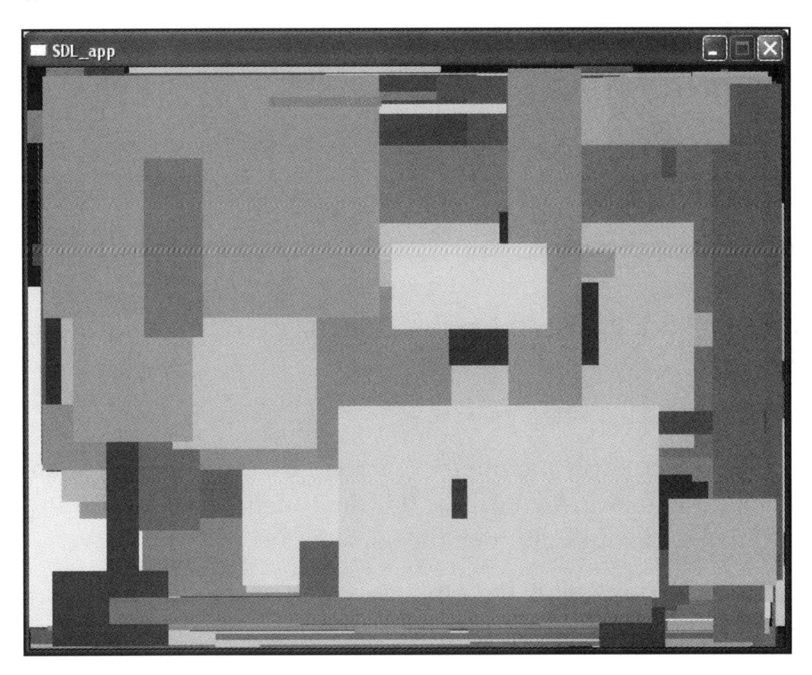

Figure 3.6 *The output of FOSDL3_3*

to go is to access the frame buffer directly. If you recall, I discussed the `pixels` member of `SDL_Surface` earlier, so you know that it is a pointer to the pixel data for the surface. This member is how you will access individual pixels on a surface.

Of course, it is never that simple (at least not in every case). Depending on where your surface exists (either in the video memory or the main memory), you may or may not have to lock the surface. Because of how SDL works, the actual surface format might be different than the surface format you see from the programming end (in other words, when SDL accommodates you with an impossible pixel format that doesn't exist on any video card).

When you want to do direct manipulation of pixel data on a surface, you go through a number of steps.

1. Determine whether the surface needs to be locked.
2. Lock the surface if necessary.
3. Manipulate the pixel data.
4. Unlock the surface if necessary.

Step 1 is rather easy. To determine whether a surface needs to be locked, you use the SDL_MUSTLOCK macro. If you had a surface pointer named pSurface, this is what it would look like.

```
if(SDL_MUSTLOCK(pSurface))
{
     //surface needs to be locked
}
```

If you do need to lock the surface, you use the SDL_LockSurface function, shown here.

```
int SDL_LockSurface(SDL_Surface *surface);
```

This function takes a single parameter (surface) that is a pointer to an SDL_Surface. The value returned will be 0 if the function is successful and -1 if it failed and could not lock the surface.

You then manipulate any pixel data that you want and follow it with a call to SDL_UnlockSurface.

```
void SDL_UnlockSurface(SDL_Surface *surface);
```

This function returns no value and takes a single parameter, a pointer to an SDL_Surface.

NOTE

Calls to SDL_LockSurface and SDL_UnlockSurface are recursive. If you call SDL_LockSurface three times in succession, you then need to call SDL_UnlockSurface three times in succession, or the surface will remain locked.

Now that you know how to lock and unlock a surface, you can expand on our little object lesson with pSurface.

```
//lock surface if needed
if(SDL_MUSTLOCK(pSurface)) SDL_LockSurface(pSurface);
//manipulate pixels here
//unlock surface if needed
if(SDL_MUSTLOCK(pSurface)) SDL_UnlockSurface(pSurface);
```

Naturally, you will want to do some error checking during the call to SDL_LockSurface, but for brevity I left it out.

> **CAUTION**
>
> **Calling `SDL_LockSurface` might, depending on which surface is being locked, cause certain system locks, so you should avoid any system calls when a lock is occurring. You should spend as little time as possible with a surface locked to avoid system freezes or decreased performance.**

The only thing left is to manipulate the individual pixels. That is the tricky part because a pixel might take up 1, 2, 3, or 4 bytes. Fortunately there is a general solution for writing to any format.

First, you need to get your color into the native pixel format. For this step, you can simply use `SDL_MapRGB`. Sure, you could convert it yourself using the information in the surface's pixel format, but why do that when a perfectly good function already exists?

Second, you need to determine where exactly in the frame buffer the pixel you want to write is. This is easily calculated by y times the pitch of the surface plus x times the bytes per pixel of the surface.

Finally, you need to copy the appropriate number of bytes from the variable storing the color onto the frame buffer. You can accomplish this with a call to `memcpy` from the variable containing the color to the memory location.

Here's how to do it in code.

```
//r,g,b are red, green, and blue components of a color we wish to write
//pSurface is the surface we are writing to
//x and y are the location of the pixel we are writing
//declare the color variable
Uint32 Color;
//convert color
Color=SDL_MapRGB(pSurface->format,r,g,b);
//pointer that we can modify
char* pData;
//grab the frame buffer
pData=(char*)pSurface->pixels;
//vertical offset
pData+=(y*pSurface->pitch);
//horizontal offset
```

```
pData+=(x*pSurface->format->BytesPerPixel);
//copy color
memcpy(pData,&Color,pSurface->format->BytesPerPixel);
```

If you want to see this code in action, you can load the project on the CD called FOSDL3_4. This example operates for the most part identically to the random rectangles example, except that the rectangle-making code has been replaced with pixel-plotting code. For a peek at what FOSDL3_4 looks like, refer to Figure 3.7.

Figure 3.7 *The output of FOSDL3_4*

If you can set one pixel, you can set a thousand pixels…or 100,000 pixels. You can draw lines, ellipses, boxes, polygons, and anything else because everything is made up of pixels. Of course, you won't get any help from SDL, but there are tons and tons of resources on the Internet and in other books that explain the algorithms for drawing any old graphical primitive you could ever want.

Blitting

The third method of creating graphics with SDL is by blitting. The word "blit" comes from the words "Block Transfer"—in the past it was typically abbreviated BLT (hold the tomato). Because BLT has no vowels in it, it was unpronounceable, so insert an "i" to make the word "blit" and continue on with life.

In order to blit, you need two surfaces (one source and one destination) and two rectangles (one each for the source and destination). Once you've got this information, you can call `SDL_BlitSurface`.

```
int SDL_BlitSurface(SDL_Surface *src, SDL_Rect *srcrect, SDL_Surface
*dst, SDL_Rect *dstrect);
```

This function takes four parameters—a pointer to the source surface (`src`), a pointer to the source rectangle (`srcrect`), a pointer to the destination surface (`dst`), and a pointer to the destination rectangle (`dstrect`). Note that `srcrect` and `dstrect` do not necessarily have to point to rectangles that are the same size (in other words, the same width and height), and these parameters can be `NULL` to indicate that the entire surface is to be used either as the source or the destination.

The return value of `SDL_BlitSurface` is an `int`. If the return value is 0, then everything is cool. If the return value is -1, there is an error; if it is –2, one of the surfaces is in video memory, which was lost, and you need to restore it.

On to another example, this time demonstrating blitting. The full code for this example is under FOSDL3_5 in the Examples folder on the CD. As usual, the code below is stripped of commenting and error checking to save space.

```
#include "sdl.h"
#include <stdlib.h>
const int SCREEN_WIDTH=640;
const int SCREEN_HEIGHT=480;
SDL_Surface* g_pDisplaySurface = NULL;
SDL_Surface* g_pBitmapSurface = NULL;
SDL_Event g_Event;
SDL_Rect g_SrcRect,g_DstRect;
int main(int argc, char* argv[])
{
     SDL_Init(SDL_INIT_VIDEO);
     g_pDisplaySurface = SDL_SetVideoMode(SCREEN_WIDTH,
          SCREEN_HEIGHT, 0, SDL_ANYFORMAT);
     g_pBitmapSurface=SDL_LoadBMP("ball.bmp");
     g_SrcRect.w=g_DstRect.w=g_pBitmapSurface->w;
```

```
	g_SrcRect.h=g_DstRect.h=g_pBitmapSurface->h;
	g_SrcRect.x=g_SrcRect.y=0;
	for(;;)
	{
		if(SDL_PollEvent(&g_Event)==0)
		{
			g_DstRect.x=rand()%(SCREEN_WIDTH-g_DstRect.w);
			g_DstRect.y=rand()%(SCREEN_HEIGHT-g_DstRect.h);
			SDL_BlitSurface(g_pBitmapSurface,
			&g_SrcRect,g_pDisplaySurface,
				&g_DstRect);
			SDL_UpdateRect(g_pDisplaySurface,0,0,0,0);
		}
		else
		{
			if(g_Event.type==SDL_QUIT) break;
		}
	}
	return(0);
}
```

As you might imagine, this example blits an image of a ball (stored in a file named ball.bmp) to random locations on the screen. After a couple of seconds, the screen looks something like Figure 3.8.

Color Keys (Transparency)

As you saw in example FOSDL3_5, the default behavior of `SDL_BlitSurface` is to simply copy a rectangular block of pixels from one surface to another. However, that is typically not good enough. More often than not, you'll have portions of the image that should be invisible when you blit, thus leaving that pixel unchanged when blitting occurs. This is done by setting a transparent color key. You can select a single color that will be ignored when blitting from one surface to another. A good color to choose is magenta (full red and full blue, no green) because it is not often used. In the image used for FOSDL3_5, the transparent pixels are represented by black.

To set a color key, you use the `SDL_SetColorKey` function, yet another SDL function that is named for exactly what it does.

```
int SDL_SetColorKey(SDL_Surface *surface, Uint32 flag, Uint32 key);
```

This function returns an `int`. In typical SDL style, 0 means success and -1 means an error. The function has three parameters—a pointer to the surface for which you are setting the color key (`surface`), a set of flags (`flag`), and a value to use as the transparent color (`key`).

There are two different flags that you can use in the `flag` parameter. One is `SDL_SRCCOLORKEY`, and the other is `SDL_RLEACCEL`. The `SDL_RLEACCEL` flag is not used by itself, so you have three different values that you can pass in the `flag` parameter: `0`, `SDL_SRCCOLORKEY`, and `SDL_SRCCOLORKEY | SDL_RLEACCEL`.

If you pass a 0, then any color key you might have had on that surface will be cleared. If you pass `SDL_SRCCOLORKEY`, the key holds the value that will be set as the transparent color. The color has to be in the native pixel format, so it is a good idea to use `SDL_MapRGB` here. If you pass `SDL_SRCCOLORKEY | SDL_RLEACCEL`, you set the color key and set up the surface to use RLE (*Run Length Encoded*) acceleration. (In other words, you encode the image so it blits faster by skipping over transparent pixels.)

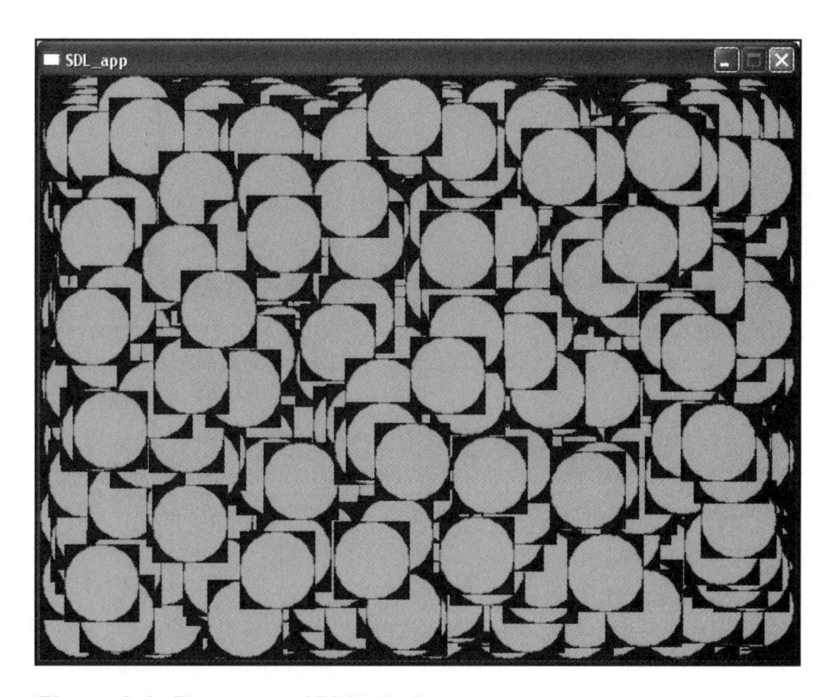

Figure 3.8 *The output of FOSDL3_5*

Just so you can see the difference, take a look at FOSDL3_6 on the CD. It is virtually identical to FOSDL3_5; I only added a single line to the program to set the color key. Because it is so similar, I'm not putting the full source in the book. The only difference is the following line, added right after the line that loads the image of the ball.

```
SDL_SetColorKey(g_pBitmapSurface,SDL_SRCCOLORKEY,0);
```

This one line makes a big difference, as you can see in Figure 3.9.

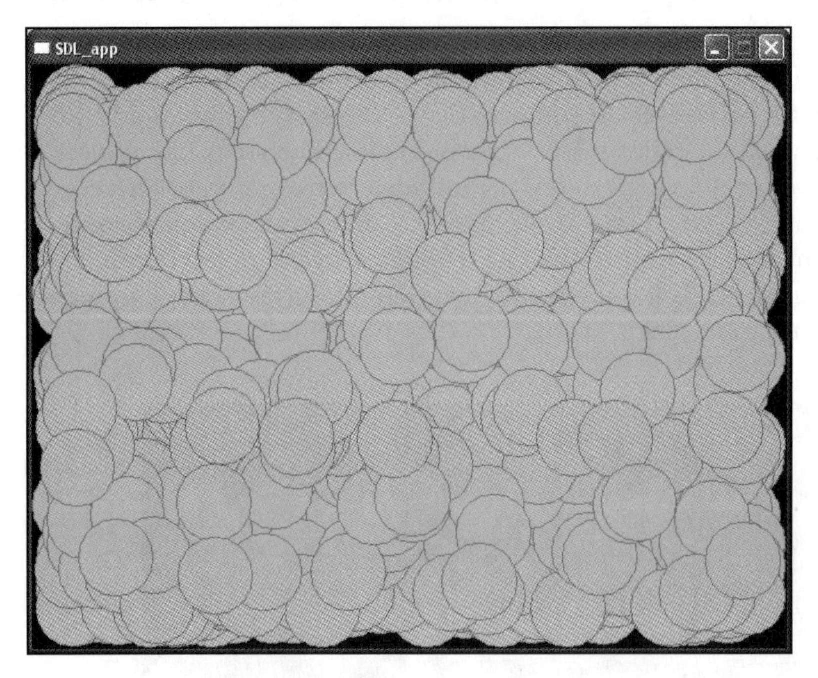

Figure 3.9 *The output of FOSDL3_6*

If you ever need to know whether the source color key is set for a surface, you can examine the `flags` member of the `SDL_Surface` representing it. `SDL_SRCCOLORKEY` will be present if there is a color key. Similarly, `SDL_RLEACCEL` will be present if you specified RLE acceleration. If `SDL_SRCCOLORKEY` is present, the color key member of the surface's pixel format will have the color key.

Clipping Output

It is quite likely that there will come a time when you need to write graphics only to a certain portion of the screen, while keeping the area around it free of graphics. SDL can help you with this. You can write to the entire screen (or the entire window, if you are running in windowed mode), but you can specify any rectangular area as the only area to which you can write until you set another rectangular area. This is quite useful if, for example, you have some sort of status panel on one side of the screen, and the rest of the screen is used for the game's play area.

In any case, this is something you should know how to do even if you never use it. To set a single rectangular area as your output area on a surface, you call the `SDL_SetClipRect` function. `ClipRect` is short for "Clipping Rectangle."

```
void SDL_SetClipRect(SDL_Surface *surface, SDL_Rect *rect);
```

This function returns no value. It takes two parameters—a pointer to a surface for which you are setting the clipping area (`surface`) and a pointer to a rectangle that describes the clipping rectangle (`rect`). If you use `NULL` for `rect`, the entire area of the surface will be the new clipping area.

The clipping area only affects blitting operations that use the surface as the destination. Color fills and pixel plotting are unaffected. To retrieve the clipping rectangle of a surface, you use the `SDL_GetClipRect` function.

```
void SDL_GetClipRect(SDL_Surface *surface, SDL_Rect *rect);
```

This has the same parameter list as `SDL_SetClipRect` except that in this case, `rect` is filled in with the current clipping rectangle used by the surface.

> **TIP**
>
> **It's okay to set a clipping area that exceeds the bounds of a surface because SDL will fix it so the clipping rectangle fits entirely on the surface.**

Here is another quick example, built from FOSDL3_6. The new example can be found in FOSDL3_7; it contains an addition of only a few lines.

```
g_ClipRect.x=32;
g_ClipRect.y=32;
g_ClipRect.w=SCREEN_WIDTH-64;
g_ClipRect.h=SCREEN_HEIGHT-64;
SDL_SetClipRect(g_pDisplaySurface,&g_ClipRect);
```

Essentially, this rectangle chops off 32 pixels from each edge of the display surface. The output of FOSDL3_7 looks like Figure 3.10.

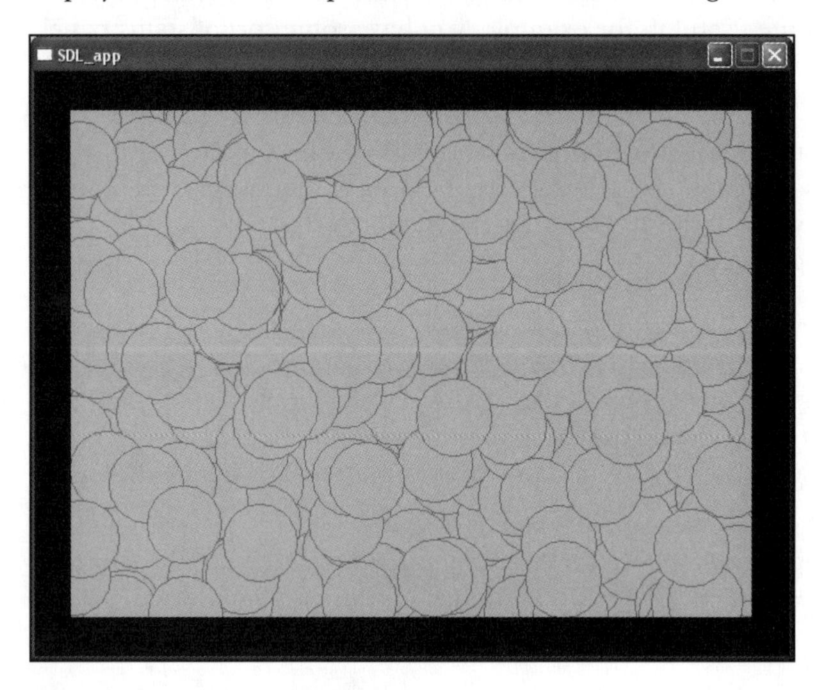

Figure 3.10 *The output of FOSDL3_7*

Other Topics

At this point, you have all of the basics for SDL's video subsystem. However, I glossed over some of the less fundamental aspects of the subsystem, and this is the part of the chapter where I will rectify that. The next few topics don't really have much to do with one another, but I would be remiss not to cover them because they are part of the subsystem.

Palettes

I briefly mentioned palettes when I covered SDL_PixelFormat. Palettes are a way of using color indirection for 8-bit surfaces.

In the age of video cards capable of 32 bits per pixel at good speeds, you might wonder why in the world you would ever limit yourself to 256 colors. There are a number of reasons.

First, even though video hardware gets better each year, a surface that has 32 bits per pixel takes up four times as much memory as one that only has 8 bits per pixel, so you can copy the same size 8-bit surface in a quarter of the time it would take you to transfer the 32-bit surface. To rephrase: 8-bit surfaces take up less space and transfer quicker. However, depending on the architecture, the hardware might actually transfer 32-bits *faster* than 8-bits in some cases!

Second, there are some devices, most notably laptops and handhelds but also older hardware, that just do better with 8 bits per pixel. If you are developing mass-market games, you don't want to limit your market.

Third, 8-bit surfaces are the only way to achieve certain cool effects. I'm talking about palette animation, otherwise known as color cycling. You can create the illusion of movement without blitting a single pixel just by switching colors around in the palette.

Of course, there are the downsides, the big one being that you only have 256 colors with which to work. This not only limits the number of colors on the screen, but it also makes it difficult to generate art.

In any case, a palette in SDL is represented by an SDL_Palette structure, which looks like this:

```
typedef struct{
  int ncolors;
  SDL_Color *colors;
} SDL_Palette;
```

This structure is quite simple. The two members are ncolors, which contains an int that specifies how many colors are in the palette (typically 256, but you could make your own smaller palettes for switching out colors) and colors, which is a pointer to an array of SDL_Color variables. These SDL_Color variables contain all of the colors in the palette.

To create a surface that has a palette, you need to specify 8 bits per pixel during the creation of that surface. If you are working in full-screen mode, you will also want to use the SDL_HWPALETTE flag because it will give you better control over the colors in the palette. Here's why: If the desktop is running in an 8-bit mode, the operating system typically reserves a handful of colors so it can display itself properly. In Windows, this handful is 20 colors—the first and last ten in the palette. That leaves 236 colors that you can set in the physical palette and remain "Windows safe." However, there is also a logical palette that consists of 256 colors that you can use on your surface. When it comes time to display the surface, the colors in the logical palette will map onto the closest color in the physical palette and be shown in that color.

Sound like a pain in the butt? It is. If you are stuck using palettes and you plan to have your game run in a window, you have your work cut out for you. I suggest that if you need to use palettes, you also use full-screen.

If you have a surface with a palette, you'll need to know how to set the colors in that palette. SDL has two functions for this; the first is SDL_SetPalette.

```
int SDL_SetPalette(SDL_Surface *surface, int flags, SDL_Color *colors,
int firstcolor, int ncolors);
```

This function returns an int. If SDL was able to set all of the colors as specified in the function call, it will return 1. If it was unable to set all of the colors, it will return 0. In the case of SDL_SetPalette, a returned value of 0 is not necessarily an error—it means that it couldn't set all of the colors, but it did set as many as it could. If you specified SDL_HWPALETTE, this function will always return 1. If you are trying to call this function on a non-8-bit surface, it will naturally return 0.

The first parameter (surface) is a pointer to a surface for which you are setting palette colors. The second parameter (flags) is one or both of SDL_LOGPAL (logical palette) and SDL_PHYSPAL (physical palette). These two flags can be combined. The third parameter (colors) is a pointer to an array of SDL_Color values. The fourth parameter (firstcolor) is the first color in the palette you want to set. Finally, the last parameter (ncolors) is how many colors you want to set.

The other function you can use to set colors in a palette is called SDL_SetColors.

```
int SDL_SetColors(SDL_Surface *surface, SDL_Color *colors, int first-
color, int ncolors);
```

As you can see, this function looks very much like `SDL_SetPalette`, with only the `flags` parameter missing. In fact, other than that, the operation of this function is identical to `SDL_SetPalette`, with an assumed `flags` value of `SDL_LOGPAL|SDL_PHYSPAL`. If you are in full-screen mode with `SDL_HWPALETTE` set, there is no reason not to use `SDL_SetColors`, but if you really like typing you can always use `SDL_SetPalette`.

Here is a quick example of using palettes. The example is named FOSDL3_8 on the CD and can be found in the usual place. This example sets a full-screen 640×480 8-bit mode, sets up a grayscale palette, and then draws a number of filled rectangles—one of each color.

For the most part, this example is identical to the others you've seen in this chapter. The only difference is the setup of the palette and the drawing of the rectangles, which is shown here.

```
//set up colors
int index;//loop variable
for(index=0;index<256;index++)
{
    //make a shade of gray
    g_PaletteColors[index].r=index;
    g_PaletteColors[index].g=index;
    g_PaletteColors[index].b=index;
}
//set the palette
SDL_SetColors(g_pDisplaySurface,g_PaletteColors,0,256);

//do color fills
SDL_Rect FillRect;
for(index=0;index<256;index++)
{
    FillRect.x=index;
    FillRect.y=index;
    FillRect.w=SCREEN_WIDTH-index;
    FillRect.h=SCREEN_HEIGHT-index;
    SDL_FillRect(g_pDisplaySurface,&FillRect,index);
}
//update the screen
SDL_UpdateRect(g_pDisplaySurface,0,0,0,0);
```

In an ideal world I would show you what this looks like here, but 8-bit surfaces being what they are, the screen captures are almost always garbled. If you want to see this example, you'll have to run it.

That's really about it for palettes. It's all about how to make a surface with one and how to manipulate the colors.

Updating the Display

All along, you have used SDL_UpdateRect to update the screen without really understanding why you are doing so. SDL has two basic ways to deal with screen updates. One is dirty rectangle screen updates (in which you use a function like SDL_UpdateRect), and the other is double buffering (which is used in full-screen mode).

In dirty rectangle updates (the default for SDL), you can specify one or more rectangles that you want to have updated. You can do this with one of two functions—SDL_UpdateRect or SDL_UpdateRects. Yes, the "s" makes a difference.

```
void SDL_UpdateRect(SDL_Surface *screen, Sint32 x, Sint32 y, Sint32 w,
Sint32 h);
void SDL_UpdateRects(SDL_Surface *screen, int numrects, SDL_Rect *rects);
```

In SDL_UpdateRect, there are five parameters. First is a pointer to the surface you want to update (screen), followed by x, y, w, and h, which describe the single rectangle you want to update. If these four values are 0, the entire surface is updated (which is what you have been doing so far).

In SDL_UpdateRects, there are only three parameters. The first (screen) is again a pointer to a surface. The second (numrects) is how many rectangles are in the array pointed to by the third parameter (rects). Those rectangles are updated for the surface. This is a good function to use if only certain portions of the screen have actually changed since the last update. There is no combining of rectangles when you use this function. The rectangles in the list are totally up to you, so if you overdraw a number of times you only have yourself to blame when your performance drops.

Finally, there is SDL_Flip. This is intended for use with full-screen double-buffered modes (in other words, modes set with SDL_DOUBLEBUF as one of the flags). However, because SDL aims to please, calling SDL_Flip when you're not double buffering simply calls SDL_UpdateRect (screen, 0, 0, 0, 0), so it's not a requirement to double buffer.

```
int SDL_Flip(SDL_Surface *screen);
```

Unlike SDL_UpdateRect and SDL_UpdateRects, this function returns a value. If it is successful, it returns 0. If it fails, it returns -1. The only parameter is a pointer to a surface (screen).

If you are double buffering, you will typically want to update the entire screen every frame prior to calling SDL_Flip—in other words, completely redraw the entire screen. If you are not using double buffering, you can just redraw those portions of the screen that need it prior to updating.

Alpha Blending

And now for perhaps the most attractive feature of SDL—alpha blending. Even if hardware support for alpha blending doesn't exist, SDL will do its best to emulate it for you. Naturally anything emulated will be a bit slower, but the fact is that SDL will do it for you so you don't have to implement it yourself.

In case you are unfamiliar with what alpha blending is, it's a way of doing translucent blitting. This is useful for a variety of effects, including glass, ghost images, teleporter effects, fading out a defeated enemy, and just about anything else you can imagine. It also has a decent "wow" factor for the user of your application. If something slowly fades out rather than just disappearing instantly, it looks much cooler.

Alpha values range from 0% to 100%, with the actual values based on how the alpha is being done. At 0%, which means zero literally, the blit will be completely transparent. At 100%, the blit will be completely opaque (just like the blits we have done in this chapter).

Essentially, the mathematics behind an alpha blend look like the following equation.

```
(Resulting_Color)=(Alpha)*(Source_Color)+(1.0-Alpha)*(Destination_Color)
```

This equation works based on Alpha being between 0.0 (0%) and 1.0 (100%). When you are using byte values (as you do in SDL), 0 is 0% and 255 is 100% or 1.0.

You can do alpha blits in one of two ways. You can specify a single alpha value for an entire surface or you can specify an alpha value for each pixel on the surface.

Per-Surface Alpha

To specify a per-surface alpha value, you simply need to call SDL_SetAlpha.

```
int SDL_SetAlpha(SDL_Surface *surface, Uint32 flag, Uint8 alpha);
```

If this function looks familiar, don't be surprised. It is essentially the same layout as SDL_SetColorKey. The return value of this function is an int. It will be 0 if it is successful and -1 if it fails. The first parameter (surface) is the surface for which you are setting a single alpha value. The second parameter (flag) is any combination of SDL_SRCALPHA and SDL_RLEACCEL. If SDL_SRCALPHA is present, an alpha value for the surface will be set. If it is not present, the alpha value for the surface will be cleared. If SDL_RLEACCEL is ored with SDL_SRCALPHA, the surface will be optimized for run length encoded acceleration (which is much the same as using SDL_RLEACCEL with a color key).

The third parameter (alpha) is an alpha value to use for the surface. It ranges from 0 to 255. You can also use SDL_ALPHA_TRANSPARENT for 0 and SDL_ALPHA_OPAQUE for 255. Another important value is 128, which has special optimizations compared to other values.

To examine whether or not a surface has an alpha value, check the flags member of SDL_Surface. If SDL_SRCALPHA is present, the alpha member of the surface's pixel format will be the per-surface alpha value.

And now for a quick example using per-surface alpha values. You can find this example under FOSDL3_9 in the Examples directory on the CD. This example is essentially the same as FOSDL3_6 (the color-keyed blitting demo) except that the surface with the ball image is given a random per-surface alpha value before it gets blitted. You can see the output of this example program in Figure 3.11.

This little example also demonstrates that you can use per-surface alpha values with color keys. This is not required, of course.

Per-Pixel Alpha

For more control over your alpha values, you can create surfaces that have a per-pixel alpha value. You can do this using either

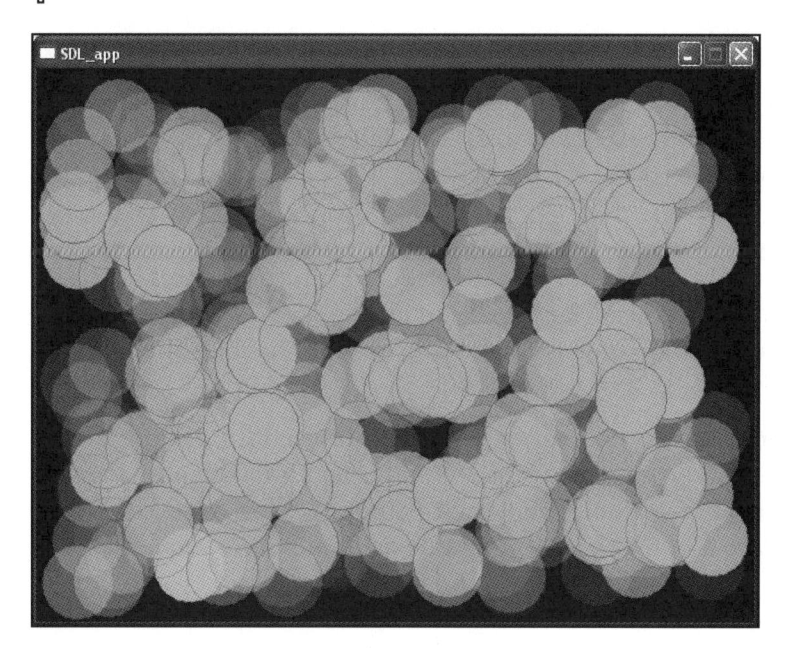

Figure 3.11 *The output of FOSDL3_9*

SDL_CreateRGBSurface or SDL_CreateRGBSurfaceFrom. Simply put some sort of alpha mask into the Amask parameters. This will cause the SDL_SRCALPHA flag to be set automatically.

Once you have created a surface with an alpha mask, you can lock it and set individual pixels much as you did with the non-alpha surface except that instead of using SDL_MapRGB to create a native pixel value, you must use SDL_MapRGBA. Also, instead of using SDL_GetRGB to unpack the pixel, you use SDL_GetRGBA. Both prototypes, shown here, operate much like you would expect them to (in other words, they work almost identically to SDL_MapRGB and SDL_GetRGB, with the addition of the alpha channel).

```
Uint32 SDL_MapRGBA(SDL_PixelFormat *fmt, Uint8 r, Uint8 g, Uint8 b,
Uint8 a);
void SDL_GetRGBA(Uint32 pixel, SDL_PixelFormat *fmt, Uint8 *r, Uint8
*g, Uint8 *b, Uint8 *a);
```

If you use per-pixel alpha values for your surfaces, you cannot use a color key or a per-surface alpha value. That's okay, though, because with per-pixel alpha, you can simply specify an alpha value of 0 for the transparent pixels.

Optimizing Alpha Surfaces

There is one last really handy function that deals with alpha surfaces (as well as with color-keyed surfaces). It is called SDL_DisplayFormatAlpha, and it is shown here.

```
SDL_Surface *SDL_DisplayFormatAlpha(SDL_Surface *surface);
```

This function takes a pointer to a surface and returns a pointer to a surface. (The returned surface is created in the process.) The pointer you get out is not the same as the pointer you put in. This function works very much like SDL_DisplayFormat.

The function creates a new surface that is optimized for blitting to the display surface, but the new surface contains an alpha channel based on a per-pixel alpha value, a per-surface alpha value, a color key, or a combination of a per-surface alpha value and a color key. Essentially, it takes a surface on which you are using alpha or a color key and creates a surface that can be blitted to the display more quickly.

If you use this function on a surface with a color key, all of the transparent pixels get an alpha value of 0 and all of the non-transparent pixels get an alpha value of 255. If you do a lot of alpha-based rendering, you'll probably get a lot of mileage out of SDL_DisplayFormatAlpha.

Overlays

And now we come to the part on overlays. An overlay is used to render data from a video file (such as an .mpg) onto a surface. Video data is formatted completely differently from surfaces, and the SDL_Overlay structure exists so you can easily draw this data onto surfaces.

First, take a look at the SDL_Overlay structure, shown here.

```
typedef struct{
  Uint32 format;
  int w, h;
  int planes;
  Uint16 *pitches;
  Uint8 **pixels;
  Uint32 hw_overlay:1;
} SDL_Overlay;
```

The first member (format) is unlike a surface's format in that it is only a single Uint32 value, specifying one of the flags shown in Table 3.3.

Table 3.3 Overlay Formats

Constant	Value	Meaning
SDL_YV12_OVERLAY	0x32315659	Planar mode: Y+V+U
SDL_IYUV_OVERLAY	0x56555949	Planar mode: Y+U+V
SDL_YUY2_OVERLAY	0x32595559	Packed mode: Y0+U0+Y1+V0
SDL_UYVY_OVERLAY	0x59565955	Packed mode: U0+Y0+V0+Y1
SDL_YVYU_OVERLAY	0x55595659	Packed mode: Y0+V0+Y1+U0

Of course, none of these constants will mean anything to you until you have a good understanding of how the various YUV formats work. Because this is the only portion of the book dedicated to overlays, I suggest that you take a gander at http://www.webartz.com/fourcc/indexyuv.htm if this topic interests you. There you will find everything you ever wanted to know about YUV formats. Typically, the format you use will depend on the sort of media from which you are rendering. You will have to research the format that you are using.

The `w` and `h` members of `SDL_Overlay` are the width and height. It's good that at least a few members of this structure are at least somewhat familiar, right?

The `planes` member specifies how many bit planes there are for this overlay. The number of planes depends on which format is being used. Think of planes as individual images that, when taken together, make up the full image.

The `pitches` member is an array that stores the pitch for each plane. Naturally, there is one pitch for each plane, demonstrating yet again that each plane is like its own image.

The `pixels` member is an array of pointers for the planes. There is one pointer for each `plane`, and a `pitch` corresponds to each pixel pointer.

And finally there is a bit flag named hw_overlay. It will be 1 if the overlay exists in hardware and 0 if it does not. Naturally, an overlay in video memory will perform better than an overlay not in video memory, but as far as programming is concerned there is really no difference in your code.

Creating an Overlay

Creating an overlay is rather easy. You simply call SDL_CreateYUVOverlay.

```
SDL_Overlay *SDL_CreateYUVOverlay(int width, int height, Uint32 format,
SDL_Surface *display);
```

This function returns a pointer to an SDL_Overlay. If you get a NULL returned, there was an error. There are four parameters. The first two (width and height) are the width and height of the overlay. (I know that comes as a shock to you.) The third parameter (format) is one of the format constants found in Table 3.3. The last parameter (display) is a pointer to a surface on which this overlay will be rendered.

Destroying an Overlay

On the flip side, to destroy an overlay (or rather, to free it), you use the SDL_FreeYUVOverlay function.

```
void SDL_FreeYUVOverlay(SDL_Overlay *overlay);
```

This function returns no value and takes as its sole parameter a pointer to an overlay created using SDL_CreateYUVOverlay.

Locking and Unlocking an Overlay

As you can see, overlays behave very much like surfaces; you just use different functions to work with them. This goes for accessing the data within the overlay's planes, too. To access an overlay's pixel data (either for writing or reading), you must first lock it, then do whatever accessing you need to do, and then unlock it.

The functions for locking and unlocking are aptly named SDL_LockYUVOverlay and SDL_UnlockYUVOverlay, respectively.

```
int SDL_LockYUVOverlay(SDL_Overlay *overlay);
void SDL_UnlockYUVOverlay(SDL_Overlay *overlay);
```

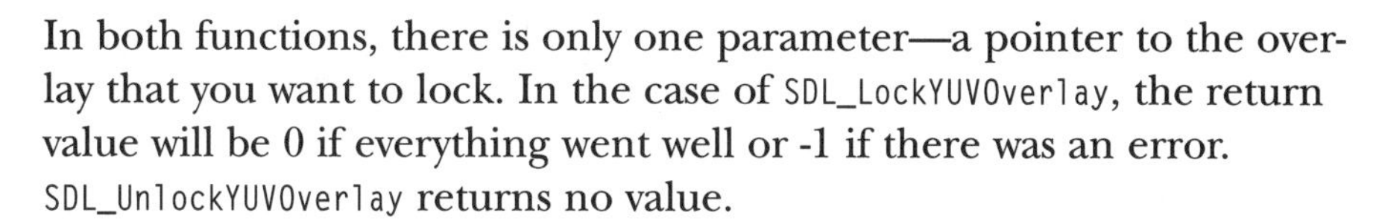

In both functions, there is only one parameter—a pointer to the overlay that you want to lock. In the case of SDL_LockYUVOverlay, the return value will be 0 if everything went well or -1 if there was an error. SDL_UnlockYUVOverlay returns no value.

Between the calls to SDL_LockYUVOverlay and SDL_UnlockYUVOverlay, you manipulate the planes however you want by accessing one of the pointers stored in the pixels member of the SDL_Overlay structure. Just like with surfaces, you must pay attention to the pitch of the plane, stored in the pitches array of the SDL_Overlay structure.

Drawing an Overlay

And finally, you would probably like to be able to draw the overlay onto the surface that you indicated during the call to SDL_CreateYUVOverlay. You do this using SDL_DisplayYUVOverlay.

```
int SDL_DisplayYUVOverlay(SDL_Overlay *overlay, SDL_Rect *dstrect);
```

This function returns 0 if it was successful, as stated in the SDL documentation. Ergo, you can assume that a non-zero return value must be an error. That would be my assumption, anyway. The documentation doesn't say either way.

While in-depth coverage of using overlays is beyond the scope of this book, I have written a simple example program using overlays called FOSDL3_10, which you can find on the CD. It creates an overlay that each frame fills with random data. The overlay is then displayed, resulting in kind of a TV snow effect. Because the machine I am working on has hardware overlays, I was unable to provide a figure for this example.

Checking Video Modes

If you plan to create full-screen applications with SDL (and I think it is highly likely that you will at some point), you might find it useful to check the availability of a particular resolution or to grab a list of modes with a particular number of bits per pixel.

If you already have a particular resolution in mind (say 640×480 with 16 bits per pixel), you can use the SDL_VideoModeOK function.

```
int SDL_VideoModeOK(int width, int height, int bpp, Uint32 flags);
```

The first three parameters (width, height, and bpp) are for the width, height, and bits per pixel on which you are checking. The final flags parameter contains the flags you want to use during the call to SDL_SetVideoMode.

If the return value is 0, there is no mode that indicates the height and width. If it is not 0, then the returned value is the number of bits per pixel that is the closest to the value given in bpp (which is often the same value).

As long as you stick to common sizes (640×480, 800×600, and 1024×768) and common bits-per-pixel values (8 and 16), you probably won't need to use SDL_VideoModeOK.

Checking individual modes is fine in some circumstances, but in others you might want to look at a list of display modes based on a particular pixel format. To do this, you use SDL_ListModes.

```
SDL_Rect **SDL_ListModes(SDL_PixelFormat *format, Uint32 flags);
```

This function takes a pointer to an SDL_PixelFormat (called format) and a Uint32 called flags (the same sort of flags as you would use during a call to SDL_SetVideoMode). If the format parameter is NULL, SDL will use the format currently used on the display.

The return value can be 0, meaning that no resolutions use that pixel format, or –1, indicating that any resolution can be used with that format. If the value is anything else, it is a list of pointers to SDL_Rects that shows the various resolutions that you can use with that format. This list is terminated by a NULL value and is sorted from largest to smallest.

Gamma

We've had alpha, there is no beta, so now we've got gamma. Video hardware abounds with Greek letters. Adjusting gamma values, when the hardware supports it, can create some interesting effects. Unfortunately, you cannot rely on gamma support being present, and this is one of the few things that SDL does not emulate.

What is gamma? Put simply, it adjusts each color channel and each value in the channel in whatever way you want. Suppose you wanted to create a negative image. You could do it pixel by pixel and set the red value to (255 - current red), the green value to (255 - current green), and the blue value to (255 - current blue). Or you could set up a gamma ramp (essentially a table of values) that maps a 0 in green to a 255 in green, a 255 in green to a 0 in green, and likewise all of the other shades of green to the appropriate negative values. You could then do the same thing for red and blue. You would not have to change the image at all.

Similarly, you could fade to white by slowly increasing the gamma values for red, green, and blue, and by decreasing fade to black. A gamma ramp is very much like using a palette for each color channel.

This all probably sounds confusing and weird, so take a look at a function for doing this and then I'll show you an example, which will make everything clear.

If you want a particular ratio to be applied equally to each value in a color channel, you can use `SDL_SetGamma`.

```
int SDL_SetGamma(float redgamma, float greengamma, float bluegamma);
```

Each of these parameter values is a floating point. There is one parameter for each of the red, green, and blue channels. These values work as multipliers, so if you specify 1.0, it means you want colors in that channel to be shown normally. If you specify 0.5, you want them diminished by 50%; if you specify 2.0, you want them doubled. Naturally, you can't get any redder than a full red of 255; the same is true for green and blue, so all values higher than 255 are treated as 255.

Now for a short example. You can find it in the Examples folder of the CD-ROM under FOSDL3_11. It is a simple example that sets a full-screen mode (640×480 at 16 bits per pixel), sets the screen to be filled with random pixels, then fades to black and back again, over and over. If your hardware doesn't support gamma it will quit almost immediately, reporting the lack of gamma support to stdout.txt.

If you want to be more hard core about your gamma values, you can use `SDL_SetGammaRamp` instead.

```
int SDL_SetGammaRamp(Uint16 *redtable, Uint16 *greentable, Uint16
*bluetable);
```

In this function, instead of setting a single multiplier value, you send three pointers to `Uint16` arrays. Each pointer must point to an array of 256 `Uint16` values. If this function fails, the return value will be -1, meaning that gamma is not supported. Using this function, you could easily create a negative image. If you want a particular color channel's lookup table to remain unchanged, you can simply specify NULL for that channel.

If you are interested in seeing what the current gamma ramp looks like, you can use SDL_GetGammaRamp.

```
int SDL_GetGammaRamp(Uint16 *redtable, Uint16 *greentable, Uint16
*bluetable);
```

This function behaves almost identically to SDL_SetGammaRamp except that the pointers passed retrieve the values of the current gamma ramp rather than setting them. If a -1 is returned, there is no gamma support.

Cursors

You have probably noticed that when an SDL application is running, there is a default cursor that looks a little different than the standard Windows cursor. If you haven't noticed this, then by all means run an SDL application now and take a look at it. Go ahead…I'll wait.

As you can see, it looks like a negative of the standard Windows cursor. Naturally, SDL has functions you can use to change the appearance of the cursor.

In theory, this means I have to introduce you to a new structure called SDL_Cursor. However, because of the various ways in which the different platforms treat cursors, the only way to refer to an SDL_Cursor is through a pointer. You never actually deal with anything inside the structure.

To create a cursor, you use SDL_CreateCursor, shown here.

```
SDL_Cursor *SDL_CreateCursor(Uint8 *data, Uint8 *mask, int w, int h,
int hot_x, int hot_y);
```

This function returns a pointer to an SDL_Cursor. The data and mask parameters contain the pixel data for the cursor, but I'll get back to them in just a moment. The w and h parameters are the width and height of the cursor. The width has to be a multiple of eight. Finally, hot_x and hot_y specify the "hot spot" of the cursor (in other words, the portion of the cursor that is actually pointing somewhere).

The data and mask are monochrome representations of the cursor image. A single bit represents one pixel in the cursor (which is why the width of the cursor must be a multiple of 8). Therefore, data and mask are two monochrome images that are combined to give you the cursor you want. Each must point to a block of data that is large enough to contain the entire cursor image. The width of a cursor in bytes is equal to the actual width of the cursor divided by 8, and the height is just the value specified for h in the function call. Therefore, the formula for the necessary size of an array is

arraysize = h * w / 8

When a cursor is drawn, the mask is drawn first. If a given bit is 0, then the pixel on screen is left as is. If a given bit is 1, then the pixel is made black.

After the mask has been drawn, the information pointed to by the data is drawn. If the bit is 1, the pixel on the screen is left alone. If the bit is 0, then white is XORed on the screen. If the pixel was already made black by the mask, it will turn out white; otherwise whatever color already existed there will be inverted.

In text form, that explanation is a little difficult to get all in one shot, so a table of values and colors should be helpful (see Table 3.4).

As a short exercise, take an image and convert it into the appropriate data for use as a cursor. In Figure 3.12, the white and black pixels should be those colors when the cursor is being used, and the gray pixels should be transparent. There are no inverted color pixels in this particular image.

The image is 32×32, so the width is okay. I'm going to make the mask first, and then the data. To make the mask, simply look at each pixel.

Table 3.4 Data and Mask Bits for Cursors

Data Bit	Mask Bit	Color
0	0	Original color (transparent pixel)
0	1	White
1	0	Inverted original color
1	1	Black

Figure 3.12 *An example cursor*

If it is intended to be transparent or inverted, place a 0 for that pixel. Otherwise, place a 1.

```
00000000000000111000000000000000
00000000001111111111000000000000
00000000111111111111110000000000
00000001111111111111111100000000
00000111110000111000011111000000
00001111100000111000001111100000
00001110000000111000000011100000
00011100000000111000000001110000
00111100000000111000000001111000
00111000000000111000000000111000
01110000000000111000000000011100
01110000000000111000000000011100
01110000000000000000000000011100
11110000000000000000000000011110
11111111111100000001111111111110
11111111111100000001111111111110
11111111111100000001111111111110
11110000000000000000000000011110
01110000000000000000000000011100
01110000000000111000000000011100
01110000000000111000000000011100
00111000000000111000000000111000
00111100000000111000000001111000
00011100000000111000000001110000
00001110000000111000000011100000
00001111100000111000001111100000
00000111110000111000011111000000
00000001111111111111111100000000
00000000111111111111110000000000
00000000001111111111000000000000
00000000000000111000000000000000
00000000000000000000000000000000
```

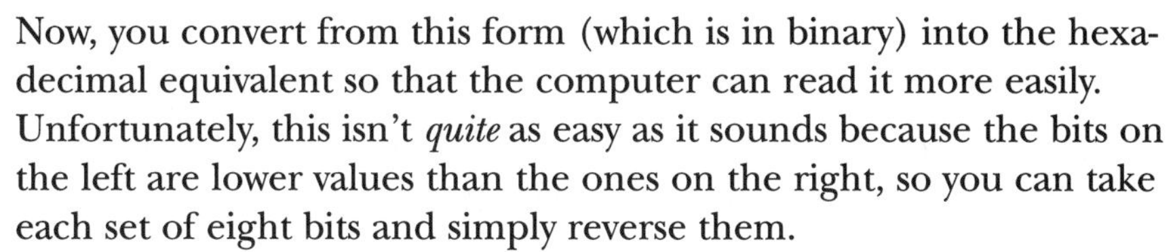

Now, you convert from this form (which is in binary) into the hexadecimal equivalent so that the computer can read it more easily. Unfortunately, this isn't *quite* as easy as it sounds because the bits on the left are lower values than the ones on the right, so you can take each set of eight bits and simply reverse them.

```
00C00100
00FC1F00
00FF7F00
80FFFF00
E0C3E103
F0C1C107
70C00107
38C0010E
3CC0011E
1CC0011C
0EC00138
0EC00138
0E000038
0F000078
FF0FF87F
FF0FF87F
FF0FF87F
0F000078
0E000038
0EC00138
0EC00138
1CC0011C
3CC0011E
38C0010E
70C00107
F0C1C107
E0C3E103
80FFFF00
00FF7F00
00FC1F00
00C00100
00000000
```

Because there are eight hex digits per row, and there are two hex digits per byte, you know that each row takes up four bytes, which easily fit into a `Uint32`. You can now take these values exactly as they are, put `0x` in front of each row, and set up an array of `Uint32` to contain your mask.

Now you can do the same thing for the data layer, except this time you only place a 1 for a black or inverted pixel.

```
00000000000000111000000000000000
00000000001111000111100000000000
00000000110000101000011000000000
00000001001111101111100100000000
00000110010000101000010011000000
00001001100000101000001100100000
00001010000000101000000010100000
00010100000000101000000001010000
00100100000000101000000001001000
00101000000000101000000000101000
01010000000000101000000000010100
01010000000000111000000000010100
01010000000000000000000000010100
10010000000000000000000000010010
10111111111100000001111111111010
10000000000100000001000000000010
10111111111100000001111111111010
10010000000000000000000000010010
01010000000000000000000000010100
01010000000000111000000000010100
01010000000000101000000000010100
00101000000000101000000000101000
00100100000000101000000001001000
00010100000000101000000001010000
00001010000000101000000010100000
00001001100000101000001100100000
00000110010000101000010011000000
00000001001111101111100100000000
00000000110000101000011000000000
00000000001111000111100000000000
00000000000000111000000000000000
00000000000000000000000000000000
```

Next, do the exact same contraction into hexadecimal digits (again, taking each byte backward), like this:

```
00C00100
003C1E00
00436100
807C9F00
```

```
60422103
9041C104
50400105
2840010A
24400112
14400114
0A400128
0AC00128
0A000028
09000048
FD0FF85F
01080840
FD0FF85F
09000048
0A000028
0AC00128
0A400128
14400114
24400112
2840010A
50400105
9041C104
60422103
807C9F00
00436100
003C1E00
00C00100
00000000
```

Now it is time to put this to the test. On the CD you will find an example called FOSDL3_12 that contains a demo program that uses this very cursor. There are a couple of functions in the program that I am about to cover, namely SDL_FreeCursor and SDL_SetCursor.

First, take a look at SDL_FreeCursor. You use this function whenever you no longer need a cursor that you created with SDL_CreateCursor.

```
void SDL_FreeCursor(SDL_Cursor *cursor);
```

This function returns no value and takes a single parameter—a pointer to the SDL_Cursor that you want to free. The function is simple enough, and I will speak no more of it.

The other function used in the example program is SDL_SetCursor. As you might infer from the name, it sets the currently active cursor.

```
void SDL_SetCursor(SDL_Cursor *cursor);
```

This function returns no value and takes a pointer to an SDL_Cursor as its parameter. If the cursor is currently visible, it will immediately change to its new appearance.

If you wanted to grab the current cursor in use in your application, you could use the SDL_GetCursor function.

```
SDL_Cursor *SDL_GetCursor(void);
```

This function takes no parameters and returns a pointer to an SDL_Cursor—the cursor currently in use. This is handy if you only want to switch cursors temporarily and then switch back later.

Finally, you can turn the cursor on and off using SDL_ShowCursor.

```
int SDL_ShowCursor(int toggle);
```

This function takes a single integer value as its parameter, which can be SDL_ENABLE, SDL_DISABLE, or SDL_QUERY. In the case of SDL_ENABLE and SDL_DISABLE, the value sets the visible or invisible state of the cursor. In the case of SDL_QUERY, no change occurs. The function returns the current state of the cursor—either SDL_ENABLE or SDL_DISABLE.

The SDL cursor functions are quite simple. While the cursors are rather primitive (only four values per pixel, one being transparent), they are still useful, especially if you want to change from the standard arrow cursor with which SDL starts. In full-screen mode, though, I imagine you will generally want to emulate your own cursors so that you can have more colors.

Summary

This was a long, long chapter, but for good reason. The video subsystem of SDL provides you with a rich set of functionality with which to generate graphics. This is a good thing, since vision accounts for 70% of most people's sensory input. Because most of the rest of the examples in the book have a heavy graphical basis, it is good that we spent this chapter on the video system.

CHAPTER 4

SDL Event Handling and the Window Manager

While the information concerning the video subsystem in Chapter 3 is what most people consider the most important aspect of a game (and indeed graphics are very important), a game cannot exist unless there is some manner of interaction. In a computer game, this means some form of user input, and in SDL it means event handling. So, arguably, event handling is even more important than graphics. Perhaps "important" isn't the proper word, though. I think a better term would be "fundamental."

This chapter is about two different SDL subsystems. First is the event-handling subsystem, which covers how SDL treats input from various sources. The second is the window manager, a rather small subsystem that is important only if your game runs inside a window. If you are going to create full-screen games every time, the window manager is less of a factor. Nevertheless, I will cover it in this chapter.

The Event-Handling Subsystem at a Glance

First, take a look at SDL's event-handling subsystem. Over the years, I have seen a number of different event-handling schemes, and most of them (especially the WIN32 way of doing it) are a bit kludgy and require way too much type casting. SDL's scheme is the best I have seen, and I think you will like it too.

I will describe briefly what an event is, just so that you and I are both on the same page. (Hah! Page. Get it? You're reading a book, which consists of pages. It's author humor. You're supposed to laugh.)

Anyway, an event is simply something that happens, such as a key press, a key release, or mouse movement. Pretty much anything that occurs to the computer that you might want to react to is an event.

Depending on the event, you will want to know not only what event occurred, but also some extra data about the event to help you decide what to make the program do. For example, when a key is pressed, you want to know not only that a key was pressed, but also which key was pressed.

Types of Events

There are 16 different types of events that you can receive using SDL. For organization and presentation purposes, I've divided these 16 events into four categories—keyboard, mouse, joystick, and system.

Keyboard Events

Keyboard events take two forms—key presses and key releases. There is also a way to set up SDL so that once a key has been pressed, it will periodically repeat the key press event. This is useful if you are making any sort of widget into which the user will input textual data.

In addition to the simple "a key has been pressed" or "a key has been released" data, a keyboard event also contains other information, such as which key has been pressed. This information includes a scan code, a special SDL key identifier, and (optionally) the ASCII or Unicode equivalent for that key. It also contains the shift state of the keyboard, such as whether Shift, Ctrl, or Alt is being held down. You will have all of the information you could possibly need to react to keyboard events.

Mouse Events

The mouse generates three different events. One is a mouse motion event, which occurs any time the mouse is moved. The other two are mouse button events—one for when a mouse button is pressed, and the other for when a mouse button is released.

In a mouse motion event, the extra data includes the current state of the mouse buttons (which is important if you are using the mouse to drag items from one place to another), the position of the mouse, and how far the mouse has moved since the last mouse event.

In mouse button events, the extra data includes which button has changed its state, the state of all of the buttons, and the position at which this button change occurred.

Joystick Events

Although joysticks are covered in Chapter 6, "SDL Joysticks," the events they generate are covered here. Joysticks generate events just like any other input device. They can generate up to five different events, depending on the joystick. These events include axis events, button events (one for a press and one for a release), hat events, and trackball events. Naturally, if the joystick in question doesn't have a hat or trackball, it won't generate those types of events.

Most of the joystick events are quite similar. Since there is no telling how many joysticks a user can have on their system, the extra information with the event always includes which device and which axis, button, hat, or trackball generated the event. Also, there is always a value to which the axis, button, hat, or trackball has changed, and that information is also stored with the joystick event.

System Events

The system events are sort of a catchall category. In this category I have placed those events that do not rely directly on user input, although most of them do depend on it indirectly.

There are six different types of system events, which vary quite widely in their aspects (unlike keyboard, mouse, and joystick events). These events are active, quit, window manager, video resize, video expose, and user events.

Active events deal with systems that can run more than one application at a time, which was difficult to do not long ago, but recently has become a staple of personal computing. Human beings can only really do one thing at a time, so a single application is considered the "active" application and typically has input focus and mouse focus. Having the focus of a particular input device means that only that application will receive data from that input device. Active events occur when an application gains or loses any of these focuses (or foci, depending on how much of a Latin nerd you are).

A *quit event* naturally occurs only when the user quits the application. When SDL is in a windowed environment, a quit event occurs when the user closes the window. In full-screen mode, you have to provide the user with some other way to quit. Quit events have no extra information stored with them.

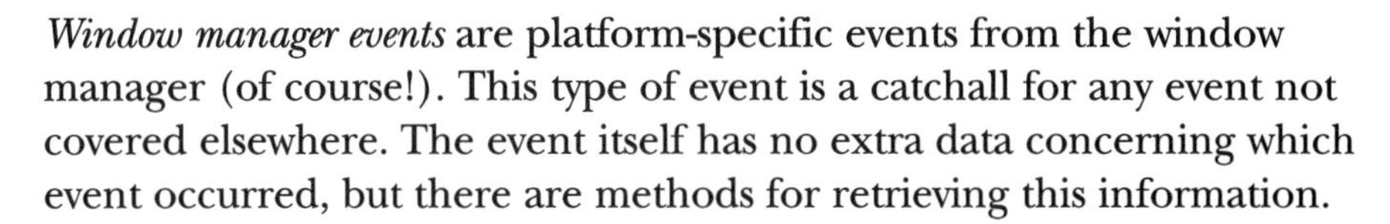

Window manager events are platform-specific events from the window manager (of course!). This type of event is a catchall for any event not covered elsewhere. The event itself has no extra data concerning which event occurred, but there are methods for retrieving this information.

A *video resize event* occurs if you are running your SDL application in a window and you have it set up so that the window can be resized. The information stored with this event specifies how wide and tall the window has become after resizing.

A *video expose event* occurs when the system has changed the screen, so your application must be redrawn. This event contains no additional data.

Finally, a *user event* is defined by you, the programmer. You can use it for any sort of message you want. You get three pieces of additional data—an `int` and two `void*` pointers—that you can use for whatever you like.

Methods of Gathering Input

Now that you have an overview of what sort of information you can get from the event-handling subsystem, you need to know how to go about getting that information. There are essentially three ways to grab event/input information from the SDL event-handling subsystem—by waiting, polling, or directly gathering.

Waiting

In most non-game applications, the program typically does absolutely nothing most of the time; it just sits there and waits for an event to occur. This is the *event-driven* model of input gathering. Although you probably won't want to use this in most games, it is typically the method of input gathering that you will use if you make editors for your game levels.

With this method, most of the program's time is spent waiting for something to happen. Once something occurs, the program reacts to it, typically redraws the screen or performs the appropriate task, and then goes back to waiting, ad infinitum.

Polling

Many games use the polling method of input gathering. The program checks often to see whether an event has occurred. If one has, the program reacts to it and looks for more events. If no event has occurred, the application will do something else for a moment (move the bad guys around, do animations, and so on) and then look for another event. With polling, you won't miss any data because you are still responding to events.

Direct

The third way of gathering data is directly from the input devices themselves. At any time, you can see whether a particular key is up or down on the keyboard, where the mouse is, the state of the mouse buttons, and the various input states of joysticks. This is the totally hard-core way of gathering input; if it is done improperly, you can miss input.

Even if you are using the direct method of gathering information about input devices, you still need to poll the event queue.

The Event-Handling Subsystem in Depth

Now that you've got the gist of how the event-handling system in SDL works, you can explore it in greater depth and actually look at the structures and functions involved in making your application respond to events.

Types of Events

Just as I did when I briefly explained the types of events that SDL can read, I will divide the discussion of the structures involved into the same four categories. In the in-depth discussion there is also a fifth category that concerns the actual `SDL_Event` structure, which ties all of the other events together into a single struct.

Keyboard Events

As you learned earlier, there are two types of keyboard events that can occur—key presses and key releases. When one of these occurs, the information about what key was pressed or released is placed into an `SDL_KeyboardEvent` structure.

```
typedef struct{
  Uint8 type;
```

```
  Uint8 state;
  SDL_keysym keysym;
} SDL_KeyboardEvent;
```

In this structure (and, to be honest, in all SDL structures that deal with events), type is the first member and it is a Uint8. All event structures have this as the first member. It tells you what kind of event has occurred. In the case of keyboard events, this value will be either SDL_KEYPRESSED or SDL_KEYRELEASED.

The state member is pretty much just a duplicate of the type. It will be either SDL_PRESSED or SDL_RELEASED. You can pretty much ignore it.

The third member is another structure that contains pertinent information about which key was pressed or released. This is what the SDL_keysym structure looks like.

```
typedef struct{
  Uint8 scancode;
  SDLKey sym;
  SDLMod mod;
  Uint16 unicode;
} SDL_keysym;
```

Generally, you should ignore the scancode member. It contains a hardware-dependent code that corresponds to the key that was pressed or released. Because you are using SDL and you likely want to maintain a high level of portability, using anything hardware-dependent is a Bad Thing.

Instead, you should use the sym member. It is of the SDLKey type, which contains SDL's code for what key was pressed. All of the constants are named logically. For letters A through Z, the constants are SDLK_a through SDLK_z. Yes, the letter is lowercase. Similarly, for 0 through 9, the constants are SDLK_0 through SDLK_9. In addition, for the function keys (of which SDL provides 15), the constants are SDLK_F1 through SDLK_F15. The numeric keypad numbers are SDLK_KP0 through SDLK_KP9. Table 4.1 summarizes these constants.

Table 4.2 shows the remaining SDLKey constants. (The reason the constants in Table 4.1 were not included is because I really prefer tables that are not more than three pages long!)

Table 4.1 Common SDLKey Constants

Key Range	Constant
A through Z	SDLK_a through SDLK_z
0 through 9	SDLK_0 through SDLK_9
F1 through F15	SDLK_F1 through SDLK_F15
Keypad 0 through 9	SDLK_KP0 through SDLK_KP9

Table 4.2 Other SDLKey Constants

Constant	Key	Character
SDLK_BACKSPACE	Backspace	
SDLK_TAB	Tab	
SDLK_CLEAR	Clear	
SDLK_RETURN	Return	
SDLK_PAUSE	Pause	
SDLK_ESCAPE	Esc	
SDLK_SPACE	Space	
SDLK_EXCLAIM	Exclamation mark	!
SDLK_QUOTEDBL	Double quotes	"
SDLK_HASH	Hash	
SDLK_DOLLAR	Dollar sign	$
SDLK_AMPERSAND	Ampersand	&
SDLK_QUOTE	Quote	'
SDLK_LEFTPAREN	Left parenthesis	(
SDLK_RIGHTPAREN	Right parenthesis	)

Table 4.2 Other SDLKey Constants

Constant	Key	Character
SDLK_ASTERISK	Asterisk	*
SDLK_PLUS	Plus sign	+
SDLK_COMMA	Comma	,
SDLK_MINUS	Minus sign	–
SDLK_PERIOD	Period	.
SDLK_SLASH	Forward slash	/
SDLK_COLON	Colon	:
SDLK_SEMICOLON	Semicolon	;
SDLK_LESS	Less-than symbol	<
SDLK_EQUALS	Equals sign	=
SDLK_GREATER	Greater-than symbol	>
SDLK_QUESTION	Question mark	?
SDLK_AT	At sign	@
SDLK_LEFTBRACKET	Left bracket	[
SDLK_BACKSLASH	Backslash	\
SDLK_RIGHTBRACKET	Right bracket	]
SDLK_CARET	Caret	^
SDLK_UNDERSCORE	Underscore	_
SDLK_BACKQUOTE	Grave	
SDLK_DELETE	Delete	
SDLK_KP_PERIOD	Keypad period	.
SDLK_KP_DIVIDE	Keypad division symbol	/
SDLK_KP_MULTIPLY	Keypad multiplication symbol	*
SDLK_KP_MINUS	Keypad minus sign	–
SDLK_KP_PLUS	Keypad plus sign	+
SDLK_KP_ENTER	Keypad Enter	

Table 4.2 Other SDLKey Constants

Constant	Key	Character
SDLK_KP_EQUALS	Keypad equals sign	=
SDLK_UP	Up arrow	
SDLK_DOWN	Down arrow	
SDLK_RIGHT	Right arrow	
SDLK_LEFT	Left arrow	
SDLK_INSERT	Insert	
SDLK_HOME	Home	
SDLK_END	End	
SDLK_PAGEUP	Page up	
SDLK_PAGEDOWN	Page down	
SDLK_NUMLOCK	Num lock	
SDLK_CAPSLOCK	Caps lock	
SDLK_SCROLLOCK	Scroll lock	
SDLK_RSHIFT	Right Shift	
SDLK_LSHIFT	Left Shift	
SDLK_RCTRL	Right Ctrl	
SDLK_LCTRL	Left Ctrl	
SDLK_RALT	Right Alt	
SDLK_LALT	Left Alt	
SDLK_RMETA	Right meta	
SDLK_LMETA	Left meta	
SDLK_LSUPER	Left Windows key	
SDLK_RSUPER	Right Windows key	
SDLK_MODE	Mode shift	
SDLK_HELP	Help	
SDLK_PRINT	Print screen	

Table 4.2 Other SDLKey Constants

Constant	Key	Character
SDLK_SYSREQ	SysRq	
SDLK_BREAK	Break	
SDLK_MENU	Menu	
SDLK_POWER	Power	
SDLK_EURO	Euro	

Now, you might look at this list and see keys shown that do not exist on your keyboard. One thing that you must keep in mind is that not all keyboards look like yours, and SDL was written to support as many keyboard types as possible. Most of the keys are available on any old keyboard but you can't guarantee that, so just be careful which keys you respond to. (It's another portability issue, but also a localization issue.)

After the `sym` member comes the `mod` member, which is a combination of bit flags that specify which modifier keys (such as Shift, Ctrl, and Alt) are pressed. Table 4.3 shows the bit flags.

It is important to note here that `KMOD_CTRL`, `KMOD_SHIFT`, and `KMOD_ALT` are not their own values. Rather, they are combinations; for example, `KMOD_CTRL` is a combination of `KMOD_LCTRL` and `KMOD_RCTRL`.

When checking for a particular modifier, you take the `mod` value stored in the event, do a bitwise and (`&`), and check for non-zero.

The final member of `SDL_keysym` is a `Uint16` called `unicode`. It contains the ASCII or Unicode value of the key being pressed or released (but not by default—it needs to be enabled to work). If the value stored in `unicode` is less than 128 (0x80), then it is an ASCII code. If it is greater than or equal to 0x80, it is a Unicode value. This is yet another localization thing.

As I stated, SDL does not translate key presses into the character equivalents by default. You need to enable this feature, using the `SDL_EnableUNICODE` function.

Table 4.3 Keyboard Modifier Constants

Constant	Meaning
KMOD_NONE	No modifiers applicable.
KMOD_NUM	Num Lock is down.
KMOD_CAPS	Caps Lock is down.
KMOD_LCTRL	Left Ctrl is down.
KMOD_RCTRL	Right Ctrl is down.
KMOD_RSHIFT	Right Shift is down.
KMOD_LSHIFT	Left Shift is down.
KMOD_RALT	Right Alt is down.
KMOD_LALT	Left Alt is down.
KMOD_CTRL	A Ctrl key is down.
KMOD_SHIFT	A Shift key is down.
KMOD_ALT	An Alt key is down.

```
int SDL_EnableUNICODE(int enable);
```

The single parameter (`enable`) is one of three values. If `enable` is 1, then translation to character values is enabled. If `enable` is 0, then it is disabled. If `enable` is -1, then the enabled state is unchanged and the function will return the previous enabled state (either 0 or 1). The -1 value is useful for querying whether or not translation is currently enabled.

Another aspect of keyboard input that you can enable or disable at your whim is key repeating. In many applications that deal with text, holding down a key will eventually generate additional characters. If that is the behavior you want your application to have, then you must use `SDL_EnableKeyRepeat`.

```
int SDL_EnableKeyRepeat(int delay, int interval);
```

The two parameters, `delay` and `interval`, specify how long after the key is pressed to wait to start the repeat and how often the character should repeat, respectively. The value returned by this function will either be 0, indicating no problem, or –1, indicating an error.

The SDL documentation suggests SDL_DEFAULT_REPEAT_DELAY and SDL_DEFAULT_REPEAT_INTERVAL for the values of delay and interval.

Mouse Events

The mouse events come in two flavors—mouse motion and mouse button. The two flavors each have their own structures for dealing with the events.

Mouse Motion Events

A mouse motion event is stored in an SDL_MouseMotionEvent, which looks like this.

```
typedef struct{
  Uint8 type;
  Uint8 state;
  Uint16 x, y;
  Sint16 xrel, yrel;
} SDL_MouseMotionEvent;
```

As with all SDL event structures, the type member specifies what type of event has occurred. In the case of a mouse motion event, this constant will only ever be SDL_MOUSEMOTION.

The state member is a combination of bit flags that tells you which mouse buttons are currently pressed, if any. Table 4.4 shows these bit flags.

Table 4.4 Mouse Button State Bit Flags

Flag	Meaning
SDL_BUTTON_LMASK	The left button is currently pressed.
SDL_BUTTON_MMASK	The middle button is currently pressed.
SDL_BUTTON_RMASK	The right button is currently pressed.

If you prefer, you can also use the SDL_BUTTON macro. By placing a 1, 2, or 3 into the macro, you will get the same values as SDL_BUTTON_LMASK, SDL_BUTTON_MMASK, and SDL_BUTTON_RMASK, respectively. Additionally, instead of 1, 2, and 3, you can use SDL_BUTTON_LEFT, SDL_BUTTON_MIDDLE, and SDL_BUTTON_RIGHT. I personally prefer constants like SDL_BUTTON_LMASK because they involve less typing.

The x and y members of SDL_MouseMotionEvent are (naturally) the x and y position of the mouse. The xrel and yrel members are the relative motion of the mouse since the last event. In some cases, the absolute position of the mouse (x and y) is the most important; other times, only the relative position (xrel and yrel) is important.

Mouse Button Events

The other two types of mouse-generated events are button presses and button releases. Because they are similar in nature, both of them are stored in an SDL_MouseButtonEvent.

```
typedef struct{
  Uint8 type;
  Uint8 button;
  Uint8 state;
  Uint16 x, y;
} SDL_MouseButtonEvent;
```

The type member, as always, stores the type of event. In the case of a mouse button event, this value will be SDL_MOUSEBUTTONDOWN or SDL_MOUSEBUTTONUP.

The button member will be one of the following three values—SDL_BUTTON_ LEFT, SDL_BUTTON_MIDDLE, or SDL_BUTTON_RIGHT.

The state member tells you whether the button stored in the button member has been pressed or released. The value will be SDL_PRESSED or SDL_RELEASED. Of course, you can get the same information from the type member.

Finally, the x and y members tell you the absolute position of the mouse when the button was pressed.

Joystick Events

To refresh your memory, the five types of joystick-generated events are axis, button up, button down, hat, and ball. Each one of these has its own structure. Again, while the events for joysticks are explained in this chapter, making use of actual joysticks is not covered until Chapter 6.

Joystick Axis Motion Event

A typical joystick will have two axes—vertical and horizontal. A joystick can also have other axes, including rudder controls, dials, and any other type of input widget that represents a changeable linear value (unlike a button, which is either on or off).

When an axis on a joystick is moved, a joystick axis motion event occurs. The data for this event is stored in an `SDL_JoyAxisEvent`.

```
typedef struct{
  Uint8 type;
  Uint8 which;
  Uint8 axis;
  Sint16 value;
} SDL_JoyAxisEvent;
```

The `type` member specifies the type of event that has occurred. In the case of a joystick axis motion event, this value will always be `SDL_JOYAXISMOTION`.

The `which` member is common to all joystick events. Because a variable number of joysticks can be attached to the system, you need a way to differentiate which joystick is generating an event. I will discuss this more in Chapter 6, but suffice it to say that the `which` member tells you which joystick generated the event.

The `axis` member tells you which axis on the joystick was moved. Because a joystick can have a number of axes, this member is quite important.

Finally, the `value` member lets you know the new value of that joystick's axis.

Joystick Button Events

There are two different button events for joysticks. Because you have already taken a look at how keyboard and mouse button events are handled, this should not be a shock to you. When a button on a joystick is pressed or released, a joystick button event is triggered and the information for the event is stored in an `SDL_JoyButtonEvent` structure.

```
typedef struct{
  Uint8 type;
```

```
  Uint8 which;
  Uint8 button;
  Uint8 state;
} SDL_JoyButtonEvent;
```

Now things should start to fall into place. The `type` member will be either `SDL_JOYBUTTONDOWN` or `SDL_JOYBUTTONUP`. The `which` member is again an identifier for the joystick that generated the event. The `button` member specifies which button on the joystick was pressed or released. Finally, the `state` member tells you the state of the button (either `SDL_PRESSED` or `SDL_RELEASED`).

Joystick Hat Position Change Event

Now for the point-of-view hat events. Not all joysticks have hats, but many of the cooler (in other words, more expensive and odd-looking) ones do. Typically, a hat is placed on top of a joystick and can be moved into one of nine positions. When the user changes the position of the hat, a joystick hat position change event occurs. The information for this event is stored in an `SDL_JoyHatEvent`.

```
typedef struct{
  Uint8 type;
  Uint8 which;
  Uint8 hat;
  Uint8 value;
} SDL_JoyHatEvent;
```

The `type` and `which` members have their usual meanings. The `type` member is `SDL_JOYHATMOTION`. The `which` member has the joystick identifier. The `hat` member tells you which hat was moved. Normally there is only one hat, but you never know with some of the crazier devices out there. Finally, the `value` member is a set of bit flags that tells you the new position of the hat. Table 4.5 lists the bit flags.

The flags account for five of the nine possible values. The other four values are combinations of these flags (see Table 4.6).

Although common sense probably dictates this, you cannot have a hat that indicates both up and down at the same time, nor can you have one that indicates both left and right at the same time.

Table 4.5 Joystick Hat Bit Flags

Flag	Meaning
SDL_HAT_CENTERED	The hat is centered (neutral position).
SDL_HAT_UP	The hat is pointing up.
SDL_HAT_RIGHT	The hat is pointing right.
SDL_HAT_DOWN	The hat is pointing down.
SDL_HAT_LEFT	The hat is pointing left.

Table 4.6 Joystick Hat Combined Flags

Flag	Value
SDL_HAT_RIGHTUP	SDL_HAT_RIGHT|SDL_HAT_UP
SDL_HAT_RIGHTDOWN	SDL_HAT_RIGHT|SDL_HAT_DOWN
SDL_HAT_LEFTUP	SDL_HAT_LEFT|SDL_HAT_UP
SDL_HAT_LEFTDOWN	SDL_HAT_LEFT|SDL_HAT_DOWN

Joystick Ball Motion Event

The final type of joystick-generated event is the ball motion event, which occurs on joysticks that have trackballs. This is different from using a trackball instead of a mouse. Both are pointing devices and both will generate mouse events. However, the joystick ball motion event is only for trackballs that are integrated into a non-keyboard and non-mouse input device.

The information in a joystick ball motion event is packed into an `SDL_JoyBallEvent`—and yes, I agree that the name of the structure does sound a little suggestive.

```
typedef struct{
  Uint8 type;
  Uint8 which;
  Uint8 ball;
  Sint16 xrel, yrel;
} SDL_JoyBallEvent;
```

The `type` member is `SDL_JOYBALLMOTION`. The `which` member is (again) the identifier for which joystick generated the event. The `ball` member tells you which ball was moved. Finally, `xrel` and `yrel` tell you how far on the horizontal and vertical axes the trackball was moved. This is the only event with two pieces of information in it. I'm not entirely sure why the joystick ball motion events weren't consolidated into the axis motion events.

System Events

The remaining six events that I arbitrarily lump into the system category don't really have any sort of relationship to one another, which is why they are all in the same category in the first place…I couldn't find a better place for them.

Several of the events, notably the quit, expose, and window manager events, are quite similar in that there is no additional information stored with them. In the case of the window manager event, however, you can glean additional information.

Quit and Expose Events

Quit and expose events are represented by two different structures, although the structures are identical except for their names. A quit event is stored in an `SDL_QuitEvent` structure, and an expose event is stored in an `SDL_ExposeEvent`.

```
typedef struct{
  Uint8 type
} SDL_QuitEvent;
typedef struct{
  Uint8 type
} SDL_ExposeEvent;
```

As you can see, both of these events store only one piece of information—the type of event that occurred. There is no additional information for either of these events. In the case of a quit event, the type member has a value of SDL_QUIT; in the case of an expose event, the value is SDL_VIDEOEXPOSE.

Although these two events are similar in aspect, they are not similar in meaning. When your application receives a quit event, you should terminate the application. When you receive an expose event, you should redraw the display.

Resize Events

If your application is running in a windowed environment, and you specified the flag that tells SDL you'd like a resizable window, it is quite likely that you will need to respond to resize events at some point. These are stored in an SDL_ResizeEvent structure.

```
typedef struct{
  Uint8 type;
  int w, h;
} SDL_ResizeEvent;
```

The type member has a value of SDL_VIDEORESIZE. The w and h members indicate the new width and height of the window. That's all I have to say about that; resize events are pretty simple.

Activation Events

Although I am pretty much treating activation events as a single event, they are in reality six related events (three sets of event pairs). You will get an activation event if your application gains or loses input focus (keyboard input) or mouse focus, or when minimization or restoration occurs. If and when any of these things occur, the information is stored in an SDL_ActiveEvent structure.

```
typedef struct{
  Uint8 type;
  Uint8 gain;
  Uint8 state;
} SDL_ActiveEvent;
```

The type member is always SDL_ACTIVEEVENT. The gain is either 0 or 1. If it is 0, something was lost; if it is 1, something was gained.

The state member tells you which item was lost or gained. If you gain or lose mouse focus, it is SDL_APPMOUSEFOCUS. If you gain or lose keyboard input, it is SDL_APPINPUTFOCUS. If the application is iconified (in other words, minimized) or restored, it is SDL_APPACTIVE.

Window Manager Events

If you want, you can receive events from the window manager. This is unnecessary most of the time, and SDL has these events disabled. The event is stored in an SDL_SysWMEvent structure.

```
typedef struct {
        Uint8 type;
} SDL_SysWMEvent;
```

Like the quit and expose events, this event structure contains only the type of event that occurred. The type member will always be SDL_SysWM. You need to use another function to receive extended information about the actual event.

> **CAUTION**
> **If you decide to respond to window manager events, you will sacrifice a great deal of your application's portability!**

I will talk more about window manager events for the Windows platform later in this chapter, in the "Window Manager Subsystem" section.

User Events

You can define your own events with the SDL_UserEvent structure. This is a generic structure that provides you with a way to store three pieces of information.

```
typedef struct{
  Uint8 type;
  int code;
  void *data1;
  void *data2;
} SDL_UserEvent;
```

The type member can be in the range of SDL_USEREVENT through SDL_NUMEVENTS-1. In the current version of SDL, these values are 24 and 31, respectively, which gives you a chance to define up to eight user event types.

The meanings and values of the code, data1, and data2 members are completely up to you.

The SDL_Event Structure

Finally, the one event structure to rule them all: SDL_Event! This is the main event structure (the only one received by the various event functions), and it contains all other types of events.

```
typedef union{
  Uint8 type;
  SDL_ActiveEvent active;
  SDL_KeyboardEvent key;
  SDL_MouseMotionEvent motion;
  SDL_MouseButtonEvent button;
  SDL_JoyAxisEvent jaxis;
  SDL_JoyBallEvent jball;
  SDL_JoyHatEvent jhat;
  SDL_JoyButtonEvent jbutton;
  SDL_ResizeEvent resize;
  SDL_ExposeEvent expose;
  SDL_QuitEvent quit;
  SDL_UserEvent user;
  SDL_SywWMEvent syswm;
} SDL_Event;
```

As you can see, this is not actually a structure—it is a union, so each of the event structures occupies the same memory. This is why the type parameter is always included as the first member of an event structure. When you read in an SDL_Event, you check its type member, which tells you what event it is and thus which other member you should be looking at. In my opinion, this is one of the best ways to handle input. Sure, in certain cases some bytes get wasted, such as with a quit or expose event, but all of the other event structures are rather small (the largest being SDL_MouseMotionEvent, with 10 bytes).

Methods of Gathering Input

Now that you've spent a while looking at how events are represented in SDL, it is time to learn how to process them. As I stated earlier, there are three distinct ways to get information from input devices—by waiting, polling, and directly gathering. Each method is suited for different types of applications. See Figures 4.1 through 4.3 for a graphical view of the three different ways to process input.

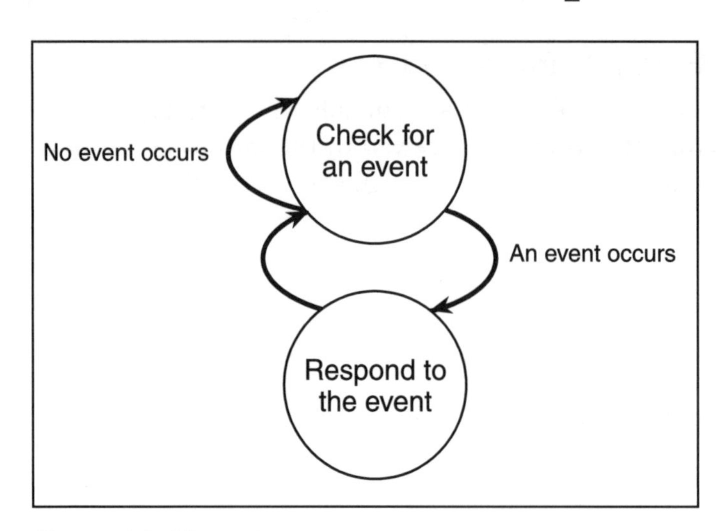

Figure 4.1 *Waiting for events*

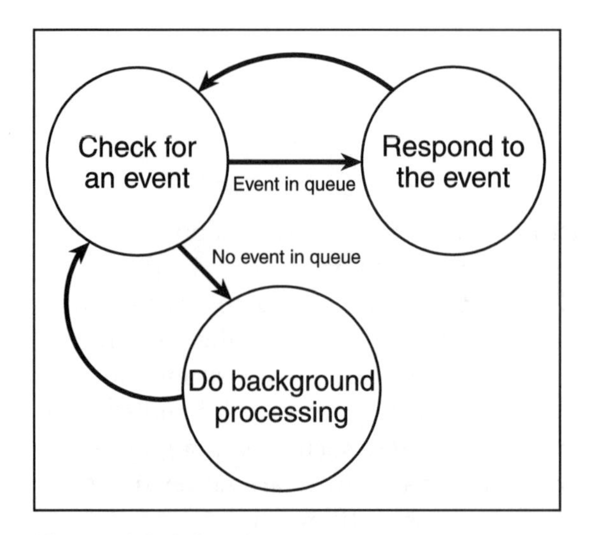

Figure 4.2 *Polling for events*

Waiting

Conceptually, the simplest method of gathering input is to wait for it. Using this method, your application spends most of its time doing absolutely nothing…it simply waits for some event to occur. When an event does occur, the application processes it and then goes back to waiting. This is typical for non-game applications.

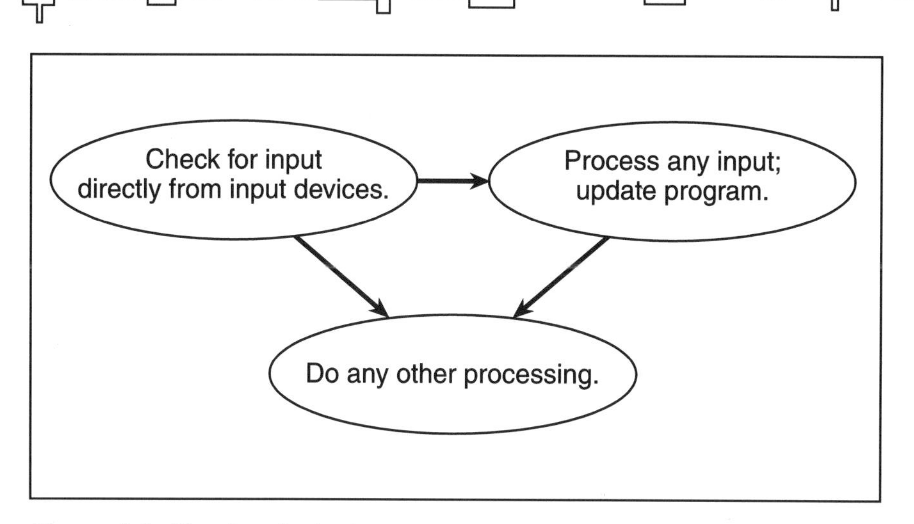

Figure 4.3 *Directly gathering input*

If you simply want your program to sit and wait for an event to occur, you use the SDL_WaitEvent function.

```
int SDL_WaitEvent(SDL_Event *event);
```

To use this function, you supply a pointer to an SDL_Event structure. When the next event occurs, this structure will be filled in with the information about that event, and will then return. If this function returns a 1, everything is fine and the event was copied into the SDL_Event structure and then removed from the event queue. If something went wrong, the function will return 0.

If for some reason you put NULL as the parameter for this function, SDL will simply wait for an event and then return. The state of the event queue will remain unchanged.

A typical event-handling loop using SDL_WaitEvent looks like this:

```
//declare an event variable
SDL_Event event;
//do this forever...
for(;;)
{
	//wait for an event
	SDL_WaitEvent(&event);
	//process the event
```

```
        //if there is a quit event...
        if(event.type==SDL_QUIT)
        {
            //...break out of the infinite loop
            break;
        }
        //if there is a key press event...
        if(event.type==SDL_KEYDOWN)
        {
            //...handle the key press event here
        }
        //other handlers for the other events go here
}
```

If you want, you could also put your event dispatching into a switch, instead of using a series of `if` statements. Or, you could put together everything into an `if…else if…else if…else` block. The structure is completely up to you.

For a simple example of an event loop that uses `SDL_WaitEvent`, be sure to check out FOSDL4_1 in the Examples folder on the CD-ROM. This example sets up a window and then waits for events. For the most common events, it reports what event occurred.

Polling

Another method of gathering input is to periodically poll the event queue. If you find that no event has occurred, have the program do something else for a moment and then check for events again. This is more typical for game applications, especially those that have background processing such as animation.

To check to see whether an event has occurred without waiting for one to occur, you use the `SDL_PollEvent` function.

```
int SDL_PollEvent(SDL_Event *event);
```

This function operates much like `SDL_WaitEvent` except that when it returns a 0, the function does not indicate an error. It simply indicates that no event was found in the queue. If `NULL` is passed in the `event` parameter, the next event is not removed from the queue.

For event loops using SDL_PollEvent, typically you will take one of two paths. You might follow these steps.

1. Check for an event.
2. If there is an event, process it and then return to Step 1.
3. If there is not an event, do something else for a little while and then return to Step 1.

This is not the only way to go about things, of course. You might follow these steps instead.

1. Check for an event.
2. If there is an event, process it.
3. Do something else for a little while.
4. Return to Step 1.

In the first scheme (which I personally prefer over the second), the program will continue to process events as long as there are events left in the queue. Only when the event queue is empty will anything else happen.

In the second scheme something else happens between events, regardless of whether there are any. I dislike this scheme because it can introduce input lag—in other words, when the state of the game is behind the current state of the input queue. I do not suggest using this scheme.

If you'd like to see a quick example of an event loop using SDL_PollEvent, check out FOSDL4_2 in the Examples folder on the CD-ROM. It is very much like FOSDL4_1; the only difference is the use of SDL_PollEvent. Because this application writes continually to stdout.txt, don't run it for very long or you will have a very large stdout.txt file!

Direct

A third method of gathering input is directly from the devices themselves. Of course, you will still have to use some method of clearing out the event queue, such as using SDL_PollEvent.

You are now going to learn how to grab input directly from the keyboard, mouse, and system. You can find the stuff on joysticks in Chapter 6.

Keyboard

To grab the current state of the keyboard, use the SDL_GetKeyState function.

```
Uint8 *SDL_GetKeyState(int *numkeys);
```

The numkeys parameter is a pointer to an int that has the number of keys for which you would like to get the state. Passing a NULL will cause SDL to give you back all of the keys. The return value is a pointer to an array of Uint8s. You should not deallocate this pointer because SDL maintains it internally.

You can index the array with the various SDLK_* constants (refer to Tables 4.1 and 4.2 earlier in the chapter). So if you are looking to check for the state of the A key, here is what you would do.

```
Uint8* kbarray;
//grab the keyboard state
kbarray=SDL_GetKeyState(NULL);
if(kbarray[SDLK_a]==1)
{
	//the A key is down
}
```

In the array, the value 1 indicates that the key is down, and 0 indicates that the key is up.

Because of how SDL works, you should call the SDL_PumpEvents function before you ever call SDL_GetKeyState.

```
void SDL_PumpEvents(void);
```

This function takes any input waiting to be added to the event queue, updates any input device states (such as key states), and then adds the event to the queue. Under normal circumstances, you don't have to call this function because other functions such as SDL_WaitInput and SDL_PollInput call it for you. However, it is crucial to call this function if you are reading information directly from input devices.

Another piece of information you can grab about the keyboard is the modifier state, which I talked about earlier when I discussed keyboard events. You can retrieve the current state of the modifier keys with a call to SDL_GetModState.

```
SDLMod SDL_GetModState(void);
```

This function takes no parameters and returns a set of bit flags. (Refer back to Table 4.3 for a review of these bit flags.) If you are simply using the keyboard as a many-buttoned gamepad, then you probably won't care about the mod state. If that's the case, just look at the key states.

If you want, you can also change the modifier state of the keyboard using the SDL_SetModState function.

```
void SDL_SetModState(SDLMod modstate);
```

This function takes a combination of the bit flags shown in Table 4.3 and returns no value. The modifier state of the keyboard is changed to the supplied value.

Now for a function for which I just could not find a good place. It is called SDL_GetKeyName, and it returns SDL's name for a particular key based on the SDLK_* constant for that key.

```
char *SDL_GetKeyName(SDLKey key);
```

I had to get that one in somewhere, and here was as good a place as any.

Mouse

You can retrieve the current state of the mouse for either the relative or absolute value. To get the absolute position of the mouse, you use SDL_GetMouseState; to get the relative position, you use SDL_GetRelativeMouseState. Both functions look quite similar.

```
Uint8 SDL_GetMouseState(int *x, int *y);
Uint8 SDL_GetRelativeMouseState(int *x, int *y);
```

Each function takes two parameters, int pointers, which get filled in with the absolute or relative x and y positions of the mouse, depending on which function you use. You can place a NULL into either of these parameters, and the values of the mouse's axes will not be returned.

The return values of these functions are the button states of the mouse, and you can use the SDL_BUTTON constants and macro to determine which buttons are pressed.

As with the keyboard state, you will want to call SDL_PumpEvents prior to calling either of these functions.

System

You can get information about the state of the system, such as whether the application is active and whether or not the application has keyboard or mouse focus, by using SDL_GetAppState.

```
Uint8 SDL_GetAppState(void);
```

This function takes no parameters and returns a Uint8. The value returned is a combination of the active SDL_APPACTIVE, SDL_APPINPUTFOCUS, and SDL_APPMOUSEFOCUS bit flags.

Trapping Events

Now that you can wait for events, poll events, and get information directly from the input devices, I'm going to show you one more way to deal with input. You can set up an event trap, which SDL calls a *filter.* This is a very powerful mechanism supplied by SDL.

First, I'm going to tell you exactly how this idea works. You can create your own function to handle events, so you can almost totally forget about the need to call SDL_PollEvent or SDL_WaitEvent. You need to create this function to follow a certain prototype because later you must send a function pointer to another function. Here's what the function pointer type looks like.

```
typedef int (*SDL_EventFilter)(const SDL_Event *event);
```

To follow this prototype, you can make a function that, for example, looks like this.

```
int MyEventFilter(const SDL_Event* event);
```

When you create this function, the event parameter is a constant pointer to an SDL_Event that contains information about an event that is about to be posted to the event queue. You can handle it in whatever way you need. If you decide to return 1, the event will still be posted to the queue; if you return 0, it won't be. You can use such a function to handle almost any event. However, it is a good idea to let the SDL_QUIT events go through and be handled by the application.

To set up your own function as an event filter, you use the SDL_SetEventFilter function.

```
void SDL_SetEventFilter(SDL_EventFilter filter);
```

The filter parameter is a pointer to a function with which you want to trap events. If you pass a NULL, then event filtering is turned off. You can also retrieve the current event filter using SDL_GetEventFilter.

```
SDL_EventFilter SDL_GetEventFilter(void);
```

This function takes no parameter and returns a pointer to the current event filter (or NULL if there is none).

Sending Events

User events will not occur unless you make them, so you need a way to send events to the event queue. The function for doing this is `SDL_PushEvent`.

```
int SDL_PushEvent(SDL_Event *event);
```

This function takes a pointer to an `SDL_Event` that contains the information about the event you want to add to the queue and returns an `int`. If the returned value is 0, everything went well and the event was added to the queue. If it is -1, the event could not be added to the queue.

You can add any sort of event to the queue; you simply have to fill out the appropriate part of the `SDL_Event` structure and then call `SDL_PushEvent`. However, if you use `SDL_PushEvent`, the event filter will not trap the event, and it will go directly to the event queue to be read by `SDL_WaitEvent` or `SDL_PollEvent`.

The Window Manager Subsystem

Now for a short section on the window manager, and then we can wrap up this chapter. The window manager allows you to do a few things, such as set the caption of the window in which your application is running, set the icon that is displayed in the corner of the application window, and set the keyboard and mouse capture state of the system.

In this section you will also find information regarding window manager events and how to handle them (at least on WIN32 systems).

Captions

Even if you are running in full-screen mode, you probably want to title the application something other than SDL_app, which is the default when you run it. This is even more important in a windowed environment. To set the caption of your application, use `SDL_WM_SetCaption`.

```
void SDL_WM_SetCaption(const char *title, const char *icon);
```

This function takes two parameters, both pointers to strings, called `title` and `icon`. The SDL documentation states that `title` becomes the application caption and icon becomes the iconic caption. In WIN32, there is really no difference, so icon ends up not being used.

You can also retrieve the caption and icon caption for the application by using SDL_WM_GetCaption.

```
void SDL_WM_GetCaption(char **title, char **icon);
```

This function takes two pointers to pointers to character arrays that get filled in with pointers to strings containing the captions. There is not much to the window manager caption thing. Two functions, and that's it.

Icons

You can set an icon for the application window using SDL_WM_SetIcon. Sure, this isn't an earth-shattering capability, but it can and does make the application look more professional and finished.

```
void SDL_WM_SetIcon(SDL_Surface *icon, Uint8 *mask);
```

This function takes two parameters. The first (icon) is a pointer to an SDL_Surface that contains the image for use as the icon. In WIN32, this image has to be 32×32 pixels in size. The second parameter (mask) is a pointer to an array of Uint8s that contains a bit mask for the image, much the same as how bit masks are used for SDL_Cursors. If you use NULL for the mask, the entire surface is used for the icon. This function must be called prior to calling SDL_SetVideoMode.

Speaking of icons and words that have icon in them, you can minimize (or iconify) an application using SDL_WM_IconifyWindow.

```
int SDL_WM_IconifyWindow(void);
```

When this function is called, SDL attempts to minimize the application. If it cannot do so, the function will return 0. If this is successful, the function will return a non-zero and the application will soon receive an active event with SDL_APPACTIVE.

Input Grab

Earlier I mentioned input focus and mouse focus. SDL has the ability to grab or capture input from these devices. When you decide to grab the input, the SDL application is the *only* application to receive events from them. This is not necessarily a bad thing, especially for games. Games are greedy little applications that don't like to share the system.

The function for grabbing input is SDL_WM_GrabInput.

```
SDL_GrabMode SDL_WM_GrabInput(SDL_GrabMode mode);
```

This function takes as a parameter the new desired grab mode and returns the current grab mode. The grab mode constants are: SDL_GRAB_ON, SDL_GRAB_OFF, or SDL_GRAB_QUERY. In the case of SDL_GRAB_ON and SDL_GRAB_OFF, that becomes the new mode. In the cases of SDL_GRAB_QUERY, the mode remains unchanged and the current mode is returned.

Events

Finally, you get to window manager events. Again, I must warn you that these are platform-specific; if you decide to respond to them, you will be limiting your portability.

Now that I've said that, take a look at window manager events as far as WIN32 is concerned. In order to even look at window manager events, you need to enable them using SDL_EventState.

```
Uint8 SDL_EventState(Uint8 type, int state);
```

This function takes two parameters—a type of event (passed in the type parameter) and a state of responding to that event. You can supply any type of event, but in the case of window manager events you would put SDL_SYSWMEVENT.

The state parameter contains one of three values—SDL_ENABLE, SDL_IGNORE, or SDL_QUERY. If the value is SDL_ENABLE, that type of event will be posted to the queue. If the value is SDL_IGNORE, it won't be posted to the queue. If the value is SDL_QUERY, the current state will be returned by SDL_EventState.

After you have turned on window manager events, you receive them as part of your event loop like other types of events. As you saw earlier, the only information about a window manager event that you get in an SDL_Event structure is simply that an event occurred. To find out more information about it, you need to use SDL_GetWMInfo.

```
int SDL_GetWMInfo(SDL_SysWMinfo *info);
```

The parameter to this function is a pointer to an SDL_SysWMInfo structure. The exact contents of this structure depend on what platform you are compiling for, which is why it's not necessarily a good idea to respond to these events, but anyway.... In WIN32, this is what SDL_SysWMInfo looks like:

```
typedef struct {
     SDL_version version;
     HWND window;                   /* The Win32 display window */
} SDL_SysWMinfo;
```

This function has two members—the version of SDL and an HWND that is the main display window for the application. If you really need to tie WIN32-specific code with this window handle, this is the way to do it. However, I really don't suggest it.

Summary

So now you've seen two more of the subsystems of SDL—the event-handling subsystem and the window manager subsystem. The event-handling subsystem is, at least in my opinion, the most important. The window manager is less important, but the ability to set the caption and icon are important for a polished look and feel.

These subsystems will be used often to make later examples more interactive (and game-like). For the most part, the only two things you need to make a computer game are a way to display graphics and the ability to get and respond to input from the user, both of which you now have. The rest is just bells and whistles.

CHAPTER 5

SDL Audio and CD-ROM

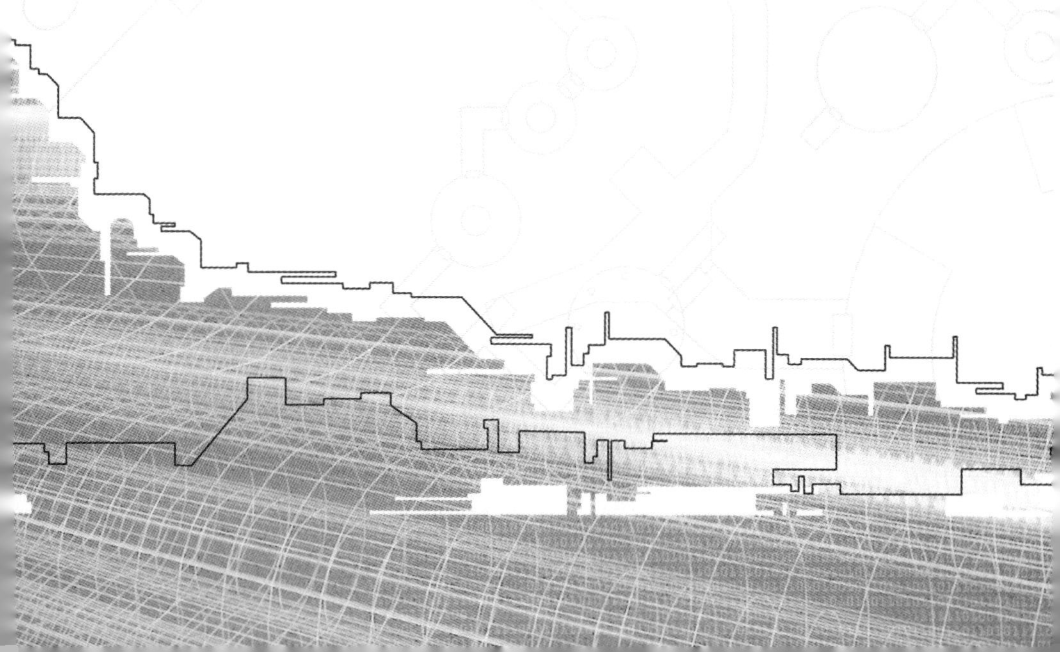

This chapter is about the two subsystems of SDL that deal with making noise—the audio and the CD subsystems. Using them, you can make your applications play .WAV files, tracks from a CD, and so on.

The SDL Audio Subsystem

After looking at the video and event-handling subsystems of SDL, the audio subsystem will seem a little crude by comparison. This is not surprising, however, because SDL is meant to work on many platforms, and there has been nowhere near the effort to standardize audio hardware that there has been to standardize video hardware. To use SDL's audio subsystem, you need to know quite a bit about how sound works.

Audio Structures

There are only two structures in SDL's audio subsystem: SDL_AudioSpec and SDL_AudioCVT. These cryptic-sounding structures stand for "audio specification" and "audio convert."

SDL_AudioSpec contains information such as the format of the sound buffer, the number of channels, the bits per channel, and so on. Here's what it looks like:

```
typedef struct{
  int freq;
  Uint16 format;
  Uint8 channels;
  Uint8 silence;
  Uint16 samples;
  Uint32 size;
  void (*callback)(void *userdata, Uint8 *stream, int len);
  void *userdata;
} SDL_AudioSpec;
```

The first member (freq) contains the audio frequency in samples per second, which directly affects how many bytes per second are streamed through your audio hardware. The size of a sample varies, depending on the format and number of channels.

In theory, the frequency can be any number, but typical values are 11025, 22050, and 44100 (in other words, 11-kHz, 22-kHz, and 44-kHz sounds). Perhaps the most commonly supported frequency is 22 kHz.

The `format` member is how the sound is formatted. It can be 8-bit or 16-bit, signed or unsigned, and in the case of 16-bit sounds, either big endian or little endian. Table 5.1 shows the possible formats.

Table 5.1 SDL_AudioSpec Formats

Constant	Meaning
AUDIO_U8	Each channel consists of a stream of Uint8s.
AUDIO_S8	Each channel consists of a stream of Sint8s.
AUDIO_U16LSB	Each channel consists of a stream of little endian Uint16s.
AUDIO_U16MSB	Each channel consists of a stream of big endian Uint16s.
AUDIO_U16	This is the same as AUDIO_U16LSB.
AUDIO_U16SYS	Depending on the system, this might be either AUDIO_U16LSB or AUDIO_U16MSB.
AUDIO_S16LSB	Each channel consists of a stream of little endian Sint16s.
AUDIO_S16MSB	Each channel consists of a stream of big endian Sint16s.
AUDIO_S16	This is the same as AUDIO_S16LSB.
AUDIO_S16SYS	Depending on the system, this might be either AUDIO_S16LSB or AUDIO_S16MSB.

The `channels` member will be either 1 or 2 for mono or stereo sound, respectively. Depending on the format, which specifies either one or two bytes per channel per sample, the size of a sample can be 1 (8-bit mono format), 2 (8-bit stereo or 16-bit mono), or 4 (16-bit stereo).

The `silence` member is a calculated value that will generate silence when written to the sound buffer. This helps when you are trying to avoid the snap, crackle, pop of the sound buffer.

The samples member is the size of the audio buffer measured in samples. The size parameter is the size of the audio buffer measured in bytes.

The callback member is a pointer to a user-defined function. You have to create one of these in order to play any audio. I told you the audio system was hard core. I'll get back to how to create such a function a little later.

Finally, userdata is a pointer to data that gets passed to the audio callback function.

SDL_AudioCVT contains information to convert sound from one format to another. I'm not going to show this structure and explain each member because most of the members are built and used only by SDL. Suffice it to say that converting audio from one format to another is a tricky business, but this structure manages to do it just fine. If you really want to take a look at this structure, you can find it in the SDL documentation.

Audio Functions

Before I move on to the audio functions, I have to explain how you must initialize SDL to use the audio subsystem, in particular for WIN32. Because of the Windows implementation of SDL (which, generally speaking, relies on DirectX), you must initialize both systems when you call SDL_Init, or else you'll have problems. Just letting you know. Now on to the functions.

Open, Pause, and Close

Just like with the video subsystem, you must do a little more setup after you initialize the audio subsystem. In the case of video, it was a call to SDL_SetVideoMode. In the case of audio, it is a call to SDL_OpenAudio.

```
int SDL_OpenAudio(SDL_AudioSpec *desired, SDL_AudioSpec *obtained);
```

This function takes two parameters—a pointer to a desired SDL_AudioSpec (which you fill out yourself) and a pointer to another SDL_AudioSpec that is filled in with the actual audio specification that is obtained. You can put a NULL in the obtained parameter, and SDL will do its best to emulate the format you placed into the desired parameter. The return value of this function will be 0 if it is successful and -1 if there was an error.

Now take a closer look at the callback member of SDL_AudioSpec. To refresh your memory, here's what it looks like.

```
void (*callback)(void *userdata, Uint8 *stream, int len);
```

This is a pointer to a function that returns no value and takes three parameters—a void* (userdata, the same as the member of the same name in SDL_AudioSpec), a Uint8* (stream), and an int (len). The stream and len parameters refer to the audio buffer that you need to fill during this callback. You fill in len bytes.

I know this all might seem a little weird (it did to me when I first looked at this subsystem), so I'll cover two more functions and then you'll do a quick example.

After you are done messing around with sound, you call SDL_CloseAudio, which looks like this:

```
void SDL_CloseAudio(void);
```

A simpler function could not exist. This function takes no parameters and returns no values. It is the proper bookend to the call to SDL_OpenAudio.

The final function that I absolutely must cover before doing any example is SDL_PauseAudio, which allows you to turn sounds on and off. Here's what it looks like.

```
void SDL_PauseAudio(int pause_on);
```

This function returns no value and takes an int as its sole parameter. If the pause_on parameter is 1, the sound is paused. If it is 0, the sound is not paused.

Now for the example, which you can find in FOSDL5_1 on the CD.

```
#include "sdl.h"
#include <stdlib.h>
const int SCREEN_WIDTH=640;
const int SCREEN_HEIGHT=480;
SDL_Surface* g_pDisplaySurface = NULL;
SDL_Event g_Event;
SDL_AudioSpec* g_SpecDesired;
SDL_AudioSpec* g_SpecObtained;
void FOSDLAudioCallback(void* userdata,Uint8* buffer,int len);
int main(int argc, char* argv[])
```

```
{
	SDL_Init(SDL_INIT_VIDEO|SDL_INIT_AUDIO);
	atexit(SDL_Quit);
	g_pDisplaySurface =
SDL_SetVideoMode(SCREEN_WIDTH,SCREEN_HEIGHT,0,SDL_ANYFORMAT);
	g_SpecDesired=new SDL_AudioSpec;
	g_SpecObtained=new SDL_AudioSpec;
	g_SpecDesired->freq=22050;
	g_SpecDesired->format=AUDIO_S16LSB;
	g_SpecDesired->channels=1;
	g_SpecDesired->samples=8192;
	g_SpecDesired->callback=FOSDLAudioCallback;
	g_SpecDesired->userdata=NULL;
	SDL_OpenAudio(g_SpecDesired,g_SpecObtained);
	delete g_SpecDesired;

	SDL_PauseAudio(0);
	for(;;)
	{
		if(SDL_PollEvent(&g_Event)==0)
		{
			SDL_UpdateRect(g_pDisplaySurface,0,0,0,0);
		}
		else
		{
			if(g_Event.type==SDL_QUIT) break;
		}
	}
	SDL_CloseAudio();
	delete g_SpecObtained;
	return(0);
}
void FOSDLAudioCallback(void* userdata,Uint8* buffer,int len)
{
	int index;
	for(index=0;index<len;index++)
	{
		buffer[index]=rand()%256;
	}
}
```

As usual, the version of code listed here lacks error checking and comments. The full version, coded the way it should be, is on the CD. Some of the more important highlights of this example are the use of the three audio functions I have discussed. First, the program sets up a desired audio spec, and then it opens the audio device. Next, it turns off audio pausing. The rest of the program simply performs screen updates in the absence of an event. The FOSDLAudioCallback function is doing all of the actual work. It simply writes random bytes into the buffer. When you run this program, you will hear random sounds. It's kind of painful, really. This is the audio version of the random pixel demo.

One last function for this section, and then I'll move on. To check the status of the audio playback, you use the SDL_GetAudioStatus function.

```
SDL_audiostatus SDL_GetAudioStatus(void);
```

This function takes no parameters and returns one of the following values: SDL_AUDIO_STOPPED, SDL_AUDIO_PLAYING, or SDL_AUDIO_PAUSED. What each one means should be reasonably obvious.

Lock and Unlock

The theory behind the audio callback function is to give you, the programmer, ultimate control over what goes into the sound buffer. In actuality, it makes you into a monkey shoveling coal into a furnace. The userdata member of SDL_AudioSpec is also passed into the callback function. It is a void*, so you can make it point to pretty much anything you want, such as audio data that you are streaming into the sound buffer one shovel-full at a time. Sound like a pain? It is.

Naturally, you will eventually want to change the data contained in whatever structure you are pointing to with userdata, unless you really want to stream the same small bit of sound data onto the sound buffer repeatedly. First, you use SDL_LockAudio to tell the callback to stop being called, and then you call SDL_UnlockAudio to tell the callback to resume. You want to do this because the audio callback likely is running in a different thread, and you don't want to change the data when another thread might be reading it. This can cause much havoc, including system locks and other types of spectacular crashes.

Fortunately, both SDL_LockAudio and SDL_UnlockAudio are extremely simple functions to remember. Take a look:

```
void SDL_LockAudio(void);
void SDL_UnlockAudio(void);
```

No parameters, no return values—it doesn't get any easier. Naturally, you don't want to keep the audio callback locked out for longer than necessary or you'll quickly be soundless, and that's just not cool.

WAV Files

Wouldn't it be nice if you had some actual data to put into the sound buffer, rather than filling it with random and painful noise? SDL's audio facilities, while a bit crude, do give you the ability to load in WAV files. The function for doing so is called SDL_LoadWAV.

```
SDL_AudioSpec *SDL_LoadWAV(const char *file, SDL_AudioSpec *spec, Uint8
**audio_buf, Uint32 *audio_len);
```

This function takes four parameters. The first (file) is a string that contains the name of the file from which you wish to load the WAV file. The second parameter (spec) is a blank SDL_AudioSpec, which this function fills with information about the WAV file, such as the format and number of channels. The third parameter (audio_buf) is filled in with a pointer to the audio data for the sound, and the last parameter (audio_len) is the length of the data pointed to by audio_buf, in bytes. This function returns the generated audio spec (the same as spec), or NULL if there was an error.

When you are done with a WAV file's data, you destroy it with a call to SDL_FreeWAV.

```
void SDL_FreeWAV(Uint8 *audio_buf);
```

The sole parameter, audio_buf, is the same pointer you retrieved from SDL_LoadWAV.

And now for an example that will play an actual sound. You can find this example under FOSDL5_2 on the CD. Because of how the audio subsystem works, I had to find a way that I could stream a sound into the audio buffer and hold a spare sound to start playing immediately afterward. This is somewhat primitive, but here's what I came up with.

```
//type for streaming wav data to sound buffer
typedef struct
{
```

```
	//pointer to current sound's data
	Uint8* m_CurrentSound;
	//length of current sound
	int	m_CurrentSoundLength;
	//pointer to next sound's data
	Uint8* m_NextSound;
	//length of next sound
	int m_NextSoundLength;
} FOSDL_AudioStream;
```

This structure contains two pointers—one for the currently playing sound and one for the sound that will be played next. Also there are two lengths, each indicating how much is left of a sound. When the callback function finishes with the first sound, it will switch to the next one and clear out the next sound's data. Because of this, the main event loop constantly has to check to see whether the next sound has been cleared and, if so, load in another sound to queue.

Since I haven't covered conversion of audio formats yet (they're coming up next), I had to create the primary sound buffer to match the data that it would be getting from the WAV file. Had I not done this, the sound would be garbled.

The callback function is also an interesting piece of work. Up until today, I'd never in my life actually had to stream data to the hardware sound buffer. In my opinion, this is a bit of a messy process. I spent a good hour refining it so that it didn't lock up my machine. Here's what my callback looks like.

```
//audio callback
void FOSDLAudioCallback(void* userdata,Uint8* buffer,int len)
{
	//cast user data to stream data
	FOSDL_AudioStream* pstrm;
	pstrm=(FOSDL_AudioStream*)userdata;

	//continue while len > 0 and at least one sound is non-empty
	while(len>0 && (pstrm->m_CurrentSoundLength>0 || pstrm-
>m_NextSoundLength>0))
	{
		//check for current sound being NULL
		if(pstrm->m_CurrentSoundLength==0)
		{
```

```
            //copy next sound to current sound
            pstrm->m_CurrentSound=pstrm->m_NextSound;
            pstrm->m_CurrentSoundLength=pstrm->m_NextSoundLength;
            //clear next sound
            pstrm->m_NextSound=NULL;
            pstrm->m_NextSoundLength=0;
        }
        //while len>0 and length of current sound>0, stream to buffer
        while(len>0 && pstrm->m_CurrentSoundLength>0)
        {
            //stream a byte to audio buffer
            *(buffer++)=*(pstrm->m_CurrentSound++);
            //decrease lengths
            len--;
            pstrm->m_CurrentSoundLength--;
        }
    }
}
```

If you follow it along, the function does customary checks to ensure that there is still sound data left to stream. When there is, it streams data one byte at a time. This short function is far from being a full-featured audio streaming engine, but some of the fundamental concepts are there. Check out FOSDL5_2 to see (or rather, hear) it work.

Converting and Mixing

Something should have bothered you a little bit about the discussion of loading and playing WAV files. I had to open the audio device to use the same format as the WAV data I was streaming to it. In the real world, you don't have this luxury. There has to be a way to take the data you will stream and convert it to the format in which it will be played. SDL can help you here.

First, you have to make a converter. This is the SDL_AudioCVT structure's sole purpose—to keep information vital for one sound format to be converted into another. While the actual details of the conversion are not important, knowing how to make it happen is. To build a converter, you use the SDL_BuildAudioCVT function.

```
int SDL_BuildAudioCVT(SDL_AudioCVT *cvt, Uint16 src_format, Uint8 src_chan-
nels, int src_rate, Uint16 dst_format, Uint8 dst_channels, int dst_rate);
```

This function takes a number of parameters. The first, cvt, is a pointer to an SDL_AudioCVT that will be filled in with the data necessary to convert sounds. The next three, src_format, src_channels, and src_rate, specify what sort of data will be put into the converter. You can get these from the SDL_AudioSpec generated by SDL_LoadWAV.

The dst_format, dst_channels, and dst_rate specify what the output of the converter will be. You can get this data from the obtained audio specification after the call to SDL_OpenAudio. If this function can create the converter, it will return 1. If it cannot, it will return -1.

You must be aware of at least a few of the members of SDL_AudioCVT. These are named buf, len, len_mult, and len_ratio.

The buf member is a pointer into which you place the data that you want to convert. After the conversion, it contains the newly converted data. The len member is the original length of your audio data, before conversion. The len_mult member helps you allocate enough size for buf. You should allocate at least len*len_mult bytes so that there is enough room to do the conversion. Finally, len_ratio, when multiplied by len after the conversion has taken place, will give you the number of bytes taken up by the sound after it has been converted.

Sound like a lot of trouble? I agree. After you have set up the buf and len members of SDL_AudioCVT, you call SDL_ConvertAudio.

```
int SDL_ConvertAudio(SDL_AudioCVT *cvt);
```

This function takes only a pointer to the SDL_AudioCVT structure. If it is able to convert the data, it returns 0. If it cannot, it returns -1.

One final function, and then we're done (or rather, I've had it) with the audio subsystem of SDL. You use the SDL_MixAudio function when you want to mix two sounds together into a single stream.

```
void SDL_MixAudio(Uint8 *dst, Uint8 *src, Uint32 len, int volume);
```

This function simply takes two pointers to audio data (dst and src), a length of the data you want to mix (len), and a volume. The volume can range from 0 to SDL_MIX_MAXVOLUME. The SDL documentation does not suggest using this function to mix more than two streams. Use it at your own risk.

Why You Don't Want to Use the SDL Audio Subsystem

Compared to other parts of SDL, the audio subsystem is very low level—it must be in order to accommodate all of the platforms on which it performs. There are much better things to use than the functions I've detailed here, which is why I have glossed over some of them a bit. In Chapter 11, I will talk about SDL_mixer, which is a much better alternative (although it uses this subsystem at its core).

The SDL CD Subsystem

You're sitting there, playing a game, and there is music playing from the CD. Background music like this has been a mainstay in the video game industry for years. However, you have to find specialized APIs to get it to work on your system.

SDL to the rescue. With SDL, you can play music from CDs. If you wanted, you could even make a CD player console with SDL. (I don't really see why you'd want to do this since there are many of these types of applications available for free on the Internet, but you could.)

The SDL CD subsystem consists of two structures and 11 functions. I divide the functions into two groups—one that is informational and one that is comprised of functions that cause the CD player to actually do something.

CD Structures

As usual, I'll start with the structures. There are two of these, and they are purely informational. The first structure is SDL_CD.

```
typedef struct{
  int id;
  CDstatus status;
  int numtracks;
  int cur_track;
  int cur_frame;
  SDL_CDtrack track[SDL_MAX_TRACKS+1];
} SDL_CD;
```

There are a number of members here. The first one, id, is a private identifier for the CD-ROM drive. Typically this will have no importance whatsoever to your application.

The second parameter, status, tells you the status of the CD drive. It will be one of the constants listed in Table 5.2.

Table 5.2 CD-ROM Status Constants

Constant	Meaning
CD_TRAYEMPTY	There is no CD in the tray.
CD_STOPPED	The CD is not playing.
CD_PLAYING	The CD is playing.
CD_PAUSED	The CD has been paused.
CD_ERROR	There has been an error.

The numtracks member specifies how many tracks are on the CD. If you've ever listened to a CD in your life, you are well aware that CD music is arranged in tracks; typically, one song is on a track. Tracks are an easy way to index the musical data.

The cur_track member tells you which track the CD is currently playing, and the cur_frame member tells you which frame the CD is currently playing. A frame is the atomic unit of measurement on a CD, much like a byte is the atomic unit of memory on a computer.

The final member is an array called track. It points to an array of SDL_CDTrack structures. This structure, shown here, gives you information about all of the tracks on the CD.

```
typedef struct{
  Uint8 id;
  Uint8 type;
  Uint32 length;
  Uint32 offset;
} SDL_CDtrack;
```

The id member of SDL_CDTrack is the track number on the CD. It ranges from 0 to 99, with 0 being the first track on the CD.

The type member tells you what sort of track this is. Since a CD can contain both computer-readable data and music data, this member will be either SDL_AUDIO_TRACK or SDL_DATA_TRACK. Naturally, you cannot play a data track.

The length and offset members measure the length of the track and where it begins, respectively. This measurement is in frames. Of course, this unit of measurement is completely useless to human beings; we are used to minutes and seconds. As luck would have it, SDL has a constant that will convert frames to seconds. It is called CD_FPS, which stands for frames per second. Dividing the length by CD_FPS will give you the length of a track in seconds, which is easily converted into minutes and seconds.

CD Functions

Again, I divide the CD functions in SDL into two groups—informational and CD playing. There are only two informational functions; the other nine actually deal with playing the CD.

Informational Functions

Before you do anything with the CD subsystem of SDL, you need to know two things—how many CD drives there are and what their names are.

Before you can use any SDL CD-ROM function, you must initialize the subsystem by including SDL_INIT_CDROM as part of the call to SDL_Init. Then you can check how many CD-ROM drives are attached to the machine with a call to SDL_CDNumDrives.

```
int SDL_CDNumDrives(void);
```

This function takes no parameters and returns the number of CD-ROM drives attached to the computer. Next, you can find out the name of the CD-ROM drive by calling SDL_CDName.

```
const char *SDL_CDName(int drive);
```

This function takes the number of the drive, which ranges from 0 to one less than the value returned by SDL_CDNumDrives. The return value is a string containing the name of the CD drive.

Now a quick example. FOSDL5_3 contains the code for this demo. It doesn't really do much; it simply initializes the CD-ROM subsystem and writes how many CD drives there are and the name of each drive. The code looks something like this:

```
#include "sdl.h"
int main(int argc, char* argv[])
{
      SDL_Init(SDL_INIT_CDROM);
      atexit(SDL_Quit);
      fprintf(stdout,"Number of CD drives:%d\n",SDL_CDNumDrives());
      for(int index=0;index<SDL_CDNumDrives();index++)
      {
            fprintf(stdout,"The name of CD Drive#%d is
%s.\n",index,SDL_CDName(index));
      }
      return(0);
}
```

On my machine, this program writes the following to stdout.txt:

```
Number of CD drives:1
The name of CD Drive#0 is D:\.
```

Your output will vary, depending on the configuration of your system.

CD Playing Functions

Now that you can find out what CD-ROM drives are available, you'll want to get information about the tracks available on the CD. To do this, you use `SDL_CDOpen`.

```
SDL_CD *SDL_CDOpen(int drive);
```

This function takes a drive number, just like `SDL_CDName` did, and returns a pointer to an `SDL_CD` that will contain all of the information about that CD-ROM. Drive 0 is the default drive for the system.

After you are done with the CD, you call `SDL_CDClose`.

```
void SDL_CDClose(SDL_CD *cdrom);
```

This function returns no value and takes as its single parameter a pointer to the `SDL_CD` structure you got from opening it with `SDL_CDOpen`.

Through experimentation I have determined that, at least on my machine, simply calling SDL_CDOpen won't give you the information you need about the number of tracks on a given CD. To get that information, you need to call SDL_CDStatus.

```
CDstatus SDL_CDStatus(SDL_CD *cdrom);
```

This function takes an SDL_CD pointer (the same one returned from SDL_CDOpen) and returns the status of the CD. These are the same statuses that were shown back in Table 5.2.

Now you have enough information to be able to look at the contents of a CD. Example program FOSDL5_4 on the CD shows how you might do this. It shows how many tracks are on the CD and lists each track's information.

And now you're actually going to play a CD. There are two different functions that you can use to do this. The first one is called SDL_CDPlay.

```
int SDL_CDPlay(SDL_CD *cdrom, int start, int length);
```

This function takes a pointer to an SDL_CD structure (cdrom), a frame at which to begin (start), and a number of frames to play (length). It returns 0 if everything went fine and -1 if there was an error. You can get the start and length parameters from looking at the audio tracks on the CD.

Of course, if you are going to play a CD, you also want to be able to stop it. The function for doing that is SDL_CDStop.

```
int SDL_CDStop(SDL_CD *cdrom);
```

This function takes a pointer to an SDL_CD structure that contains the information about the CD you are using. The return value is 0 for success and -1 for failure.

In FOSDL5_5, I have created a small application that will randomly shuffle the songs on a CD. It's actually a pretty neat little program and a low-memory footprint compared to commercial programs that do the same thing. Check it out on the CD-ROM. (I'm actually using the program as I'm writing this.)

There is another function that you can use to play music from a CD. It is called SDL_CDPlayTracks, and it looks like this:

```
int SDL_CDPlayTracks(SDL_CD *cdrom, int start_track, int start_frame,
int ntracks, int nframes);
```

This function takes a number of parameters. The first (cdrom) is a pointer to the SDL_CD structure representing the CD drive. The second parameter (start_track) is the starting track to begin playing. The third parameter (start_frame) is the first frame of the starting track to begin playing. This is in relation to the starting track, so if you want to begin at the start of the track, put 0. The fourth parameter (ntracks) is how many tracks you want to play. The final parameter (nframes) is how many frames of the last track you want to play. If you want to play the entire track, put the length of that track. SDL_CDPlayTracks returns 0 if there is no problem. If an error occurs, you'll get a -1.

You could easily rewrite FOSDL5_5 to use SDL_CDPlayTracks instead of SDL_Play. In fact, you'd only have to change a single line.

In order to have a full-featured CD playing program, there are just a few other things that you must be able to do. One is to pause and resume CD playing, and the other is to eject the CD. All three of the functions for doing these things are rather similar.

```
int SDL_CDPause(SDL_CD *cdrom);
int SDL_CDResume(SDL_CD *cdrom);
int SDL_CDEject(SDL_CD *cdrom);
```

Each of these functions takes a pointer to an SDL_CD structure, and the return values are 0 for success or -1 for an error. The SDL_CDPause function pauses the playing CD. SDL_CDResume restarts the play. Finally, SDL_CDEject ejects the CD tray.

Summary

After reading this chapter, you probably guessed that I'm not a big fan of the SDL audio subsystem. This would be true—I'm not. Luckily, there is a promising SDL add-on library in development at the time of this writing called SDL_sound.

On the other hand, I do really like the CD subsystem. It has all of the features anyone would need to play music from a CD, with such a simple interface that doing it takes mere minutes.

In Chapter 11, you will take a look at SDL_mixer, which is much better than the audio subsystem of SDL.

CHAPTER 6

SDL Joysticks

In Chapter 4, I talked a bit about joysticks, primarily about the events related to them. This chapter deals with joysticks themselves, and how to set them up so that you can read events from them.

Joysticks at a Glance

As far as SDL is concerned, a joystick is any game controller attached to your machine that is not the system's keyboard or mouse. This can be anything from a game pad to a flight yoke to a racecar steering wheel.

As you learned in Chapter 4, SDL divides the type of information that you can get from a joystick into four categories, each represented by its own type of event. These four types are axes, buttons, hats, and balls.

An axis has a range of values. Most joysticks have at least two axes—one horizontal and one vertical. Typically, these axes are used to control the position or speed of something on the screen. A button has two states—up and down. They are commonly used to trigger some sort of event, such as a gun firing. A hat has eight states. It typically is used to change the point of view within the game. Finally, a ball typically is used to select options, although it has other uses as well.

Of course, I don't intend to tell you how to use an axis, button, hat, or ball on a joystick. I'm a proponent of being unconventional and creative.

There is only one structure to know about in the joystick subsystem of SDL. It is called `SDL_Joystick`, and the members are hidden from you as a programmer. You can get all the information you need to know through functions.

As far as functions in the SDL joystick subsystem go, there are three types. One type of function opens and closes access to a particular joystick attached to the system. It also enumerates joysticks so that you can examine which ones are attached to the system.

Another type of function allows you to examine various types of information you can get from the joystick, such as how many axes, buttons, and so on the joystick has.

The third type of function allows you to check on the state of the joystick's buttons, axes, hats, and balls. This is similar to the "direct access" method of gathering input from the keyboard or mouse.

Gathering Information about Joysticks Attached to the System

Before you can use joysticks in an application, you have to ask a number of questions. How many joysticks are attached to the system? What are the names of these joysticks? How many axes do each of these joysticks have? How many buttons? How many hats and/or trackballs?

To answer the question of how many joysticks are attached to the system, you call `SDL_NumJoysticks`.

```
int SDL_NumJoysticks(void);
```

This function takes no parameters and returns how many joysticks are attached to the system. That was an easy question to answer.

To learn the names of the joysticks, which can be important if you offer customizable controls as part of your game, you call `SDL_JoystickName`.

```
const char *SDL_JoystickName(int index);
```

This function takes an `index` into the joystick list. Valid values are 0 to one less than the value returned by `SDL_NumJoysticks`. This function returns a string that contains the name of the joystick.

To answer any of the other questions, such as how many axes, buttons, hats, or balls are on the joystick, you first must open access to the joystick. You do this with `SDL_JoystickOpen`.

```
SDL_Joystick *SDL_JoystickOpen(int index);
```

This function takes an `index` into the joystick list, just as `SDL_JoystickName` did. The returned value is a pointer to an `SDL_Joystick` structure. The implementation details for `SDL_Joystick` are not important. You simply need to have a pointer to an `SDL_Joystick` in order to work with a joystick.

For every open, there is a close. When you are done with a joystick that you have opened, you need to close it, just like everything else in SDL. The function for doing so is called (you guessed it!) `SDL_JoystickClose`.

```
void SDL_JoystickClose(SDL_Joystick *joystick);
```

This function returns no value and takes a pointer to an `SDL_Joystick`. It closes access to the joystick.

Finally, you might like to check whether a particular joystick in the list is currently opened. To do so, you use `SDL_JoystickOpened`.

```
int SDL_JoystickOpened(int index);
```

This function takes an `index` into the joystick list, similar to `SDL_JoystickOpen`, and returns either 1 (indicating that the joystick is opened) or 0 (indicating that the joystick has not been opened).

Once you have your `SDL_Joystick` pointer, you can ask how many axes, buttons, hats, or trackballs the joystick has by using one of the following four functions. Figure 6.1 shows a picture of a joystick with its anatomy labeled.

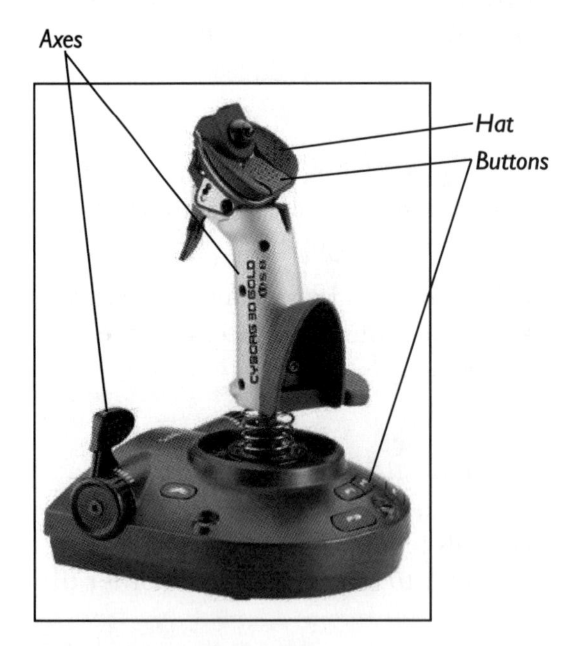

Figure 6.1 *Joystick anatomy*

```
int SDL_JoystickNumAxes(SDL_Joystick *joystick);
int SDL_JoystickNumButtons(SDL_Joystick *joystick);
int SDL_JoystickNumHats(SDL_Joystick *joystick);
int SDL_JoystickNumBalls(SDL_Joystick *joystick);
```

Each of these functions, which are all named appropriately, take only a pointer to an `SDL_Joystick` (the one you obtained from `SDL_JoystickOpen`) and return the number of input widgets of that particular type the joystick has.

Naturally, as with any subsystem of SDL, you must first initialize it in your call to `SDL_Init` by using the `SDL_INIT_JOYSTICK` bit flag.

Now for a short example. You can find it on the CD-ROM under FOSDL6_1, in the Examples folder.

```
#include "sdl.h"
#include <stdlib.h>
SDL_Joystick* g_pStick;
int main(int argc, char* argv[])
{
      SDL_Init(SDL_INIT_JOYSTICK);
      atexit(SDL_Quit);
      if(SDL_NumJoysticks()==0)
      {
           fprintf(stdout,"There are no joysticks attached to the system.\n");
      }
      else
      {
           fprintf(stdout,"Number of Joysticks: %d\n\n",SDL_NumJoysticks());
           for(int index=0;index<SDL_NumJoysticks();index++)
           {
                 fprintf(stdout,"Joystick Index: %d\n",index);
                 fprintf(stdout,"Joystick Name: %s\n",SDL_JoystickName(index));
                 g_pStick=SDL_JoystickOpen(index);
                 fprintf(stdout,"Number of axes:
                 %d\n",SDL_JoystickNumAxes(g_pStick));
                 fprintf(stdout,"Number of buttons:
                 %d\n",SDL_JoystickNumButtons(g_pStick));
                 fprintf(stdout,"Number of hats:
                             %d\n",SDL_JoystickNumHats(g_pStick));
                             fprintf(stdout,"Number of balls:
```

```
                %d\n",SDL_JoystickNumBalls(g_pStick));
                SDL_JoystickClose(g_pStick);
                fprintf(stdout,"\n");
            }
    }
    fprintf(stdout,"\nTerminating program normally.\n");
    return(0);
}
```

This program is very simple. It examines how many joysticks are attached to the system, goes through and opens each one, and returns information about each of the input widgets. When I ran the example on my system, this is what it spit out.

```
Number of Joysticks: 1


Joystick Index: 0
Joystick Name: Microsoft PC-joystick driver
Number of axes: 2
Number of buttons: 6
Number of hats: 0
Number of balls: 0
```

As you can see, I have only one joystick attached to my system. It's actually a game pad, but I'm using a default Microsoft driver. It has two axes, six buttons, and no hats or trackballs. If I had a number of other joystick-type input devices attached, they also would have been listed here.

The joystick subsystem is rather simple to use to look at the devices attached to the system. As you will read in a moment, it is just as easy to get data from joysticks.

Getting Data from Joysticks or Other Input Devices

When you are getting joystick data, you have two choices. These choices are not mutually exclusive and can be used together, but you will want to primarily use one or the other.

One choice, as I discussed in Chapter 4, is to use events. I won't bother recounting the event structures dealing with joysticks here because they were covered back in Chapter 4. However, you do need to enable joystick events if you plan to use them. The function for doing so is called SDL_JoystickEventState.

```
int SDL_JoystickEventState(int state);
```

This function takes an int value—SDL_ENABLE, SDL_IGNORE, or SDL_QUERY. Passing SDL_ENABLE or SDL_IGNORE will turn on or off, respectively, the joystick event polling state. This is the suggested way to handle joystick input. Passing SDL_QUERY will cause this function to return the current state of joystick event polling.

When joystick event polling is enabled, joystick events will be read automatically whenever there is a call to SDL_PollEvent or SDL_WaitEvent. If you choose not to use joystick events, you will have to update joystick information manually, using SDL_JoystickUpdate.

```
void SDL_JoystickUpdate(void);
```

This function takes no parameters and returns no values. It updates all opened joysticks. It gets called automatically when you have joystick event polling enabled.

After you have updated the joysticks, you can read directly the values for the input widgets on the joysticks using one of the accessor functions.

If you want to read the value of a particular axis, you use SDL_JoystickGetAxis.

```
Sint16 SDL_JoystickGetAxis(SDL_Joystick *joystick, int axis);
```

This function takes two parameters. The first (joystick) is a pointer to an SDL_Joystick. The second (axis) is the number of the axis you want to read. The returned value is the current position of the axis, which can range from –32,768 to 32,767.

To read the state of a button on a joystick, you use SDL_JoystickGetButton.

```
Uint8 SDL_JoystickGetButton(SDL_Joystick *joystick, int button);
```

This function takes a pointer to an SDL_Joystick (called joystick) and a button index (button). It returns 0 if the button is not pressed and 1 if it is.

For point-of-view hats, the accessor function is SDL_JoystickGetHat.

```
Uint8 SDL_JoystickGetHat(SDL_Joystick *joystick, int hat);
```

This function takes a pointer to an SDL_Joystick (joystick) and the index of the hat (hat). It returns the current position of the hat. Just like hat events (detailed in Chapter 4), this returned value is a combination of bit flags.

Finally, you can retrieve how far a trackball has moved since the last update with a call to SDL_JoystickGetBall.

```
int SDL_JoystickGetBall(SDL_Joystick *joystick, int ball, int *dx, int *dy);
```

Since trackballs have two return values, this function is a bit of an oddball compared to the other accessor functions. The first two parameters (joystick and ball) are again pointers to the SDL_Joystick you are looking at and the ball from which you want data. The dx and dy parameters are pointers to ints that are filled with the relative motion of the trackball. The return value is 0 if successful and -1 if there was an error.

Here is another short example, just to demonstrate getting information from a joystick, and then you'll be done with joysticks. The example is called FOSDL6_2.

```
#include "sdl.h"
#include <stdlib.h>
const int SCREEN_WIDTH=640;
const int SCREEN_HEIGHT=480;
SDL_Surface* g_pDisplaySurface = NULL;
SDL_Event g_Event;
SDL_Joystick* g_pStick;
int g_nStickButtons;
int g_StickAxis[2];
SDL_Rect g_FillRect;
int main(int argc, char* argv[])
{
	SDL_Init(SDL_INIT_VIDEO|SDL_INIT_JOYSTICK);
	atexit(SDL_Quit);
	g_pDisplaySurface =
	SDL_SetVideoMode(SCREEN_WIDTH,SCREEN_HEIGHT,0,SDL_ANYFORMAT);
	g_pStick=SDL_JoystickOpen(0);
	g_nStickButtons=SDL_JoystickNumButtons(g_pStick);
	SDL_JoystickEventState(SDL_ENABLE);
```

```
    for(;;)
    {
        if(SDL_PollEvent(&g_Event)==0)
        {
            g_FillRect.x=g_FillRect.y=0;
            g_FillRect.w=SCREEN_WIDTH;
            g_FillRect.h=SCREEN_HEIGHT;

SDL_FillRect(g_pDisplaySurface,&g_FillRect,SDL_MapRGB(g_pDisplaySurface-
    >format,0,0,0));
            g_FillRect.x=g_FillRect.y=0;
            g_FillRect.w=256;
            g_FillRect.h=256;

SDL_FillRect(g_pDisplaySurface,&g_FillRect,SDL_MapRGB(g_pDisplaySurface-
    >format,0,128,0));
            g_FillRect.x=g_StickAxis[0]+128-2;
            g_FillRect.y=g_StickAxis[1]+128-2;
            g_FillRect.w=g_FillRect.h=5;

SDL_FillRect(g_pDisplaySurface,&g_FillRect,SDL_MapRGB(g_pDisplaySurface-
    >format,255,255,255));
            for(int index=0;index<g_nStickButtons;index++)
            {
                g_FillRect.x=256;
                g_FillRect.y=16*index;
                g_FillRect.w=g_FillRect.h=16;
                if(SDL_JoystickGetButton(g_pStick,index))
                {

SDL_FillRect(g_pDisplaySurface,&g_FillRect,SDL_MapRGB(g_pDisplaySurface-
    >format,255,0,0));
                }
                else
                {

SDL_FillRect(g_pDisplaySurface,&g_FillRect,SDL_MapRGB(g_pDisplaySurface-
    >format,128,128,128));
                }
            }

            SDL_UpdateRect(g_pDisplaySurface,0,0,0,0);
```

```
            }
            else
            {
                    if(g_Event.type==SDL_QUIT) break;
                    if(g_Event.type==SDL_JOYAXISMOTION)
                    {
                            if(g_Event.jaxis.axis<2)
                            {

        g_StickAxis[g_Event.jaxis.axis]=g_Event.jaxis.value>>8;
                            }
                    }
            }
        }
        SDL_JoystickClose(g_pStick);
        return(0);
}
```

This example uses a combination of event polling and accessor functions to get joystick input. There is a graphical display that shows the position of the first two axes of the joystick and all of the buttons. Not bad for a five-minute program. Figure 6.2 shows the output of this program as I was testing it.

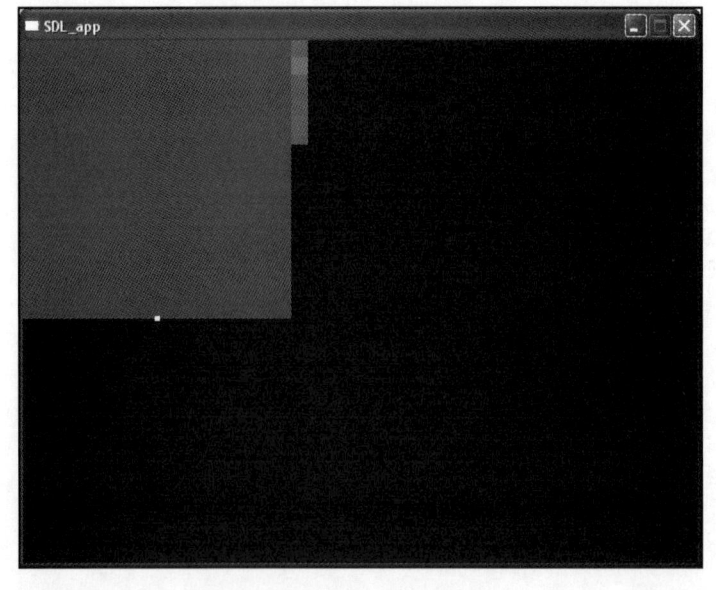

Figure 6.2 *Output of FOSDL6_2*

Summary

That wraps up the joystick subsystem. There really isn't all that much to it. Generally speaking, you just need to open up the joystick, enable events, and respond from there as with any other sort of event.

CHAPTER 7

SDL Threads and Timers

You have looked at a number of the SDL subsystems. Thus far, all of the subsystems could be perceived by one of the five senses. Video and the window manager can be perceived by sight, audio and CD playing can be perceived by hearing, and event handling and joysticks can be perceived by touch.

In this chapter, you come to two subsystems that cannot be perceived by any of the senses. I'm talking about threads and timers. I discuss these two subsystems as though they were one, since they are very similar in terms of what you can accomplish with them.

Multitasking and multithreading have been buzzwords of the computer world for quite a while. For example, at this very moment, in addition to my word processor I have open my e-mail, the table of contents for this book, the file folder in which the book's files are stored, the SDL online documentation, and ICQ. In recent years, we have come to take this ability to multitask for granted, but it was not so long ago that such things were virtually impossible.

Each "task" that I have open on my machine can have subtasks, which do their little part to work for the team. These might be semi-autonomous threads, shoveling coal in the background, or they might be periodically time-based. In any case, they can be intrinsic to a successful game or application.

SDL Threads and Timers at a Glance

In threads and timers, you have five distinct types of entities. They are threads, timers, mutexes, semaphores, and condition variables. Two of these entities, threads and timers, deal with running other code concurrently with the main thread (the application or game). The other three deal with communication between the main thread and the other threads, and between the other threads themselves.

A thread is a semi-autonomous running piece of code. If your main thread were a super villain, each of the threads would be a henchman. Most of the time, henchmen have nothing to do so they sit around, play solitaire, drink coffee, and grumble with the other henchmen about how poorly they are treated and paid by the super villain. This is also true of threads. Most of the time they do nothing but wait for a particular condition. When that condition occurs, the thread goes into action, takes care of whatever business is required, and then goes back to waiting again.

A timer is a periodic event. For example, if you needed to create a blinking cursor, you could set up a timer that goes off every 100 milliseconds (ms) to change a Boolean variable from false to true or true to false. You could then read that variable and know whether or not the cursor was visible.

A mutex is a simple way to communicate between threads. It exists in one of two states—locked or unlocked. When a mutex has been locked by one thread, and another thread tries to lock it, the second thread will have to sit and wait until the first thread unlocks the mutex. In this way, threads can work together sequentially on a task.

A semaphore (named for a form of flag communication still used by the navies of the world) is similar in concept to a mutex, except that it can have more values than just locked or unlocked. It has a numeric value that, depending on whether it is positive, negative, or zero, allows threads to either wait or do whatever it is they are doing. Semaphores are a more robust way to schedule events than mutexes.

Finally, a condition variable works with mutexes. It tells threads when to begin their tasks. Condition variables are just another way to communicate between threads.

I know that some of these entities, such as mutexes, semaphores, and condition variables, might seem a little odd if you are unfamiliar with multithreaded programming. Although this book is not about multithreading (a much larger topic than I could possibly cover in a small book like this), I shall try my best to give you a decent overview of how you can use these entities.

Timers

I'll begin with the easiest entity to program—the timer. A timer is nothing more than a function that is called after a certain period of time has elapsed. Typically, the function doesn't do much before returning. To create a timer, you use `SDL_AddTimer`.

```
SDL_TimerID SDL_AddTimer(Uint32 interval, SDL_NewTimerCallback callback,
void *param);
```

> **NOTE**
>
> **Before using timers, you have to initialize them with the `SDL_INIT_TIMER` bit flag during your call to `SDL_Init`.**

This function takes three parameters. First is `interval`, which is the number of milliseconds that should pass between calls to the timer function. The second is `callback`, which is a pointer to the timer function that needs to be called each interval. The last is `param`, which is a pointer to whatever data the timer will need each time it is called. This function returns an `SDL_TimerID`, which you should keep somewhere so that you can later remove the timer.

The callback function must look like this:

```
Uint32 TimerCallback(Uint32 interval, void *param);
```

> **TIP**
>
> **Just because you specified a 23-ms timer interval (to pick a number out of the air), don't expect that the timer interval is actually 23 ms. Systems vary, but the granularity of the timer is typically 10 ms, so when you want to create a timer, round up or down to the nearest 10 ms.**

You can name the function however you like, of course. The parameters are `interval`, which contains the current interval in use by the timer, and `param`, which is the same pointer that is passed to `SDL_AddTimer`. Your function must return a `Uint32`. This value will be the new interval.

When you want to remove a timer, you call `SDL_RemoveTimer`.

```
SDL_bool SDL_RemoveTimer(SDL_TimerID id);
```

This function takes as its sole parameter the ID of the timer you want to remove. This is the same ID that is returned by the call to `SDL_AddTimer`. The return value is an `SDL_bool`, the value of which will be either `SDL_TRUE` or `SDL_FALSE`, indicating whether or not the timer was successfully removed.

You will find an example called FOSDL7_1 on the CD. In this example, a timer is used to clear the screen to a random color every second. Of course, the timer itself does not manipulate the video; instead, it sets a Boolean flag that the main application checks for and clears when there are no events occurring.

The ability to set up timers is not the only way that SDL can help you with timing. There are also functions for checking how much time has passed since SDL was initialized, as well as a function that you can use simply to wait for a specified period of time.

To check how many milliseconds have passed since SDL was initialized, you can call `SDL_GetTicks`.

```
Uint32 SDL_GetTicks(void);
```

This function takes no parameters and returns the number of milliseconds since library initialization occurred. Typically, if you want to wait a specified number of milliseconds (for example, 500), you would do something like this:

```
//grab initial time
Uint32 time_initial=SDL_GetTicks();
//wait until 500 ms have passed
while((SDL_GetTicks()-time_initial)<500);
```

Or, you can tell SDL to wait for a specified number of milliseconds with a call to `SDL_Delay`.

```
void SDL_Delay(Uint32 ms);
```

With this function, you supply a number of milliseconds as the parameter, and the function will wait that many milliseconds before returning. The equivalent code using `SDL_GetTicks` is

```
SDL_Delay(500);
```

In games, timing often becomes critical, so the use of timers and other timing functions becomes rather important.

Threads

Timers are neat, but they are limited. Threads provide a much more powerful way to have more than one thing happening at a time in your programs. (Of course, this isn't really true on a single-processor system; only a single thread can be executing at any one time.) However, because threads are more powerful, you need to be more careful with them.

A thread will run concurrently with your main application, at least in theory. It shares with the main application all global memory, file descriptors, and so on. The problem comes in when you try to keep your thread from messing with something that it shouldn't be messing with, such as video memory or sound. For one thing, a thread should never, ever mess with video memory. When a thread is running, there should be some sort of mechanism by which the thread communicates with the main application, and there should be a way for the main application to regulate a thread's actions.

Before you get to those issues, however, take a look at how to create a thread. The function for doing so is called `SDL_CreateThread`.

```
SDL_Thread *SDL_CreateThread(int (*fn)(void *), void *data);
```

This function takes two parameters. The first (`fn`) is a pointer to a function that makes up the thread. The second is a `void*` that is the data passed to the thread's function. The return value of this function is a pointer to an `SDL_Thread`.

The thread function, which you create yourself, looks like this:

```
int FOSDL_ThreadFunction(void* data);
```

This function takes a pointer to a `void*`. This parameter is the same as the `data` parameter passed to `SDL_CreateThread`. The return value of this function is an `int` and can mean whatever you want it to mean. When this function returns, the thread dies.

If for any reason you need to stop the thread and you cannot wait for its function to return, you can use `SDL_KillThread`. Yes, it sounds a little bit violent, but nobody yet has picketed for the rights of threads.

```
void SDL_KillThread(SDL_Thread *thread);
```

This function takes the `SDL_Thread` pointer of a thread and proceeds to destroy that thread.

If you are more patient and less likely to go about slaying threads haphazardly, you can use SDL_WaitThread to wait until a thread's function terminates, allowing it to die in peace.

```
void SDL_WaitThread(SDL_Thread *thread, int *status);
```

This function takes a pointer to an SDL_Thread (thread) and a pointer to an int (status) and returns no value. The function waits for the thread to terminate. When it does, the value returned by the thread's function is placed into the int pointed to by status. If you don't particularly care about the return value, you can pass NULL as status, and the return value will be ignored.

Each thread, in addition to having an SDL_Thread pointer, also has a 32-bit thread ID, which you can use to organize threads and communication between them. To grab the thread ID of the current thread (from within a thread's function), you use SDL_ThreadID.

```
Uint32 SDL_ThreadID(void);
```

This function simply returns the 32-bit identifier for the thread. It takes no parameters. To retrieve the thread's ID from outside of the thread itself, you first need to have the SDL_Thread pointer, and then you can call SDL_GetThreadID.

```
Uint32 SDL_GetThreadID(SDL_Thread *thread);
```

This function takes a pointer to an SDL_Thread and returns that thread's 32-bit identifier.

I'll get to an example using threads in a little while. First, you need to learn how to control and communicate with them.

NOTE

Threads, as well as mutexes, semaphores, and condition variables, are not automatically included when you #include sdl.h. You also have to #include SDL_thread.h in order to use them. On the other hand, you don't have to initialize them with a bit flag sent to SDL_Init.

Mutexes

The simplest form of thread regulation is performed using a mutex. As I discussed earlier, a mutex, once created, is in one of two states—

locked or unlocked. Once a mutex is locked, nothing else can lock it again until it is unlocked by whatever had previously locked it.

Creating a mutex is quite simple. You just make a call to `SDL_CreateMutex`.

```
SDL_mutex *SDL_CreateMutex(void);
```

This function takes no parameters and returns an `SDL_mutex` pointer. It's as easy as that. Poof! You've got a mutex.

When you want to destroy the mutex later, it's just as easy. You simply call `SDL_DestroyMutex`, and all of the mutexes of the world run in fear!

```
void SDL_DestroyMutex(SDL_mutex *mutex);
```

This function takes a pointer to an `SDL_mutex` and destroys that mutex.

To lock a mutex, you call `SDL_mutexP`. This function deviates from the normal SDL "apt name" theme, but who am I to judge? Here's what the function looks like.

```
int SDL_mutexP(SDL_mutex *mutex);
```

This function takes a pointer to a mutex and returns 0 for success and -1 if an error occurred. There is also a handy macro called `SDL_LockMutex` that you can use in place of `SDL_mutexP`, so the following two lines of code are equivalent.

```
SDL_mutexP(pMutex);
SDL_LockMutex(pMutex);
```

I much prefer the second option, since it makes the code easier to read, but the choice is ultimately up to you.

`SDL_mutexP` does one of two things, depending on the current state of the mutex it is being called upon to lock. If the mutex is currently unlocked, `SDL_mutexP` will lock it and return. If the mutex is currently locked, `SDL_mutexP` will wait until it is unlocked, then relock it and return.

On the flip side, there is `SDL_mutexV`, which unlocks a mutex.

```
int SDL_mutexV(SDL_mutex *mutex);
```

This function, like `SDL_mutexP`, takes a pointer to a mutex and returns 0 if successful or -1 for an error. This function unlocks a mutex; it doesn't really matter if the mutex was locked prior to the call to `SDL_mutexV`. There is also a handy macro for this function, called `SDL_UnlockMutex`.

In FOSDL7_2 (which you can find in the Examples folder on the CD), there is a short example that uses threads and a mutex. This is a very simple example, but it demonstrates what you can do with a thread and a mutex.

I won't post the entire program here because much of it is just the simple SDL shell you have been looking at throughout the book. However, I will show you two snippets that deal with threads.

The following code exists in the main application, prior to moving into the event loop.

```
g_pMutex=SDL_CreateMutex();
SDL_LockMutex(g_pMutex);
g_pThread=SDL_CreateThread(FOSDL_ThreadFunction,NULL);
SDL_UnlockMutex(g_pMutex);
SDL_WaitThread(g_pThread,NULL);
```

Here I create a mutex, lock it, and then proceed to create the thread. After I have created the thread, the mutex is unlocked, and the application waits for the thread to terminate.

The other part in this program that deals with threads is the thread function itself, shown here.

```
int FOSDL_ThreadFunction(void* data)
{
      fprintf(stdout,"Thread %d: Initialized!\n",SDL_ThreadID());
      fprintf(stdout,"Thread %d: Attempting to lock mutex.\n",SDL_ThreadID());
      SDL_LockMutex(g_pMutex);
      fprintf(stdout,"Thread %d: Mutex is locked.\n",SDL_ThreadID());
      fprintf(stdout,"Thread %d: Unlocking mutex.\n",SDL_ThreadID());
      SDL_UnlockMutex(g_pMutex);
      fprintf(stdout,"Thread %d: Terminating.\n",SDL_ThreadID());
      return(0);
}
```

This thread doesn't do much; it simply reports to `stdout` whatever it happens to be doing at the time. Its first task is to lock the mutex but, as you recall, the mutex is already locked by the main application before this thread is created, so the thread must wait until the application unlocks it before continuing. Then the thread unlocks the mutex and terminates.

As you can see, a mutex is a great way to create a thread but not have it actually start until the main application says so. This is sort of like an "on your mark...get set..." type of mutex, with the unlocking of the mutex being the "go."

Semaphores

The limitation of the mutex is that it only has two states, locked and unlocked. This is good for simple multithreading applications, but insufficient for more than two threads performing tasks at the same time. And so there are semaphores. As you will see, semaphores can act very much like mutexes but with more flexibility.

A semaphore, like a mutex, has an internal state. However, instead of just having two states, it can have as many states as you like (although this implementation has a total of 2^32 states, the maximum that will fit into a `Uint32`). When the state is 0, the semaphore behaves like a locked mutex, and any further attempt to lock it will wait until the semaphore has been unlocked by whatever has locked it.

To create a semaphore, you use the `SDL_CreateSemaphore` function.

```
SDL_sem *SDL_CreateSemaphore(Uint32 initial_value);
```

This function takes the initial value for the state of the semaphore and returns a pointer to an `SDL_sem`.

To destroy a semaphore, you call `SDL_DestroySemaphore`.

```
void SDL_DestroySemaphore(SDL_sem *sem);
```

This function takes a pointer to an `SDL_sem`, previously created by `SDL_CreateSemaphore`, and returns no value.

Semaphores do not use the terms *lock* and *unlock*; instead, they use *wait* and *post*. Don't be fooled—these terms are equivalent to lock and unlock when you are dealing with mutexes. When you wait on a semaphore, if the current value is greater than 0, it is decreased by one and the function returns. If the value of the semaphore is 0, the wait will bide its time until the value is greater than 0, and then it will decrement the value and return. When you post a semaphore, its value goes up by one (allowing something that is waiting for it to do something).

To wait on a semaphore, you use the `SDL_SemWait` function.

```
int SDL_SemWait(SDL_sem *sem);
```

This function takes a pointer to a semaphore and returns 0 if it is successful or -1 if it fails. The function waits until the semaphore pointed to by sem has a positive value, then it decrements the value and returns.

If the thread you have waiting for a semaphore has something else it can do in the meantime, you might want to use SDL_SemTryWait instead.

```
int SDL_SemTryWait(SDL_sem *sem);
```

This function similarly takes a pointer to a semaphore and returns either 0 or –1, depending on the success. However, instead of waiting until the semaphore has a positive value, it will return immediately. If the semaphore has a 0 value, it will return SDL_MUTEX_TIMEOUT. If a 0 is returned, then the semaphore's value is decreased by one.

Finally, you can wait for a semaphore with a timeout value. To do this, you use SDL_SemWaitTimeout.

```
int SDL_SemWaitTimeout(SDL_sem *sem, Uint32 timeout);
```

This function takes two parameters—a pointer to an SDL_sem (sem) and a timeout value in milliseconds (timeout). This function will return 0 for success, -1 for an error, or SDL_MUTEX_TIMEOUT, which represents the number of milliseconds elapsed and the fact that the function was not able to decrement the semaphore's value.

After waiting on a semaphore, conceptually doing the same thing as locking a mutex, you will want to increment the value of the semaphore by calling SDL_SemPost.

```
int SDL_SemPost(SDL_sem *sem);
```

This function takes a pointer to an SDL_sem and returns 0 or –1, depending on success or failure.

Finally, you can examine the value of a semaphore using the SDL_SemValue function.

```
Uint32 SDL_SemValue(SDL_sem *sem);
```

This function takes a pointer to an SDL_sem and returns the current value held by that semaphore.

Now for a quick semaphore example. You can find this example on the CD under FOSDL7_3. I will show only the portions that deal with threads and semaphores.

The first bit deals with creating the semaphores and threads. Here's what the code looks like.

```
//create semaphore
g_pSemaphore=SDL_CreateSemaphore(0);
//create three threads
g_pThread[0]=SDL_CreateThread(FOSDL_ThreadFunction,(void*)1);
g_pThread[1]=SDL_CreateThread(FOSDL_ThreadFunction,(void*)2);
g_pThread[2]=SDL_CreateThread(FOSDL_ThreadFunction,(void*)3);
//wait for a second
SDL_Delay(1000);
//post to the semaphore
SDL_SemPost(g_pSemaphore);
```

This bit of code creates a semaphore with an initial value of 0, which means that anything waiting for the semaphore will have to wait until it gets posted. Then the code creates three threads. (I'll get to the thread function in a moment.) After that, the main application waits for a second, so that all of the threads can be initialized, and then posts to the semaphore so that the threads can start running.

The thread function, which is identical for all three threads, is shown here.

```
//thread function
int FOSDL_ThreadFunction(void* data)
{
	//grab thread number
	int threadnumber=(int)data;
	//wait for semaphore
	fprintf(stdout,"Thread %d: Initialized.\n",threadnumber);
	fprintf(stdout,"Thread %d: Waiting for semaphore.\n",threadnumber);
	SDL_SemWait(g_pSemaphore);
	//post to semaphore
	fprintf(stdout,"Thread %d: Done waiting for semaphore.\n",thread-
number);
	fprintf(stdout,"Thread %d: Posting semaphore.\n",threadnumber);
	SDL_SemPost(g_pSemaphore);
	//wait for semaphore again before terminating
	fprintf(stdout,"Thread %d: Waiting for semaphore before terminating.
\n",threadnumber);
```

```
        SDL_SemWait(g_pSemaphore);
        //terminate
        fprintf(stdout,"Thread %d: Terminating.\n",threadnumber);
        SDL_SemPost(g_pSemaphore);
        //return 0
        return(0);
}
```

Each thread waits for the semaphore twice, once on startup and once on termination. It reports the progress of the function to stdout.txt. The basic rundown of the sequence of events follows.

1. Thread 1 is created and begins waiting for the semaphore.
2. Thread 2 is created and begins waiting for the semaphore.
3. Thread 3 is created and begins waiting for the semaphore.
4. The main application posts to the semaphore.
5. Thread 1 finishes waiting for the semaphore, posts to it, and waits for it again.
6. Thread 2 finishes waiting for the semaphore, posts to it, and waits for it again.
7. Thread 3 finishes waiting for the semaphore, posts to it, and waits for it again.
8. Thread 1 finishes waiting for the semaphore, posts to it, and then terminates.
9. Thread 2 finishes waiting for the semaphore, posts to it, and then terminates.
10. Thread 3 finishes waiting for the semaphore, posts to it, and then terminates.

As you see, you can do some fancy scheduling of threads using a semaphore. You could also post twice from the main application, and then two of the three threads would be doing something at the same time. It's enough to make your head swim.

Condition Variables

Finally, we come to condition variables. Condition variables work together with mutexes to keep things properly timed between threads.

Unlike mutexes and semaphores, condition variables don't have any states whatsoever. I'll show you what I mean in a few moments. First, you need to know how to create and destroy condition variables.

To create a condition variable, you call SDL_CreateCond.

```
SDL_cond *SDL_CreateCond(void);
```

This function takes no parameters and returns a pointer to an SDL_cond. That's really about it. Since a condition doesn't have an internal value (like a semaphore) and can neither be locked nor unlocked (like a mutex), you just need this pointer to be able to use the condition variable.

When you are done with a condition variable, you destroy it by calling SDL_DestroyCond.

```
void SDL_DestroyCond(SDL_cond *cond);
```

This function takes a pointer to an SDL_cond and returns no value. It destroys the condition variable that you created earlier with a call to SDL_CreateCond.

Okay, that's all well and good, but then how do you use condition variables? As I stated earlier, you use condition variables in conjunction with mutexes. You wait for a condition variable to give off a signal, which causes a mutex to become unlocked. To wait for a condition variable to signal, you use either SDL_CondWait or SDL_CondWaitTimeout.

```
int SDL_CondWait(SDL_cond *cond, SDL_mutex *mut);
int SDL_CondWaitTimeout(SDL_cond *cond, SDL_mutex *mutex, Uint32 ms);
```

In both cases, the mut parameters are pointers to an SDL_mutex, and this mutex must be locked prior to the call to SDL_CondWait or SDL_CondWaitTimeout. When the condition variable pointed to by the cond parameter is signaled, the mutex is unlocked and the function returns. In the case of SDL_CondWaitTimeout, if the number of milliseconds specified in the ms parameter passes before a signal occurs, the function returns but the mutex remains locked. When this function returns, you get a 0 if a signal occurred, a -1 if there was an error, or SDL_MUTEX_TIMEDOUT (for SDL_CondWaitTimeout).

You can have any number of threads waiting for a condition variable to be signaled. When signaling, you choose whether you want only one of the threads waiting for the condition variable to continue doing something or whether you want all of them to start. If you just want one thread (the next one waiting for the condition variable) to start, you use SDL_CondSignal. If you want them all to start again, you use SDL_CondBroadcast.

```
int SDL_CondSignal(SDL_cond *cond);
int SDL_CondBroadcast(SDL_cond *cond);
```

In both cases, these functions take pointers to an SDL_cond and cause one or more signals. SDL_CondSignal will cause the first mutex waiting on the condition to be unlocked. SDL_CondBroadcast will cause all of the mutexes waiting on the condition to be unlocked. The functions return 0 if successful and -1 if there is an error.

Condition variables are sort of weird. For one thing, they don't contain a value, as you might assume that anything called a variable would. However, proper use of condition variables can greatly enhance the organization of a multithreaded application.

Portability Problems

Just a quick caveat about threads, timers, and portability. Under WIN32, they are no problem to use (and in fact they make several jobs a lot easier). Just keep in mind that multithreaded programs might have issues when you attempt to port them to another operating system. You have been warned.

Summary

Well, this has been an odd little chapter. Threads and timers are powerful assets to any developer's arsenal, and programming multithreaded applications is rather system-specific for most operating systems. SDL, although it has not completely perfected the ability to do cross-platform multithreading, is darn close, and that's a Good Thing.

Now we have covered every last subsystem of SDL. I left very little uncovered, and I'm sure you'll run into those few things in the SDL documentation. But now you need to move on to other things, such as some of the add-on SDL libraries that help out with common tasks.

PART TWO

Add-On Libraries

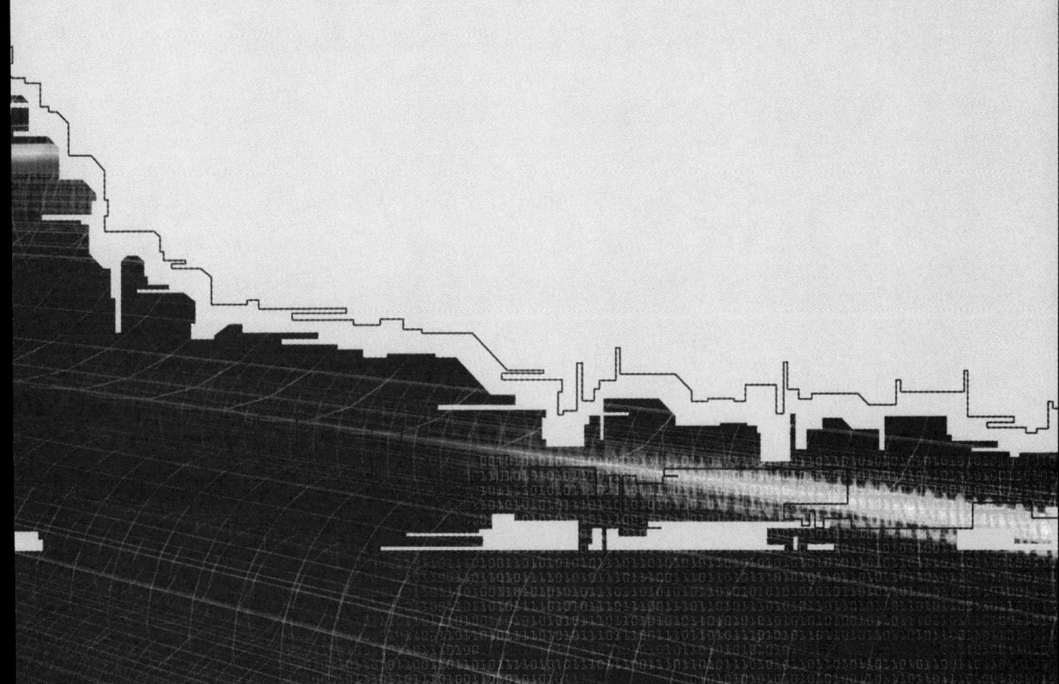

CHAPTER 8

SDL_image

And now for something completely different! A chapter that talks about only one function. Yes, you heard right! This chapter is about SDL_image, an add-on library that you can use with SDL. There is only one function within this library that you will have a use for, even though the library includes several functions.

What, you might ask, do SDL_image and the function in question do? Simply put, they allow you to load an image from almost any type of file, including BMP, PNM, XPM, LBM, PCX, GIF, JPEG, PNG, and TGA. In SDL itself, you are only allowed to load BMP files. As we all know, BMP files can be on the large side, so it is nice to have the ability to load something else.

Installation and Setup

Before you can use SDL_image, you need to install it and set it up. There is a file called SDL_image-devel-1.2.2-VC6.zip under the LIBS directory on the CD-ROM. This file contains the libraries and include files for SDL_image. You should unzip it somewhere clever. I chose to unzip it into a folder called C:\SDLDEV\SDL_image-1.2.2, with the folder that contains the libraries and include files for SDL itself. I like to keep things organized like that. Of course, you should always check for the latest version of SDL_image at http://www.libsdl.org/libraries.php.

Next, make sure that VC++ can see the appropriate directories for SDL_image's library and include files (under Tools, Options). This is similar to the process you went through to set up the environment for SDL in Chapter 1.

Finally, when you want to use SDL_image, you have to make sure that you are linking to sdl_image.lib in addition to the usual sdl.lib and sdl_main.lib. Furthermore, you will need to have jpeg.dll, libpng1.dll, zlib.dll, and sdl_image.dll available to your application, either in the application folder itself or in a system folder somewhere. For now, I suggest putting these DLLs into the same folder as the project you are writing.

Does this sound like a lot of work just to be able to load image files other than BMPs? Perhaps it is, but if you have a large number of BMPs, their size will dwarf the paltry 346 KB that are taken up by all of the DLLs combined. Using a smaller file format will actually cut the size of your application's resources even though you are adding four extra DLLs.

Using SDL_image

As I stated, there is really only one function from SDL_image that you should need to use. It is called `IMG_Load`.

```
SDL_Surface * IMG_Load(const char *file);
```

This function takes a string that holds the name of a graphics file that you want to load. If successful, it will return a pointer to an `SDL_Surface` that contains that newly loaded image. If there is some sort of problem, the function will return `NULL`.

This function looks very much like `SDL_LoadBitmap`. The only difference is that it can load images other than those with a .bmp extension.

As a quick example, take a look at FOSDL8_1 on the CD-ROM. It loads a sample image (the SDL now! logo from http://www.libsdl.org) and puts it in the application window. This image is in GIF format, thus demonstrating that SDL_image can load non-BMP image files. Take a look at Figure 8.1 to see what the application looks like.

Summary

There isn't much to say about SDL_image, since I discussed only one function. There are other functions that you can take a look at in SDL_image.h, but for the life of me I don't know of any good reason to call any of them.

Figure 8.1 *Output of FOSDL8_1*

CHAPTER 9

SDL_TTF

SDL does many things for you. It allows you to manipulate graphics, play sounds, gather input from a variety of input devices, and do things with threads and timers. One function that it truly lacks, though, is the ability to draw text on the screen.

Now, I have my own theories about how important text and fonts are to a game. I personally think that in many cases, text is overused. One of the big issues is localization. Not everyone speaks English, so it is a good idea to minimize the amount of text that is used on the screen and replace text items with icons. Of course, I've seen this sort of thing taken too far as well. In any case, there is a time and a place for text, and if you are using SDL, you will want to use SDL_ttf.

Setup and Installation

Installing and setting up SDL_ttf is much like installing and setting up SDL or SDL_image. There is a file called SDL_ttf-devel-2.0.5-VC6.zip under the LIBS folder on the CD-ROM. Unzip this file somewhere suitable (such as C:\SDLDEV\SDL_TTF-2.0.5), and then add the include and library files to the list of directories for VC++. The process is similar to the process for adding the SDL libs and include files that you read about in Chapter 1. Always be certain to check for updates to SDL_ttf on http://www.libsdl.org/projects/SDL_ttf.

> **NOTE**
> If you are particularly hard core, you might want to build SDL_ttf yourself. If this is the case, you will also need FreeType 2.0 or later. You can find the software at http://www.freetype.org.

Additionally, you will need to place SDL_ttf.dll either in a system directory or into your project directory when you write a program that uses SDL_ttf.

Using SDL_ttf

The SDL_ttf library has 31 callable functions. I divide these functions roughly into four categories—initialization, creation/destruction, information, and rendering. All SDL_ttf functions start with TTF_.

Initialization

Like SDL itself, SDL_ttf first needs to be initialized. The function for doing this is TTF_Init. Likewise, after the program ends, it needs to be uninitialized by calling TTF_Quit.

```
int TTF_Init(void);
void TTF_Quit(void);
```

TTF_Init will return 0 if all went well and -1 if an error occurred. TTF_Quit does not return any value. You will likely want to initialize SDL_ttf in much the same way you initialized SDL.

```
if(TTF_Init()==0)
{
        atexit(TTF_Quit);
}
```

It's nice to keep things all together like this, so you don't have to remember to put the call to TTF_Quit at the end of the program.

Creation and Destruction

The creation and destruction functions deal with making and unmaking fonts. The structure that keeps font information is called TTF_Font. The implementation details are completely hidden, however, so you only ever have to deal with pointers to TTF_Font objects.

There are two ways to create a font—by calling TTF_OpenFont or by calling TTF_OpenFontIndex.

```
TTF_Font * TTF_OpenFont(const char *file, int ptsize);
TTF_Font * TTF_OpenFontIndex(const char *file, int ptsize, long index);
```

In both cases, these functions return pointers to a newly created TTF_Font object. The first parameter of each is a string that specifies the file name of a TTF file to load. The second parameter of each is the point size you desire for the font. If you have ever worked with a word processor, you should be familiar with point sizes of fonts. If you aren't, one point is 1/72 of an inch. Since computer monitors vary widely, it has been established that 72 pixels make up an inch, although the actual measurement may vary. Therefore, point size equals pixel size, at least as far as computer graphics are concerned.

In the case of TTF_OpenFontIndex, there is a third parameter called index. This is for TTF files with more than one font in them; the index specifies which font you want to load.

Like everything else in SDL, you need to destroy a font when you are done using it by calling TTF_CloseFont.

```
void TTF_CloseFont(TTF_Font *font);
```

This function takes a pointer to a TTF_Font object and destroys it. There is no return value.

Information

Now, without getting into a big discussion about fonts and how typesetters do their jobs, I will tell you that a font has a number of informative statistics that might be useful to know at times. To make use of any of this information, you need to know just a small amount of font jargon.

The first (and simplest) bit of jargon is the size of the font. This is the height that characters in the font can be. It is usually equal to the point size of the font (which you specify in your call to TTF_OpenFont or TTF_OpenFontIndex). If this number is not quite the same as the point size, it will be very close. To retrieve the size of a font, you call TTF_FontHeight.

```
int TTF_FontHeight(TTF_Font *font);
```

This function takes a pointer to a TTF_Font and returns an int that represents the height or size of the font in pixels.

If you have ever written something down on ruled paper (and chances are that you have), you know that some letters, such as g, q, and p, dip down below the line, while other letters, such as m, n, and b, stay above it. The line upon which you are writing is called the *base line.* Various letters that have portions written above the line have an *ascent,* and letters that have portions below the line have a *descent.* For all of the letters of a font to fit properly when they are outputted, the font has a total ascent and descent to accommodate all of the letters. The ascent value plus the descent value equals the height of the font. For a better picture of the anatomy of a font, take a look at Figure 9.1.

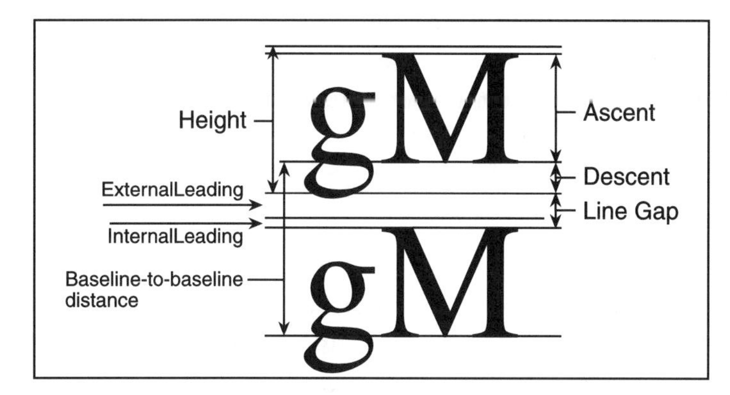

Figure 9.1 *Anatomy of a font*

To retrieve the ascent of a font, you use the TTF_FontAscent function; to retrieve the descent of a font, you use TTF_FontDescent.

```
int TTF_FontAscent(TTF_Font *font);
int TTF_FontDescent(TTF_Font *font);
```

Each of these functions takes a pointer to a TTF_Font object and returns the applicable information about the font. Most of the time, you won't really care about the ascent or descent of the font you are working with, but for those times when you really need to know, the functions are there for you.

Another more useful feature of fonts is the style, which includes whether or not the font is bold, italicized, or underlined. To retrieve the current style of a font, you use TTF_GetFontStyle. To set the current style of a font, you use TTF_SetFontStyle.

```
int TTF_GetFontStyle(TTF_Font *font);
void TTF_SetFontStyle(TTF_Font *font, int style);
```

TTF_GetFontStyle takes a pointer to a TTF_Font object and returns a combination of bit flags that represent the style of the font. This combination of bit flags can include TTF_STYLE_BOLD, TTF_STYLE_ITALIC, and TTF_STYLE_UNDERLINE. If none of these styles are present, the value will be TTF_STYLE_NORMAL (otherwise known as 0 or no style).

TTF_SetFontStyle takes a pointer to a TTF_Font object and a combination of these same bit flags and returns no value. It sets the font style appropriately.

Another useful bit of information is how much space to skip between lines of text. If you are only drawing a single line of text this won't be of any importance, but it can be helpful when you are dealing with large pieces of text that have multiple lines. The function for retrieving the amount of space recommended between lines of text is called TTF_FontLineSkip.

```
int TTF_FontLineSkip(TTF_Font *font);
```

This function takes a pointer to a TTF_Font object and returns the number of pixels that should be skipped between lines of text.

A *glyph* is a generic term for an element of a font. It can be a letter, a numeral, a punctuation mark, or none of the above, as in many of the Dingbat-type fonts. Each glyph has a number of metrics associated with it. To grab the metrics for a particular glyph, you use TTF_GlyphMetrics.

```
int TTF_GlyphMetrics(TTF_Font *font, Uint16 ch,int *minx, int *maxx,int
*miny, int *maxy, int *advance);
```

This function takes a number of parameters. The first parameter is a pointer to a TTF_Font (font), which is par for the course as far as SDL_ttf is concerned. The second parameter (ch) is an index into font glyphs. In a typical font, this is the ASCII or Unicode value of a glyph in the font. The rest of the parameters (minx, maxx, miny, maxy, and advance) are pointers to ints that are filled with the appropriate values upon the function's return. This function is handy for determining the size of an individual glyph.

And while we are on the topic of measuring the sizes of things, knowing how much space a string of text will take up is often quite useful. There are three functions for doing this, depending on how your strings are represented. They are TTF_SizeText, TTF_SizeUTF8, and TTF_SizeUNICODE.

```
int TTF_SizeText(TTF_Font *font, const char *text, int *w, int *h);
int TTF_SizeUTF8(TTF_Font *font, const char *text, int *w, int *h);
int TTF_SizeUNICODE(TTF_Font *font, const Uint16 *text, int *w, int
*h);
```

> **NOTE**
> We will essentially ignore UTF8 and UNICODE functions, but it is important to know that they do exist when localization becomes an issue. Within this book, I will simply use the standard text functions that contain strings with ASCII values.

These functions take a pointer to a TTF_Font (font), a string containing the text you want to size (text), and two pointers to ints that are filled with the width and height needed for the string to be rendered.

Rendering

The remaining functions in SDL_ttf are concerned with rendering either individual glyphs or text. Glyphs and text can be rendered one of three ways—solid, shaded, or blended. Generally speaking, the result is almost the same no matter which way you render. Rendering text or glyphs solid is the fastest way, but it has the lowest quality (however, the quality is still not bad at all). Rendering shaded gives you a little higher quality, but it is not quite as fast as solid. Finally, blended is the highest quality and is the slowest.

To render solid text or glyphs, you use one of the following four functions.

```
SDL_Surface * TTF_RenderGlyph_Solid(TTF_Font *font,Uint16 ch, SDL_Color
fg);
SDL_Surface * TTF_RenderText_Solid(TTF_Font *font,const char *text,
SDL_Color fg);
SDL_Surface * TTF_RenderUTF8_Solid(TTF_Font *font,const char *text,
SDL_Color fg);
SDL_Surface * TTF_RenderUNICODE_Solid(TTF_Font *font,const Uint16
*text, SDL_Color fg);
```

As usual, the first parameter is a pointer to a TTF_Font. The second parameter is either the number of the glyph you want to render (in TTF_RenderGlyph_Solid) or a pointer to a string that you want to render (in all other cases). The final parameter (fg) is the color in which you would like the text or glyph rendered. The return value is a pointer to a newly created 8-bit SDL_Surface. On this surface, color index 0 is the transparent background, and color index 1 is the color specified in fg.

After solid rendering, the rest of the rendering functions are a breeze because they all follow much the same pattern. Here are the shaded functions.

```
SDL_Surface * TTF_RenderGlyph_Shaded(TTF_Font *font,Uint16 ch,
SDL_Color fg, SDL_Color bg);
SDL_Surface * TTF_RenderText_Shaded(TTF_Font *font,const char *text,
SDL_Color fg, SDL_Color bg);
SDL_Surface * TTF_RenderUTF8_Shaded(TTF_Font *font,const char *text,
SDL_Color fg, SDL_Color bg);
SDL_Surface * TTF_RenderUNICODE_Shaded(TTF_Font *font,const Uint16
*text, SDL_Color fg, SDL_Color bg);
```

As you can see, they are quite similar to the equivalent solid rendering functions, except for the addition of another `SDL_Color` parameter called `bg`. This extra parameter specifies the background color for the surface that will be created. (It becomes color index 0.) The rest of the colors on the surface are various shades between `fg` and `bg`, creating a more smoothly rendered, anti-aliased look for the text. (This shading is why this takes a little more time than solid rendering.) The only real problem with shaded rendering is that there is no transparent color, so it is only suitable for rendering onto a solid-color background.

And finally, you have the blended functions.

```
SDL_Surface * TTF_RenderGlyph_Blended(TTF_Font *font,Uint16 ch,
SDL_Color fg);
SDL_Surface * TTF_RenderText_Blended(TTF_Font *font,const char *text,
SDL_Color fg);
SDL_Surface * TTF_RenderUTF8_Blended(TTF_Font *font,const char *text,
SDL_Color fg);
SDL_Surface * TTF_RenderUNICODE_Blended(TTF_Font *font,const Uint16
*text, SDL_Color fg);
```

Other than the names of the functions, these have the same parameters as the equivalent solid rendering functions. The difference lies in what kind of surface is created in response to the function call. Whereas solid rendering will give you an 8-bit palettized surface, blended rendering will give you a 32-bit surface with per-pixel alpha information. This makes for very high-quality font rendering, although it is a bit slower than either the solid or blended rendering.

Once you have rendered your text, thus creating a new surface, you simply use that surface as you would any other, blitting it to the frame buffer and so on.

As you might imagine, creating a surface every time you want text drawn is not the most efficient way to render text, so this might not be the method you would choose if your application were text heavy. However, SDL_ttf is low-level enough that you can simply store all of the glyphs on their own surfaces and render from them. If you only have a few static pieces of text, SDL_ttf is not a bad thing to use.

There are a couple of quick examples on the CD-ROM, entitled FOSDL9_1 through FOSDL9_3. The three example programs demonstrate solid, shaded, and blended text rendering. The three examples look very similar, and you probably won't even see what the difference is unless you take a screen shot and zoom in to see the anti-aliasing.

For your viewing pleasure, Figure 9.2 shows the screen from FOSDL9_3. As I stated earlier, FOSDL9_1 and FOSDL9_2 look much the same.

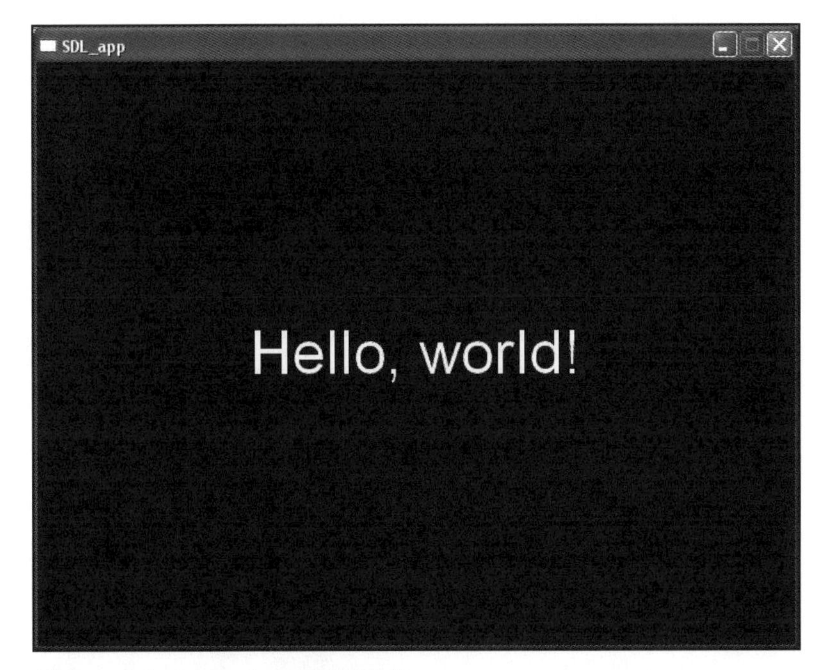

Figure 9.2 *Screen from FOSDL9_3*

Summary

It's nice to know that for all of your font rendering needs, you can turn to SDL_ttf. In the past, I've had to roll my own font-rendering engine more than once, and I think it's really cool that I don't have to do that anymore. In addition, SDL_ttf is incredibly simple to learn and use, much like the rest of SDL.

CHAPTER 10

SDL_NET

Welcome to perhaps my favorite of all of the SDL add-on libraries—SDL_net. Even if you have never done network programming, you should find it very easy to use because once again, the creators of this library have taken the word "simple" to heart.

In this chapter, you will take a look at SDL_net and put together a simple application that demonstrates a small portion of what SDL_net can do for you. Taking the information above and beyond that level is, naturally, up to you.

As a comparison, when you were learning to use the video subsystem of SDL, once you knew how to plot a single pixel, the entire world of video was yours for the taking. In networking, once you know how to send a packet (which is just a simple stream of bytes) from one machine to another, the entire networking system is yours.

A Few Networking Basics

There are a couple of terms that you really need to know before you can delve into SDL_net. If you are an Internet junkie or you play online multiplayer games (like me), most of these terms should be at least somewhat familiar to you.

The first term is *IP address.* The IP stands for Internet Protocol and is just a standard way to identify a computer on the Internet. Your IP address is written as a series of four numbers separated by dots, such as 127.0.0.1. Each of the numbers is in the 0 through 255 range, meaning that an IP address is really just four bytes. Your IP address identifies your computer and, to some extent, where you are in the world.

The second term is *socket.* A socket is simply a connection from one computer to another, or from one IP address to another. The socket allows you to communicate with other machines and surf the Internet.

The third and fourth terms are *client* and *server.* These deal more with what kind of role a computer plays in the network. A server typically does not have a user sitting in front of it, and a client does. A server's role is to process and respond to requests for information. A client is simply a machine that makes those requests of a server.

The last term is *host.* A host is the machine that is central to a game (or really anything that deals with a network) and holds the information that other clients request. (The host can be a client as well.)

Now for a few words on how various types of networks work. The simplest form of network, shown in Figure 10.1, contains two computers, A and B, connected to each other.

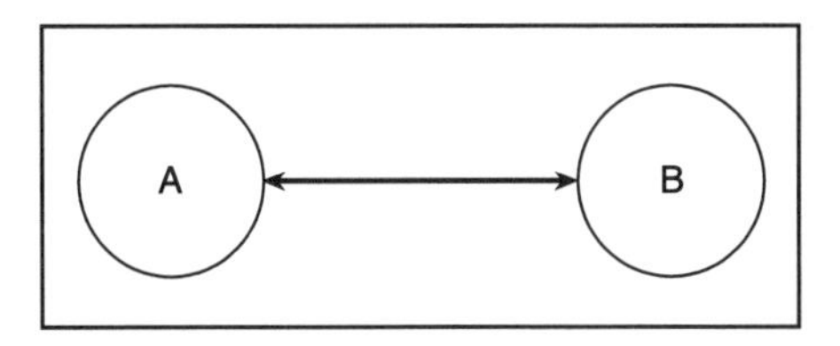

Figure 10.1 *The simplest possible network*

In Figure 10.1, either A or B might be a server or both might be clients. One connection exists between them, which is all that is required. For simplicity, suppose that they are both client machines, so this is a peer-to-peer network. A peer-to-peer network is simply a network in which there are no servers.

You can continue to add more machines to come up with the network in Figure 10.2, which has four machines—A, B, C, and D.

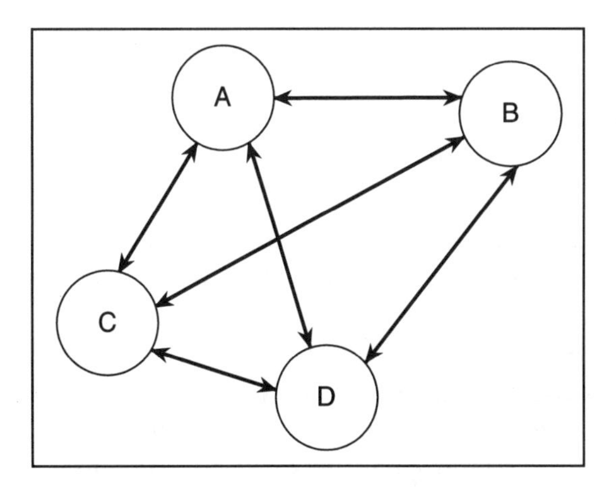

Figure 10.2 *A four-machine peer-to-peer network*

As you can see in the diagram, each machine has a separate connection to the other three machines, for a total of six connections. As you add more machines, there are even more connections. In case you were interested, a peer-to-peer network with *N* machines in it has a number of connections equal to (N)×(N–1)/2. Even in a modest ten-machine network, this is 45 connections; at 20 machines, there are 190 connections. The lesson here is that peer-to-peer is only a good idea if there are very few computers in the network, usually no more than eight to ten.

In a larger network, it is best to have a client-server setup, as shown in Figure 10.3.

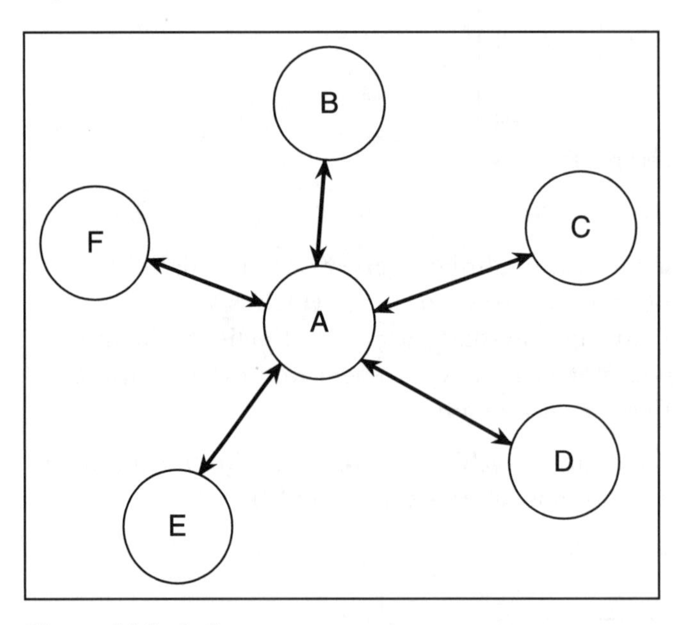

Figure 10.3 *A client-server network*

In the diagram, computer A is the server, and all of the other machines connect only to it. The client machines send data to A, which in turn updates the information on the other machines as needed. This requires you to give one machine the role of server (and typically, that is the *only* role the machine plays), but in return you get fewer connections. There are six machines in the diagram and only five connections—one for each client machine. In a peer-to-peer network with the same number of machines, you would have 15 connections.

Now comes the trade-off. Since a given client machine in the setup only speaks with the server, communication between client machines is indirect. Information first has to be sent to the server and is then passed along to other clients. Thus, the message has to be sent twice instead of just once, which is slightly less efficient than sending information directly.

Of course there are other considerations, such as the placement of the host. As I said earlier, the host machine has all of the information for the game being played. If for some reason it drops off the network, all of the other machines are then dropped because there is no place from which to get information. In a client-server setup, the server acts as the host machine; if a client drops off, the other clients are not disrupted. (Of course, if the server goes down all of the clients are out of luck anyway, but that's just how things go; servers tend to be more robust machines anyway.)

The long and short of it is that when you are designing a game that has multiplayer capabilities, you need to decide what sort of scheme to use. For a game in which people connect directly to one another over the Internet or through a local network, peer-to-peer is often fine. However, if you want a nice lobby-style chat room where people can hook up and play a game, you'll probably want to go with a client-server setup. Often, you will need to include the ability to use both.

Setup and Installation

For convenience, I have included SDL_net on the CD. You can find it in the LIBS folder, in a file called SDL_net-devel-1.2.4-VC6.zip. You simply unzip it somewhere (I chose C:\SDLDEV\SDL_net-1.2.4), and then add the directories to VC++'s include and library directories, much as you did for SDL itself.

Since newer versions (revisions, really) of SDL_net crop up quite often, you might want to check http://www.libsdl.org for a more recent version.

SDL_net at a Glance

There are four distinct portions of SDL_net, each associated with a different fundamental structure. These are IP address, TCP socket, UDP socket, and socket sets.

IP Address

An IP address keeps track of the computers to which you are talking. Each computer is identified by a 4-byte IP address and a port number (a 16-bit identifier) over which communication takes place. An IP address is abstracted in SDL_net with the `IPaddress` structure.

TCP Socket

You use a TCP (*Transfer Control Protocol*) socket to make a connection between two computers (IP addresses). There are basically two types of TCP sockets—servers and clients. Using TCP guarantees that you will receive the messages in the order that they were sent. TCP sockets are abstracted in SDL_net by the `_TCPSocket` structure, but are more commonly referenced by the `TCPSocket` pointer type.

UDP Socket

UDP (*User Datagram Protocol*) sockets are similar to TCP sockets. The main difference is that a UDP socket does not guarantee delivery of packets in the order they were sent. UDP sockets are abstracted in SDL_net by the `_UDPSocket` structure, but are more commonly referenced by the `UDPSocket` pointer type.

Socket Sets

Socket sets are very much what they sound like—collections of sockets. They are typically used by the server to listen for any incoming data from clients. The socket sets are abstracted in SDL_net by the type `_SDLNet_SocketSet`, but are more commonly referenced by the pointer type `SDLNet_SocketSet`.

SDL_net in Depth

Now that you have briefly looked at how SDL_net works, take a more in-depth view of how the structures and functions look and how to use them.

Initialization

Like SDL, you need to initialize SDL_net before you can use it. The function for doing this is `SDLNet_Init`.

```
int  SDLNet_Init(void);
```

You'll get non-zero if SDL_net fails to initialize. When you are done with SDL_net, you use SDLNet_Quit.

```
void SDLNet_Quit(void);
```

Typically, you do the atexit trick when initializing SDL_net, like this:

```
if(!SDLNet_Init())
{
     atexit(SDLNet_Quit);
}
```

Initialization is a piece of cake. It's the rest of the functions that are harder, and they aren't even that much more difficult.

IPaddress

An IP address represents the location of your computer as well as other computers to which a networking application is talking. The IPaddress structure looks like this:

```
typedef struct {
     Uint32 host;                 /* 32-bit IPv4 host address */
     Uint16 port;                 /* 16-bit protocol port */
} IPaddress;
```

The host member is a Uint32 that contains the four bytes that identify a computer. There are also special values—INADDR_ANY(0) and INADDR_NONE(0xFFFFFFFF). You use INADDR_ANY for server sockets and INADDR_NONE when a host cannot be resolved.

The port member is a Uint16 and can in theory be any number. Certain ports are used by certain types of applications, such as 80 for Web browsers, 21 for FTP programs, and 6667 for chat applications. You just want to stay away from the numbers commonly used by other types of applications.

There are two functions in SDL_net that deal with IP addresses alone. (There are other functions, but they deal with sockets; we'll get to them in due time.) The first function is SDLNet_ResolveHost. You use this function to find the IP address of a server to which you will connect or to create the IP address for making a server.

```
int SDLNet_ResolveHost(IPaddress *address, char *host, Uint16 port);
```

This function returns an int. If it returns 0, the IP address could not be resolved. The first parameter (address) is a pointer to an IPAddress structure. This is filled with the data from the resolved host. The second parameter (host) is a string containing the address to which you want to connect. This could be anything from 192.168.0.1 (if you are connecting to something on a LAN) to www.gamedev.net, or any other way of describing someplace to connect. The last parameter (port) is the port to try to see whether the host is listening on it.

When creating an IPaddress for a server socket, you put NULL as the host, which makes the IPaddress's host member equal to INADDR_ANY.

If you want to retrieve the string identifier associated with a particular IP, you use SDLNet_ResolveIP.

```
char * SDLNet_ResolveIP(IPaddress *ip);
```

This function takes a pointer to an IPaddress structure and returns a string identifier. If ip->host is INADDR_ANY, this will return the name of your computer on your LAN. If not, SDL_net will find the name of whatever the IP address points to and retrieve it.

Now for a quick sample program so you can look at these things before I move on to sockets. You can find this example under FOSDL10_1 on the CD.

```
#include "sdl.h"
#include "sdl_net.h"
#include <stdlib.h>
int main(int argc,char* argv[])
{
	if(SDL_Init(SDL_INIT_EVERYTHING)==-1)
	{
		return(0);
	}
	atexit(SDL_Quit);
	if(SDLNet_Init())
	{
		return(0);
	}
	atexit(SDLNet_Quit);
	IPaddress ip;
	SDLNet_ResolveHost(&ip,NULL,16);
```

```
    fprintf(stdout,"Local Host: %s\n",SDLNet_ResolveIP(&ip));
    SDLNet_ResolveHost(&ip,"www.gamedev.net",16);
    fprintf(stdout,"Remote Host: %s\n",SDLNet_ResolveIP(&ip));
    return(0);
}
```

This example simply resolves a NULL host and reports the name of your computer to stdout, and then resolves www.gamedev.net, resolves that name from the IP again, and reports it again to stdout.txt.

TCPSocket

A TCPSocket is a pointer type, defined as follows in SDL_net.h.

```
typedef struct _TCPsocket *TCPsocket;
```

The _TCPSocket structure has its definition hidden from programmers, which is fine. You don't really need to know how it works. If for some reason you want to know, you can check out the source code for SDL_net, downloadable from http://www.libsdl.org.

Before you can start sending data to another computer, you must first open a socket. The computer with which you open up the socket must have a server socket, so at some point you will also need to open a server socket. You use the same function to create both types of sockets—SDLNet_TCP_Open.

```
TCPsocket SDLNet_TCP_Open(IPaddress *ip);
```

This function takes a pointer to an IP address (ip) and returns a TCPSocket. If the return value is NULL, something went wrong. If ip.host is either INADDR_NONE or INADDR_ANY, a server socket will be created. If not, the function will attempt to connect to the server.

Naturally, if you open a socket you must close it later. The function for doing this is SDLNet_TCP_Close.

```
void SDLNet_TCP_Close(TCPsocket sock);
```

This function takes a TCPSocket and returns no value. It closes an open TCP socket; whether or not it is a server socket is immaterial.

Now for a few words about the differing roles of server sockets (those created with an INADDR_ANY or INADDR_NONE host) and non-server sockets, a.k.a. client sockets. Suppose, for example, that you were making a chat application in which you can choose within the program to be a server or to connect to a remote server. On the server end, you need a server socket as well as a number of client sockets, one for each of the other computers connected to your server. As a client, you only need a single client socket with which to communicate with the server.

Why is this? Because the only thing that a server socket does is listen for requests from other computers to join the session. You do not use server sockets to send or receive data. When a server socket has data that is ready to be read in, you use SDLNet_TCP_Accept.

```
TCPsocket SDLNet_TCP_Accept(TCPsocket server);
```

This function takes a TCPSocket (it must be a server socket) and returns a TCPSocket. This returned value is a connection to a remote computer that used SDLNet_TCP_Open to connect to the computer with the server socket.

After you have done this to connect to a new computer, you can find out the IP address of that computer by calling SDLNet_GetPeerAddress.

```
IPaddress * SDLNet_TCP_GetPeerAddress(TCPsocket sock);
```

This function takes a TCPsocket and returns a pointer to an IPaddress. If a server socket is supplied to this function, it will return NULL.

And now for the functions that actually allow for communication. The first one is SDLNet_TCP_Send.

```
int SDLNet_TCP_Send(TCPsocket sock, void *data, int len);
```

This function takes a non-server TCPsocket (sock), a void* that points to data (data), and an int that specifies the length of the data to be sent (len). This function returns the amount of data actually sent. If the return value is not equal to len, there was an error.

On the flip side, there is SDLNet_TCP_Recv, which receives data from another computer.

```
int SDLNet_TCP_Recv(TCPsocket sock, void *data, int maxlen);
```

This function takes a non-server TCPsocket (sock), a pointer to a buffer that has been allocated for data (data), and the maximum length of that buffer (maxlen). The value returned by this function represents how much actual data was read in, which will be less than or equal to maxlen. If it is 0 or less, there was an error.

Believe it or not, with merely eight functions and two structures, you can make almost any sort of networked application you can imagine. SDL_net makes it that easy.

UDPsocket

SDL_net also has functions that allow you to use UDP to send messages over a network. I'm not going to cover them here because I think that TCPsockets do the job perfectly well.

SDLNet_SocketSet

The last type you are going to look at in SDL_net is the SDLNet_SocketSet. Socket sets are used with either TCP or UDP sockets (it really does not matter which) to look for data coming to that socket. SDLNet_SocketSet, like TCPsocket, is just a pointer type, and the actual struct is hidden from view. There is also another type associated with SDLNet_SocketSet called SDLNet_GenericSocket.

```
typedef struct {
     int ready;
} *SDLNet_GenericSocket;
```

This type is meant to cast other types of sockets and is used to store any type of socket in a socket set.

To use a socket set, you must first allocate it. This is done using SDLNet_AllocSocketSet.

```
SDLNet_SocketSet SDLNet_AllocSocketSet(int maxsockets);
```

This function takes as a parameter the number of sockets you want to have in the set and returns the socket set.

Naturally, when you are done, you want to deallocate the socket set using SDLNet_FreeSocketSet.

```
void SDLNet_FreeSocketSet(SDLNet_SocketSet set);
```

This function returns no value and takes as its parameter a socket set that you want to deallocate.

To add a socket to a socket set, you use SDLNet_AddSocket.

```
int SDLNet_AddSocket(SDLNet_SocketSet set, SDLNet_GenericSocket sock);
```

This function takes a socket set (set) and an SDLNet_GenericSocket (sock). Even though this function takes an SDLNet_GenericSocket, you can add other types of sockets to it through casting. SDL_net has a couple of macros to help you in this matter. If you are adding a TCPsocket, you can use SDLNet_TCP_AddSocket instead. For UDP, it is similar.

To remove a socket from a set, you use SDLNet_DelSocket.

```
int SDLNet_DelSocket(SDLNet_SocketSet set, SDLNet_GenericSocket sock);
```

This function takes a socket set (set) and a generic socket (sock) and removes that socket from the socket set. Like SDLNet_AddSocket, you can replace it with SDLNet_TCP_DelSocket if you are dealing strictly with TCPsockets, to avoid casting.

Now for the actual important task done by socket sets…checking the sockets for data. You accomplish this with a call to SDLNet_CheckSockets.

```
int SDLNet_CheckSockets(SDLNet_SocketSet set, Uint32 timeout);
```

This function takes a socket set (set) and a Uint32 timeout value (timeout). The timeout value can be 0, which means that the socket set will just do a quick poll. The return value is the number of sockets in the set that have data ready, or -1 if there was an error.

After you call SDLNet_CheckSockets, you can see whether an individual socket has data ready by calling SDLNet_SocketReady, which isn't really a function; it's a macro.

```
#define SDLNet_SocketReady(sock) \
        ((sock != NULL) && ((SDLNet_GenericSocket)sock)->ready)
```

You'll have an example that uses SDL_net in Chapter 16, "Networking Components." For now, you just need to become familiar with these functions. There is also a decent example in the SDL_net source code (which you can find at http://www.libsdl.org)—one that makes a very simple chat program.

Summary

As you have seen, SDL_net is really quite simple. With it, you can make multiplayer games on multiple platforms a reality, which I can tell you is no small feat. I will talk more about networked applications in Chapter 16, so don't despair.

CHAPTER 11

SDL_mixer

Back in the Bronze Age, sound was not as important to games as it is today. Back then, we pumped everything through a television speaker (and the TVs of the day weren't that great), or worse—through a PC speaker, which had a hard time even going "beep."

With SDL, there is indeed an audio subsystem, which you looked at back in Chapter 5. Unfortunately, it is not nearly as developed as some of the other SDL subsystems. Fortunately, someone came along, saw this lacking feature, and decided that SDL_mixer would be a good idea.

Why SDL_mixer Is Better Than the SDL Audio Subsystem

SDL_mixer is much better than the audio subsystem. It has built-in functionality for handling multiple sound effects at the same time, as well as music. Plus, if you are really hard core, you can specify your own way to mix music and hook various events (such as sound endings) into your program with function pointers.

The big benefit is not that you can mix your audio data yourself—it is that you don't have to do so. Also, SDL_mixer has support for loading WAV files, VOC files, and a number of different music formats.

Setup and Installation

Before you begin using SDL_mixer, you need to install the library. Under the LIBS directory on the CD, there is a file named SDL_mixer-devel-1.2.4-VC6.zip. If you unzip this file somewhere suitable (such as C:\SDLDEV\SDL_mixer), you can set up your development environment.

To do this, you add C:\SDLDEV\SDL_mixer\include to the list of include directories under Tools, Options, and add C:\SDLDEV\SDL_mixer\lib to the list of library directories. This is similar to the process for setting up SDL itself, as well as the other add-on libraries.

When you create a project that uses SDL_mixer, you must add SDL_mixer.lib to the list of libraries to which you want to link, and you must have SDL_mixer.dll somewhere that the program can find it (either in the workspace directory or in a system directory somewhere).

SDL_mixer at a Glance

Just to get going, take a brief look at the many functions of SDL_mixer, divided up by general area of interest. For a graphical view, see Figure 11.1.

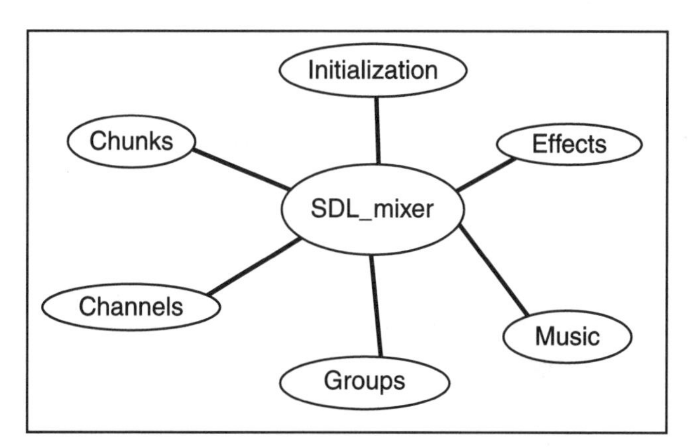

Figure 11.1 *Graphical overview of SDL_mixer*

Initialization

There are two initialization functions for SDL_mixer. One opens up the audio device (relying on the audio subsystem of SDL, which must be initialized prior to the function call), and the other closes it. Initialization functions for SDL and its brethren are never a big sweat.

Chunks

All sound effects are abstracted as chunks. You will only ever work with pointers to chunks. Chunks can be loaded from files on disk or from memory. Typically, you will load from either a WAV or a VOC file.

Channels

A channel allows more than one sound effect to be played at a time. Each channel can play a different chunk at one time. You get to pick the number of channels that are available to you, and you can change this number on the fly. You can play a channel, thus associating a chunk with it. There are a number of options for playing chunks, including a specific number of loops, a specific amount of time to play, and whether or not to fade in the chunk. You can also use a specific channel number to play a sound or let SDL_mixer look for a free one. Once the sound is playing, you can pause, resume, or halt a channel. When halting channels, you can also choose to fade the channel out over time. You can even specify a callback to trigger whenever a channel is done playing.

Groups

You can section off your channels into a number of groups, and then use a specific group of channels as a pool from which to pull when you want a specific type of sound to be played. For example, you might want to separate channels that are used to play sound effects, such as explosions, from the channels used to play voice effects. You can also use groups to treat channels collectively. You can cause all of the channels in a group to stop or fade out. Groups are handy for organizing your channels.

Music

Music is treated somewhat like sound effects (and somewhat not). For one thing, you can only have one piece of music playing at a time; it is not separated into channels and groups. There are functions for loading music from a variety of file types, including MP3. Once you have loaded a piece of music, you can play, pause, resume, stop, fade in or out, and change the position within the music.

Effects

For those of you who are especially hard core, you can deal with special effects that change the way your chunks sound. You can use some of the built-in effects or define your own. You'll take a look at the built-in effects near the end of this chapter, as well as a rough outline of how you might use your own, but this is a book on SDL, not sound engineering.

SDL_mixer in Depth

Now that you have a good conceptual overview of how SDL_mixer is constructed, take a look at the SDL_mixer functions in greater detail. All SDL_mixer functions start with Mix_ to differentiate them from SDL functions and other add-on library functions. Prior to using any SDL_mixer function, you must call SDL_Init with SDL_INIT_AUDIO as one of the bit flags. SDL_mixer does not replace the audio subsystem; it simply adds more functionality.

Initialization

Like any other SDL add-on library, you must initialize SDL_mixer before you can use it. However, there is no Mix_Init function; you simply start doing stuff. The first thing you will want to do is call Mix_OpenAudio.

```
int Mix_OpenAudio(int frequency, Uint16 format, int channels, int
chunksize);
```

This opens the audio device and initializes the rest of the SDL_mixer API. This must be the first SDL_mixer function called in an application. The four parameters are frequency (in Hz), format (any of the constants for audio format discussed back in Chapter 5), number of channels (either 1 for mono or 2 for stereo), and the chunk size (for which the SDL documentation suggests that you use 4096). The function returns -1 for an error or 0 for success. This function does essentially the same job as SDL_OpenAudioSpec.

There are a couple of constants, notably MIX_DEFAULT_FREQUENCY (which equals 22050) and MIX_DEFAULT_FORMAT (which equals AUDIO_S16SYS), that you can use if you aren't too picky about frequency and format. MIX_DEFAULT_CHANNELS is the same as 2.

Naturally, once you are done with SDL_mixer, you call Mix_CloseAudio.

```
void Mix_CloseAudio(void);
```

No parameters, no return values—this function simply closes the audio device. You can even make this function yet another that you add to the atexit chain.

Since you can't actually be sure that the audio device was opened with the frequency, format, number of channels, and so on that you specified, you will probably find it useful to call Mix_QuerySpec after you call Mix_OpenAudio.

```
int Mix_QuerySpec(int *frequency,Uint16 *format,int *channels);
```

This function will return 0 if there is an error and non-zero on success. The values pointed to by frequency, format, and channels are filled with the appropriate data for the currently open audio stream.

TIP

You can access SDL_SetError and SDL_GetError through Mix_SetError and Mix_GetError. The functionality remains unchanged.

Chunks

All of the sound data that you use in your application will be chunks, which are abstracted as a structure called Mix_Chunk.

```
typedef struct {
    int allocated;
    Uint8 *abuf;
    Uint32 alen;
    Uint8 volume;
} Mix_Chunk;
```

This is a relatively simple structure. It has a flag that tells you the chunk has been allocated (allocated), a Uint8 buffer for the audio data (abuf), a Uint32 that specifies the length of the buffer (alen), and a Uint8 that specifies the volume of the chunk (volume).

You will likely never work with Mix_Chunk directly; more often than not, you will work only with Mix_Chunk pointers. Of course, you can work with Mix_Chunk directly if you so desire. That is why the structure is available to you. Most of the time, you will simply load chunks in from WAV files. The function for doing so is Mix_LoadWAV.

```
Mix_Chunk *Mix_LoadWAV(char *file);
```

This function takes a string containing a file name and returns a Mix_Chunk pointer. If an error occurs, the return value will be NULL.

Alternatively, you can load a WAV file that has already been loaded in the memory with a call to Mix_QuickLoad_WAV.

```
Mix_Chunk *Mix_QuickLoad_WAV(Uint8 *mem);
```

The mem parameter is a Uint8 pointer that points to memory that contains the contents of a WAV file. There are some severe warnings in the documentation for SDL_mixer that make me think you might not want to use this function unless you are *very* sure of yourself.

Another hard-core function is Mix_QuickLoad_RAW.

```
Mix_Chunk *Mix_QuickLoad_RAW(Uint8 *mem, Uint32 len);
```

This function takes a pointer to raw data in memory (mem) and the length of the raw data (len). This is definitely a "you-should-really-know-what-you-are-doing-first" sort of function.

As with everything in SDL or its add-on libraries, after you are done with a chunk you need to free it. To do so, you use the Mix_FreeChunk function.

```
void Mix_FreeChunk(Mix_Chunk *chunk);
```

This function takes a pointer to a chunk and returns no value. If the buffer for the chunk was allocated, it will be freed. If the chunk buffer was not allocated, it won't be freed.

Finally, if you want to set or get the volume for a chunk, you use Mix_VolumeChunk.

```
int Mix_VolumeChunk(Mix_Chunk *chunk, int volume);
```

This function takes a pointer to a chunk (chunk) and an int with a volume level (with a valid range of 0 to MIX_MAX_VOLUME, which equals 128).

Channels

Before you can start playing sounds you need to look at channel functions, because all sound-effect mixing is based on channels. Channels are used for sound effects only; music is unaffected.

Allocation

The first and most important decision you need to make is how many channels you want to have available. If there are a large number of sound effects that might be playing simultaneously, you might want a nice, high number. If the number of sounds is relatively sparse, a lower number is more appropriate.

You use Mix_AllocateChannels to pick the number of channels available for sound-effect mixing.

```
int Mix_AllocateChannels(int numchans);
```

This function takes the number of channels (numchans) that you want to allocate and returns the number of channels allocated. You can call this function as often as you want, changing the number of channels available at a given time. However, it is not a good idea to do this too frequently. If you specify a lower number of channels than the last call, the higher-number channels will be stopped. Allocating zero channels will stop all channels.

Playing Channels

The whole point of SDL_mixer is to play sounds and, more importantly, to properly mix them, so you naturally would expect a function or two dedicated to playing sounds. SDL_mixer has four such functions. The first of these is called Mix_PlayChannel.

```
int Mix_PlayChannel(int channel, Mix_Chunk *chunk, int loops);
```

This function takes the channel number on which to play the sound (channel), a Mix_Chunk pointer (chunk) that represents the sound to be played, and the number of times to loop the sound (loops). If you put a -1 in the channel parameter, SDL_mixer will search for an available channel and use it. If you put -1 in loops, the sound will loop forever. If you want a sound to play only a single time, place 0 in the loops parameter.

You can also play a channel for a specified number of milliseconds using Mix_PlayChannelTimed.

```
int Mix_PlayChannelTimed(int channel, Mix_Chunk *chunk, int loops, int ticks);
```

The parameter list is much the same as for Mix_PlayChannel, with the addition of the ticks parameter, which specifies the number of milliseconds you want the sound to be played. Naturally, if looping the correct number of times falls short of this time limit, the sound will end normally. You can put -1 in the ticks parameter to cause the channel to play indefinitely (subject to the length of all of the loops). A -1 for loops or channel means the same thing as it does for Mix_PlayChannel.

Another way to play sounds is to cause them to fade in. This can be a nice effect, especially during some sort of transition. There is also fading out, which I will cover a little later in this chapter. The first function I'm going to show you is Mix_FadeInChannel.

```
int Mix_FadeInChannel(int channel, Mix_Chunk *chunk, int loops, int ms);
```

This function takes a channel number (channel), a pointer to a Mix_Chunk (chunk), and a number of loops (loops), just like Mix_PlayChannel. In addition, there is an ms parameter, which specifies the number of milliseconds from the start of the sound (at a volume of 0) to full volume. A -1 for loops or channel means the same thing as it does for Mix_PlayChannel.

Another option is to set a period of time for the sound to play. The function for doing this is Mix_FadeInChannelTimed.

```
int Mix_FadeInChannelTimed(int channel, Mix_Chunk *chunk, int loops,
int ms, int ticks);
```

All of the parameters except for ticks operate in the same manner as the same parameters in Mix_FadeInChannel. The ticks parameter operates exactly the same as it did for Mix_PlayChannelTimed.

Now for a quick little example, in the form of FOSDL11_1. In this example, one sound (a WAV file containing a song) is played continuously. Whenever a key is pressed, another song is played along with it. The really neat part of the whole thing is that the format of both sounds differs from the format of the audio device. Sweet.

Pausing and Resuming

Any complete audio API needs a way to pause and resume sound effects. SDL_mixer has functions for both—Mix_Pause and Mix_Resume.

```
void Mix_Pause(int channel);
void Mix_Resume(int channel);
```

Each of these channels takes a channel number as a parameter, and neither function returns a value. If -1 is set as the channel parameter, then all channels are paused or resumed as they apply to the function being called. These functions are easy enough that I don't need to include an example.

Stopping

One might think that the trivial task of stopping a sound would require only a single function. This is not the case. SDL_mixer has four entire functions dedicated to this task. Naturally, they don't all stop sounds the same way (and one of them doesn't stop sounds at all; it simply determines what to do once a sound stops).

The first of these functions, Mix_HaltChannel, is most like what you would expect for a function for stopping sounds.

```
int Mix_HaltChannel(int channel);
```

This function takes a channel number (channel) to stop playing. If you place a -1 in channel, all channels will be stopped. The function returns 0. Yes, always—so the return value is completely useless, and you might as well pretend that this function returns void.

The next function on the list is Mix_ExpireChannel. This function specifies a particular delay before causing a channel to stop playing.

```
int Mix_ExpireChannel(int channel, int ticks);
```

The function takes a channel number (channel) and a number of milliseconds (ticks) before the channel should be halted. It returns the number of channels that are going to expire. Putting -1 in channel causes all channels to expire.

You can also cause a sound to fade out prior to halting by calling Mix_FadeOutChannel.

```
int Mix_FadeOutChannel(int which, int ms);
```

This function takes a channel number to fade out (which) and a number of milliseconds over which to do the fade (ms). If which is -1, all channels will be faded out.

Finally, there is Mix_ChannelFinished.

```
void Mix_ChannelFinished(void (*channel_finished)(int channel));
```

This function takes a pointer to a callback function with a single int parameter that returns void (channel_finished). The function to which this points will be called whenever a channel is halted, either naturally or through a call to one of the stopping functions. The documentation warns never to call an SDL_mixer function or SDL_LockAudio from the callback.

Information Functions

While playing sound effects, there are a number of questions that you no doubt might like to ask about a particular channel. Is a sound playing? Is this channel paused? Is this channel being faded? If so, how? What chunk is being played on this channel?

SDL_mixer has functions to answer each of these questions. I will start with the "Is this channel playing?" question, which is answered by `Mix_Playing`.

```
int Mix_Playing(int channel);
```

This function takes a channel number (`channel`) and returns whether or not it is currently playing something. A return value of 0 means that a channel is not playing, and 1 means that it is. If you pass -1 in the `channel` parameter, the number of channels being played at the moment will be returned instead.

The "Is this channel paused?" question is answered by `Mix_Paused`.

```
int Mix_Paused(int channel);
```

Like `Mix_Playing`, this function takes a channel number (`channel`) and returns a 0 if the sound is not playing or a 1 if it is playing. If a -1 is passed for the `channel` parameter, the number of paused channels is returned.

To see whether or not a particular channel is fading (-1 is *not* valid in this case), you use `Mix_FadingChannel`.

```
Mix_Fading Mix_FadingChannel(int which);
```

This function takes a channel number (`which`) and returns one of three constants. `MIX_NO_FADING` means the channel isn't being faded either way. `MIX_FADING_OUT` means that the channel is fading out, and `MIX_FADING_IN` means that the channel is fading in.

The final question, "What chunk is a channel playing?" is answered by `Mix_GetChunk`.

```
Mix_Chunk* Mix_GetChunk(int channel);
```

This function takes a channel number (`channel`) and returns the chunk most recently played on it. The channel is not necessarily playing at the moment; you should use `Mix_Playing` to check for that.

Groups

It is often useful and advisable to place channels into a group and reserve one group of channels for sound effects (SFX) and one group of channels for voice effects (VOX), or something similar so that you can divvy up the channels for different tasks.

But before doing that, you will want to set up a reserve of channels that will not be used by default when a chunk is played using the -1 channel. To do this, you use Mix_ReserveChannels.

```
int Mix_ReserveChannels(int num);
```

This function takes a number of channels in the range of 0 to num–1 to reserve. The return value is the number of reserved channels, which should be the same as num provided that many channels were originally allocated.

The next step is to place channels into a group. You can either do this individually by channel number or by a range of channels. To do this with a single channel, you call Mix_GroupChannel.

```
int Mix_GroupChannel(int which, int tag);
```

This function takes a channel number (which) and a group number (tag). It returns 1 if it is successful and 0 if it is not. The channel number is tagged as a part of that group. If you tag a channel to be of group -1, it essentially removes the group.

If you wanted to reserve eight channels, four each for SFX and VOX, you could use Mix_GroupChannel.

```
Mix_ReserveChannels(8);//reserve eight channels
Mix_GroupChannel(0,1);//group 1 is SFX
Mix_GroupChannel(1,1);
Mix_GroupChannel(2,1);
Mix_GroupChannel(3,1);
Mix_GroupChannel(4,2);//group 2 is VOX
Mix_GroupChannel(5,2);
Mix_GroupChannel(6,2);
Mix_GroupChannel(7,2);
```

Of course if you are assigning ranges like this, it is much more efficient to call Mix_GroupChannels.

```
int Mix_GroupChannels(int from, int to, int tag);
```

This function takes a starting channel (from), an ending channel (to), and a group number to assign (tag). The return value is the number of channels added to the group. To rewrite the short snippet of code just presented, you would simply do this:

```
Mix_ReserveChannels(8);//reserve eight channels
Mix_GroupChannels(0,3,1);//group 1 is SFX
Mix_GroupChannels(4,7,2);//group 2 is VOX
```

Okay, so you can set up groups. That doesn't do you a darn bit of good unless you can somehow make use of these groupings. For one thing, you might want to know how to determine the number of channels in a particular group. For that, you can ask Mix_GroupCount.

```
int Mix_GroupCount(int tag);
```

This function takes a group number (tag) and returns the number of channels in that group. If there are no channels, it will return 0. If tag is -1, it will return the total number of channels.

It would also be useful to know whether a channel in the group is available to play a sound. For this, you look to Mix_GroupAvailable.

```
int Mix_GroupAvailable(int tag);
```

This function takes a group number (tag) and returns an available channel within that group. If no available channel can be found, it will return -1.

And how about what channel in the group has been playing for the longest or shortest amount of time? This is useful if you have a limited number of channels and you need to stop the oldest channel to play a new sound. The functions for checking this are Mix_GroupOldest and Mix_GroupNewer.

```
int Mix_GroupOldest(int tag);
int Mix_GroupNewer(int tag);
```

Each of these functions takes a group number (tag). In the case of Mix_GroupOldest, the longest-playing channel is returned. (-1 is returned if there are no channels in the group or if no channels in the group are playing.) In the case of Mix_GroupNewer, the shortest-playing channel is returned. (-1 is returned if no channels exist in the group or if no channels are playing.)

Finally, some really useful items—the ability to fade out or halt an entire group (if you suddenly want your SFX or VOX to stop because the user has turned them off). To fade out a group of channels over time, you use Mix_FadeOutGroup.

```
int Mix_FadeOutGroup(int tag, int ms);
```

The tag parameter specifies which group you want to fade out, and ms specifies the number of milliseconds you want it to take. This function returns the number of channels that will be faded out.

To halt all of the channels in a group, you use Mix_HaltGroup.

```
int Mix_HaltGroup(int tag);
```

This function takes a group number (tag) to halt. All of the channels in that group are halted. This function always returns 0 so don't bother checking it.

Music

Music in SDL_mixer is treated differently than sound effects. It is not played on a channel (or rather, there is a single channel reserved exclusively for music), and none of the sound effect functions affect it. You use the Mix_Music type when dealing with music, which does not reveal any implementation details to the programmer and is always referred to with a pointer.

Loading and Freeing

Like chunks, you have to load music from a file and free it when you are finished. The only real difference in setting up to play music is that you don't have to allocate any mixer channels, since the music portion of SDL_mixer doesn't require them.

To load a piece of music, you call Mix_LoadMUS.

```
Mix_Music *Mix_LoadMUS(const char *file);
```

This function takes a string containing a file name (file) and returns a pointer to a Mix_Music object. A NULL will be returned if there is an error. The types of music files allowed is varied. You can have MIDI, MP3, MOD, WAV, or others.

When you are finished with the piece of music, you have to free it by calling Mix_FreeMusic.

```
void Mix_FreeMusic(Mix_Music *music);
```

This function takes a pointer to Mix_Music and frees it. It returns no value.

Playing Music

Of course, the first thing you'll want to do once you have the ability to load music is to play it. There are several functions for doing so. The first of these functions is Mix_PlayMusic.

```
int Mix_PlayMusic(Mix_Music *music, int loops);
```

This function takes a pointer to a Mix_Music (music) and a number of loops (loops) to play it. Using -1 for the loops parameter will cause perpetual looping. This function returns -1 if there is an error and 0 if there is no error. Unlike with sound effects, putting 0 for loops will cause the music to never play.

If you would rather fade in the music gradually (the folks who wrote SDL_mixer seem to really like fades), you can use Mix_FadeInMusic.

```
int Mix_FadeInMusic(Mix_Music *music, int loops, int ms);
```

This function takes a pointer to a Mix_Music (music), a number of loops (loops), and a number of milliseconds (ms) over which to fade the music. Again, 0 will cause the music not to be played at all, and -1 will cause infinite loops. This function returns -1 for an error and 0 for success.

Yet another way to play music is to start at a given position for the first loop of the music. You use Mix_FadeInMusicPos to do this.

```
int Mix_FadeInMusicPos(Mix_Music *music, int loops, int ms, double position);
```

This function takes a pointer to a Mix_Music (music), a number of loops to play it (loops), a number of milliseconds over which to fade it in (ms), and a starting position (position). It returns 0 on success and -1 on failure. If loops is -1, it plays forever. If it is 0, it never plays. The position parameter has different meanings depending on what type of music you are playing. Normally it means the number of seconds, but not always.

Finally, if you want to be totally hard core about it, you can mix your own darn music. This is not suggested unless you really know what you are doing. The function for doing so is Mix_HookMusic.

```
void Mix_HookMusic(void (*mix_func)(void *udata, Uint8 *stream, int len),
void *arg);
```

This function takes a pointer to a function (mix_func) that takes a void*, a Uint8*, an int that returns no value, and a void* named arg that is passed to this mixer function. When more music needs to be loaded, you call the callback function and do whatever to mix in additional music.

I don't know about you, but the entire reason for me to use SDL_mixer is so that I *don't* have to mix my own sounds and music. But I guess it's a nice thing to have, just in case.

Anyway, FOSDL11_2 on the CD is a little example program that loads in a music file (an .xm MOD file) and plays it perpetually. It's kind of neat and only requires about four actual function calls to make the music stuff work.

Music Settings

Like channels, you can pause and resume music. In addition, you can restart music from the beginning, change the volume, and set the current position within the piece of music. You can also set up an external music player if you want.

First, take a look at how to pause and resume music. The functions for doing so are Mix_PauseMusic and Mix_ResumeMusic.

```
void Mix_PauseMusic();
void Mix_ResumeMusic();
```

Neither of these functions takes a parameter or returns a value. Mix_PauseMusic causes music to be suspended in a paused state, and Mix_ResumeMusic restores the playing state of the music.

If you suddenly feel a need to start the music over from the beginning, you call Mix_RewindMusic.

```
void Mix_RewindMusic();
```

This function takes no parameters and returns no value.

If you want to set the current position of the music to anywhere but the beginning, you can call Mix_SetMusicPosition.

```
int Mix_SetMusicPosition(double position);
```

This function takes a double called position. The meaning of this parameter depends on the type of music being played. If it is a MOD file, position is the pattern number and fractions are dropped. If it is an OGG file, position is the number of seconds from the beginning of the music. If it is an MP3 file, position is the number of seconds to jump forward. (You cannot jump backward.)

If you want to change the volume at which the music is playing, you use Mix_VolumeMusic.

```
int Mix_VolumeMusic(int volume);
```

The volume parameter should be in the range of 0 to MIX_MAX_VOLUME. If it is -1, the volume will not be changed. The return value is the previous volume of the music, so this function operates as both a setter and a getter.

Finally, you use Mix_SetMusicCMD to set up another program to play your music for you.

```
int Mix_SetMusicCMD(const char *command);
```

This function takes a string, which contains a command line expression for playing music. It returns -1 if there is an error and 0 if there is none. I'm not going to go any further into how to use this function.

Stopping Music

To stop music, you can choose to simply stop it immediately or to fade it out. Additionally, you can set up a callback function to notify you when the music has ended.

To stop music that is currently playing, you use Mix_HaltMusic.

```
int Mix_HaltMusic();
```

This function takes no parameter and always returns 0.

If you prefer to fade out the music over time, you can use Mix_FadeOutMusic.

```
int Mix_FadeOutMusic(int ms);
```

This function takes a number of milliseconds (ms) over which to fade out the music. If an error occurs, this function returns -1; otherwise, it returns 0.

Finally, you can set up a callback to notify you when music has finished playing. The function for doing so is Mix_HookMusicFinished.

```
void Mix_HookMusicFinished(void (*music_finished)());
```

This function takes a single parameter, a pointer to a function that returns no value and takes no parameters. Mix_HookMusicFinished returns no value. Whenever the music stops, the callback function is called.

Gathering Information

Just like with channels, there are a number of questions that you will need to ask of music within your code. What sort of music is playing? Is music currently playing? Is the music currently paused? Is the music being faded? If so, how? What callback function is called when the music finishes playing?

The type of music playing (MOD, OGG, or MP3) can be important, especially if you are trying to set the position of the music using Mix_SetMusicPosition. To find out the music type, you can call Mix_GetMusicType.

```
Mix_MusicType Mix_GetMusicType(const Mix_Music *music);
```

This function takes a single parameter—a pointer to a Mix_Music object (which can be NULL if you are trying to determine what type of music is currently playing). It returns the type of music, which is one of the following constants: MUS_CMD, MUS_WAV, MUS_MOD, MUS_MID, MUS_OGG, MUS_MP3, or MUS_NONE. If the return value is MUS_CMD, it means that the external player is operating. If the value is MUS_NONE, no music is playing (if you passed NULL to Mix_GetMusicType). In all other cases, the constants indicate from what kind of file the music came.

If you want to see whether music is currently playing, you use the Mix_PlayingMusic function.

```
int Mix_PlayingMusic();
```

This function takes no parameters and returns 1 if music is playing and 0 if no music is playing.

If you are interested in seeing whether the music is currently paused, you use Mix_PausedMusic.

```
int Mix_PausedMusic();
```

This function takes no parameters and returns 0 if the music has not been paused and 1 if it has. It works very much like Mix_PlayingMusic.

If you want to know whether music is being faded and how, Mix_FadingMusic is the function for you.

```
Mix_Fading Mix_FadingMusic();
```

This function takes no parameters and returns MIX_NO_FADING, MIX_FADING_OUT, or MIX_FADING_IN. It works much like Mix_FadingChannel.

Finally, to determine what callback is fired off when the music is finished, you can use the Mix_GetMusicHookData function.

```
void *Mix_GetMusicHookData();
```

This function takes no parameters and returns a pointer to the function that is called when music ends.

Effects

The last topic on the list is special effects. This portion of SDL_mixer is broken down into two parts. One part is stock effects, such as panning and other positional 3D sound effects, and the other part deals with setting up your own special effects. Effects are carried out on individual channels (or on all channels at once by specifying MIX_CHANNEL_POST as the channel number).

An important facet of all special effects deals with the idea of registration. When each effect is set up, it is registered on a particular channel, meaning essentially that it affects that channel. This state remains until the effect is unregistered.

Stock Effects

With stock effects (those built into SDL_mixer), you can set the panning (in other words, set the volume from each of the speakers separately), set the distance at which the sound is heard (which essentially just decreases the volume of the sound), set the position from which the sound comes (which is really just a clever trick with panning), and reverse the left and right stereo channels.

If you want to set the panning, you use Mix_SetPanning.

```
int Mix_SetPanning(int channel, Uint8 left, Uint8 right);
```

This function takes a channel number (channel), a volume to use for the left speaker (left), and a volume to use for the right speaker (right). The volume levels range from 0 (silent) to 255 (loud). This function will return non-zero if it is successful and 0 if there is an error. To unregister this effect, call it with 255 in both left and right.

If you want to make a channel sound as though the noise is coming from far away, you use Mix_SetDistance.

```
int Mix_SetDistance(int channel, Uint8 distance);
```

This function takes a channel number (channel) and a desired distance (distance). It returns 0 if there is an error and non-zero otherwise. The distance ranges from 0 (nearest or loudest) to 255 (farthest or quietest). To unregister this effect, call it with a distance of 0.

You can also use Mix_SetPosition to achieve a rough simulation of 3D sound.

```
int Mix_SetPosition(int channel, Sint16 angle, Uint8 distance);
```

This function takes a channel number (channel), an angle at which the sound is supposed to appear (angle), and a distance (distance). It returns non-zero on success and 0 on error. The angle parameter is 0 if you want the sound to come from right in front of you, 90 if you want it to appear to come from your right, 180 if you want it to appear to come from behind you, and 270 if you want it to appear to come from your left. To unregister this effect, call it with an angle and distance of 0.

Figure 11.2 shows the angles of the 3D sound.

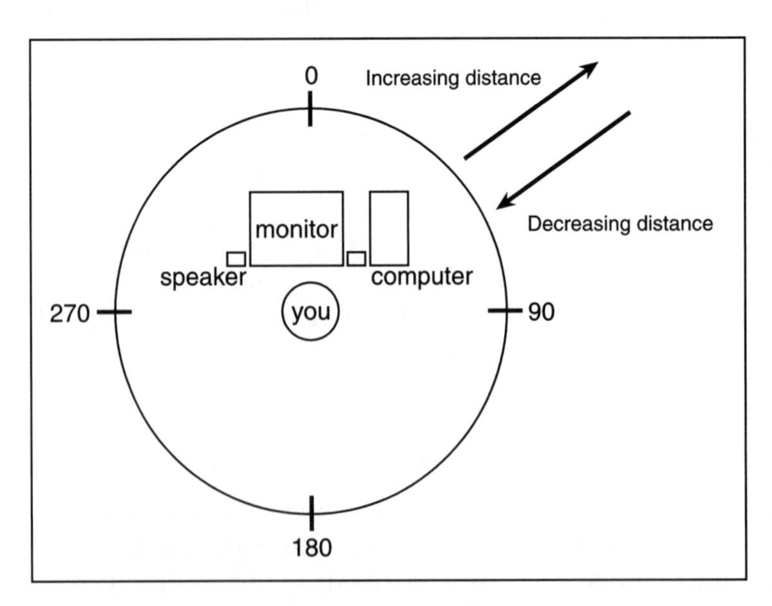

Figure 11.2 *Sound angles and distance effects*

Finally, there are times when you might want to reverse a stereo sound and have the left portion of the sound come from the right speaker and vice versa. You can use `Mix_SetReverseStereo` to achieve this effect.

```
int Mix_SetReverseStereo(int channel, int flip);
```

This function takes a channel number (`channel`) and a `flip` flag. If `flip` is non-zero, the effect is turned on; if it is 0, the effect is turned off and is unregistered. This function returns non-zero on success and 0 on error.

Hard-Core Special Effect Functions

If you want, you can use SDL_mixer to create your own special effects. You can register special effect functions on individual channels (or onto the post-mix phase), unregister effects, unregister all effects on a channel, and even set up your own post-mix mixer.

Before I get to the functions for registering and unregistering effects, you should take a look at how it is done. I'm not actually going to explain the theory behind what you need to do to create a special effect because I am not a sound engineer, but I will show you the functions you'll need if you really want to do something like that.

First, take a look at a type called `Mix_EffectFunc_t`, which is used for mixing special effects.

```
typedef void (*Mix_EffectFunc_t)(int chan, void *stream, int len, void
*udata);
```

As you can see, this is a function pointer type. It takes a channel number (`chan`), a pointer to a stream of sound data (`stream`), a length in bytes of that stream (`len`), and a pointer to some user data (`udata`). The `udata` parameter typically points to some sort of temporary data workspace that is used to make the special effect happen. The `stream`, `chan`, and `len` parameters manipulate the data going to that channel's stream. The idea here is much like putting your own sound data into the data stream, as you did back in Chapter 5.

If the user data pointer is being used for temporary storage, you will want some way to clean it up after a sound has finished playing. There is also a function pointer type to supply a callback function for doing this. The data type is `Mix_EffectDone_t`.

```
typedef void (*Mix_EffectDone_t)(int chan, void *udata);
```

This function pointer type points to functions that take a channel number (chan) and a pointer to user data (udata). The goal of the function is to clean up any temporary data that might have been used by the special effect.

Now that we have cleared that up, you can look at the function for registering a special effect on a channel—Mix_RegisterEffect.

```
int Mix_RegisterEffect(int chan, Mix_EffectFunc_t f, Mix_EffectDone_t
d, void *arg);
```

This function takes a channel number (chan), a special effect function (f), an effect finished function (d), and a user data pointer (arg). The arg parameter will be sent along to the effect callback and the effect done callback. Yes, I agree that it is bad form to use something like f and d for parameter names, but I was not consulted when SDL_mixer was created. This function returns non-zero on success and 0 on failure.

To unregister an effect from a channel, you use Mix_UnregisterEffect.

```
int Mix_UnregisterEffect(int channel, Mix_EffectFunc_t f);
```

This function takes a pointer to an effect function callback and unregisters it from the channel. This function returns 0 on error and non-zero otherwise.

If you suddenly want to get rid of all effects on a channel, you use Mix_UnregisterAllEffects.

```
int Mix_UnregisterAllEffects(int channel);
```

This function removes all of the effects from a channel (including the stock effects). It returns non-zero for success and 0 for failure.

Finally, for the super hard core, you can set a post-mix operation, which takes place after all other special effects and normal mixing have occurred. You use the Mix_SetPostMix function to do this.

```
void Mix_SetPostMix(void (*mix_func)(void *udata, Uint8 *stream, int
len),void *arg);
```

This function takes a function pointer to a mixing function (mix_func) and a user data pointer (arg). The callback function takes a user data pointer (udata) that is fed from arg, a stream pointer (stream), and a length in bytes of the stream (len).

Summary

And that is SDL_mixer. While it is actually rather easy to use, it has much power that you can use to customize the manner in which sounds are played in your application or game. Plus, it is a damn sight better than the audio subsystem of SDL by itself...thank goodness.

PART THREE

SDL Game Application Framework in C++

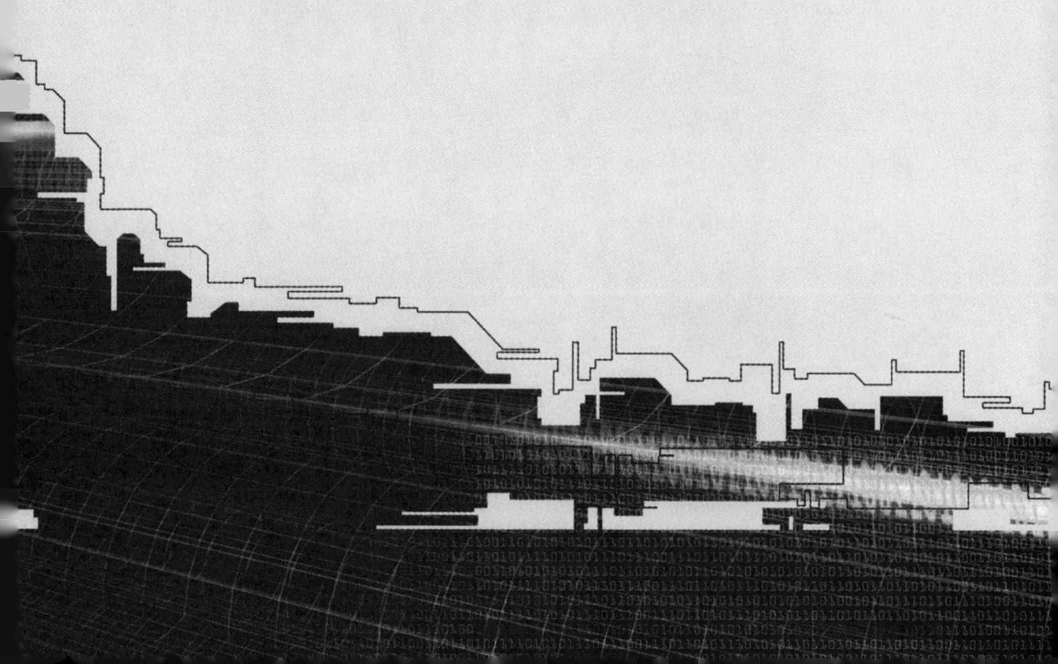

CHAPTER 12

Framework Overview

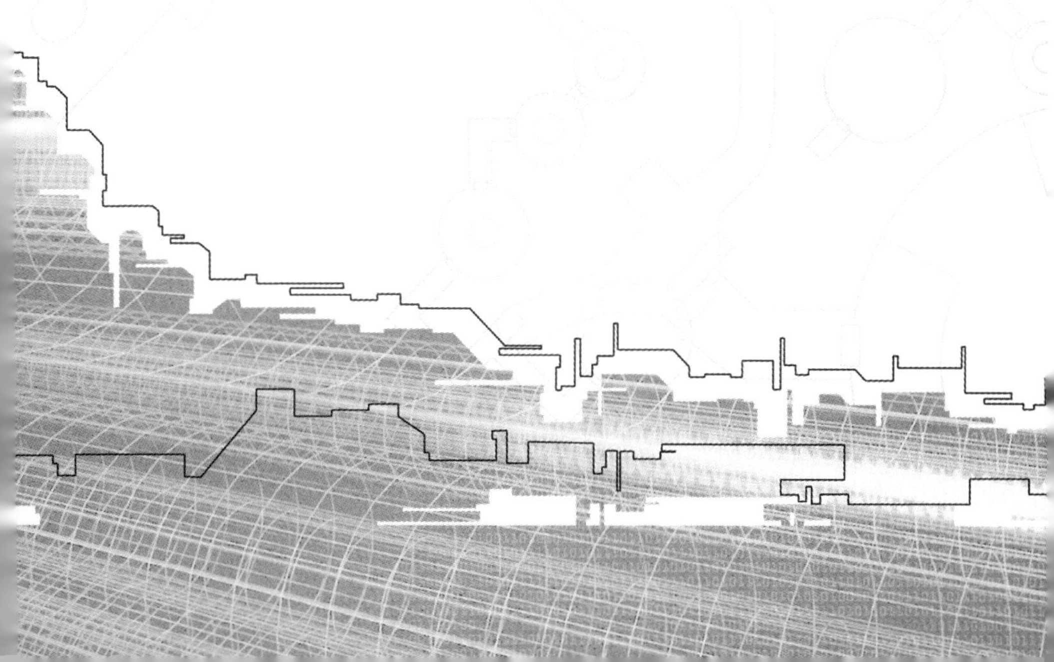

In the five chapters following this one, I will show you an example object-oriented framework that you can use to rapidly develop games and applications. None of the material shown in these chapters is a part of SDL or any related library, although the code certainly makes heavy use of SDL and the other libraries I have covered up to this point.

Because there are five chapters dedicated to the framework, each chapter is dedicated to a particular group of components. Some components are simpler than others (naturally), others are more fundamental to the way the framework works, and still others are optional.

So why is the framework even here in the first place? To make game development faster once the framework is complete. At the end of each chapter, there will be an example application using the new part of the framework.

The five sections of the framework are the core, video, audio, networking, and user interface components. The rest of this chapter contains a brief overview of each.

Core Components

The core components of the framework are absolutely fundamental to its operation, so I am covering them first. Five classes comprise the core components—the message handling class (`CMessageHandler`), the application class (`CApplication`), the event-handling class (`CEventHandler`), the thread-managing class (`CThread`), and the timer-managing class (`CTimer`). Figure 12.1 shows the basic structure of the core components. Not a single one of these classes is meant to be used as is; instead, each one is meant to have classes that do something useful derived from it. Core components are covered in Chapter 13.

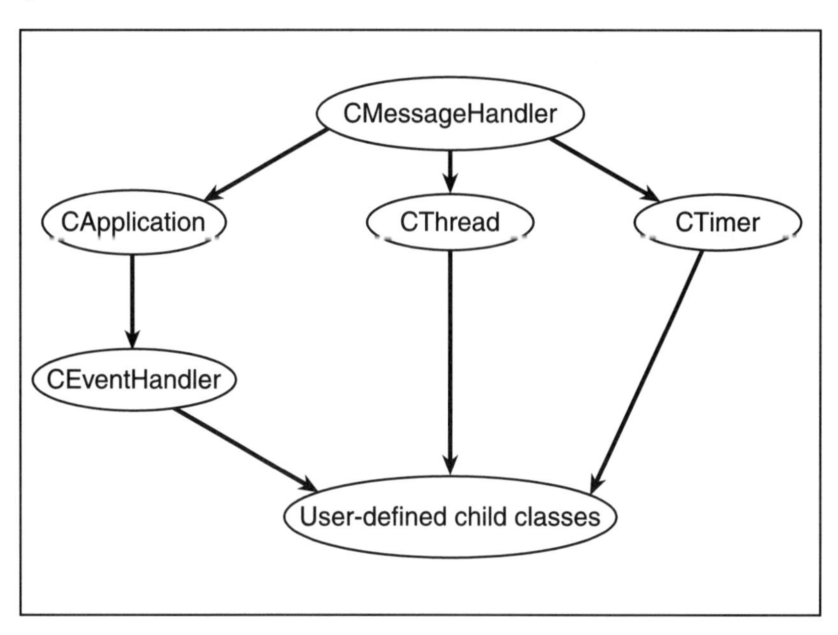

Figure 12.1 *The core component structure*

Video Components

The video components of the framework abstract some of the fundamental types for working with raster graphics, including points (`CPoint`), rectangles (`CRectangle`), and colors (`CColor`). In addition, there is a class that abstracts an SDL_Surface (`CCanvas`) and a couple of classes that assist in the management of blittable areas of a surface (`CImage` and `CImageSet`). Figure 12.2 shows the structure of the video components, which are covered in Chapter 14.

Audio Components

The audio components of the framework are essential if you want a nice, easy way to play sound effects and music. These classes abstract SDL_mixer entities. There is a class for opening and closing the audio device (`CAudio`), a class for loading and playing music (`CMusic`), a class for loading sound effects (`CSound`), and a class for encapsulating a sound

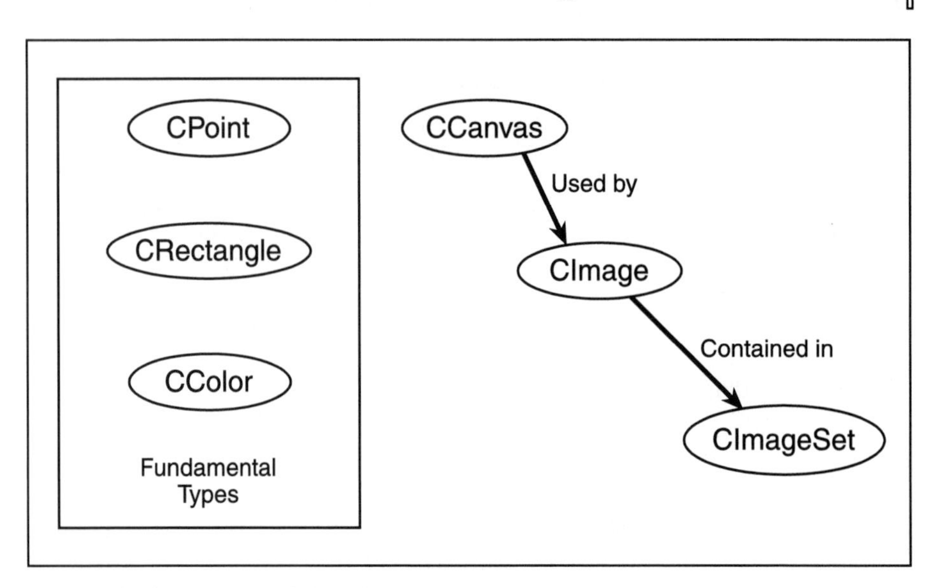

Figure 12.2 *Structure of the video components*

effect channel (`CChannel`). Together, they make up a reasonably complete abstraction of SDL_mixer. I left out abstracting channel groups and special effects because the channel groups were rendered unnecessary by the components I built and special effects are beyond the scope of this book. The audio components are covered in Chapter 15.

Networking Components

The networking components of the framework are for multiplayer capabilities. These classes abstract SDL_net entities. Components include classes for abstracting IP addresses (`CIPAddress`) and classes for abstracting TCP sockets (`CTCPSocket`, `CHostSocket`, and `CClientSocket`). Static structures for keeping track of all of the sockets in use in the networking application are also part of the `CTCPSocket` class.

User Interface Components

Don't forget user interface components, which are perhaps the most important of all. The UI components don't correspond directly to any SDL entity, but they do use the video and event subsystems quite heavily. The primary component is `CControl`, which is the base class for all other controls. It provides a hierarchy for all child controls. The other components are the child controls themselves—`CButton`, `CTextBox`, `CLabel`, and `CRadioButton`—which abstract specific types of controls and are based on `CControl`.

Summary

Now that you've got a small overview of what you're going to be doing for the next five chapters, let's just get to it and start building a nice application framework that you can use to make games.

CHAPTER 13

Core Components

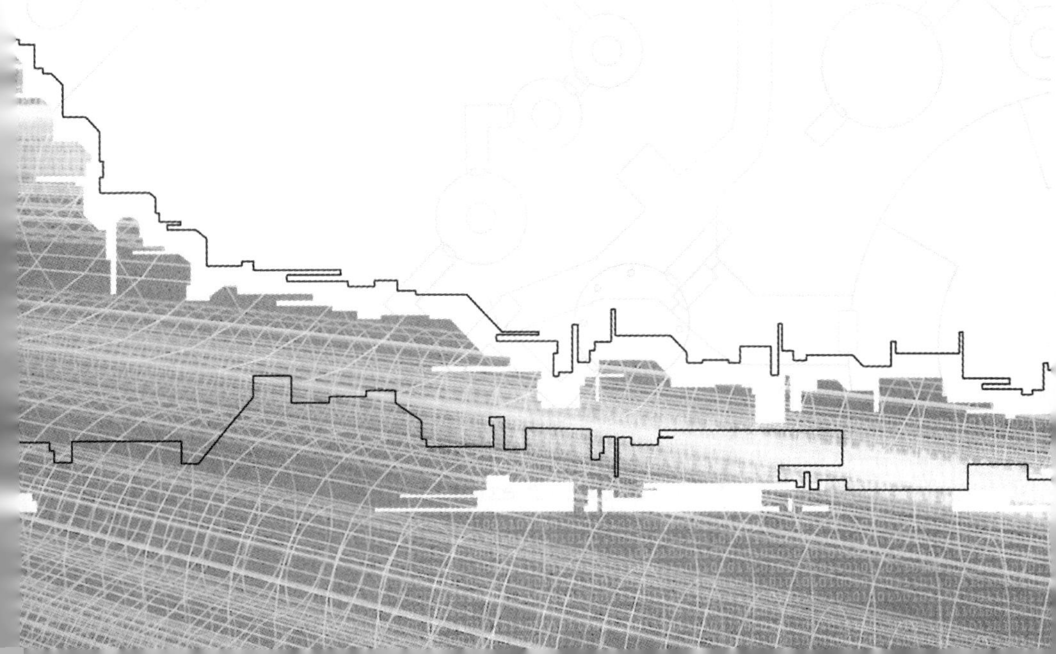

You simply cannot build a house without first pouring a foundation, and the same is true of any application framework. There are certain tasks to which you simply must attend. In a typical SDL application, certain function calls and tasks are mandatory. Figure 13.1 depicts a typical flow diagram for an SDL application.

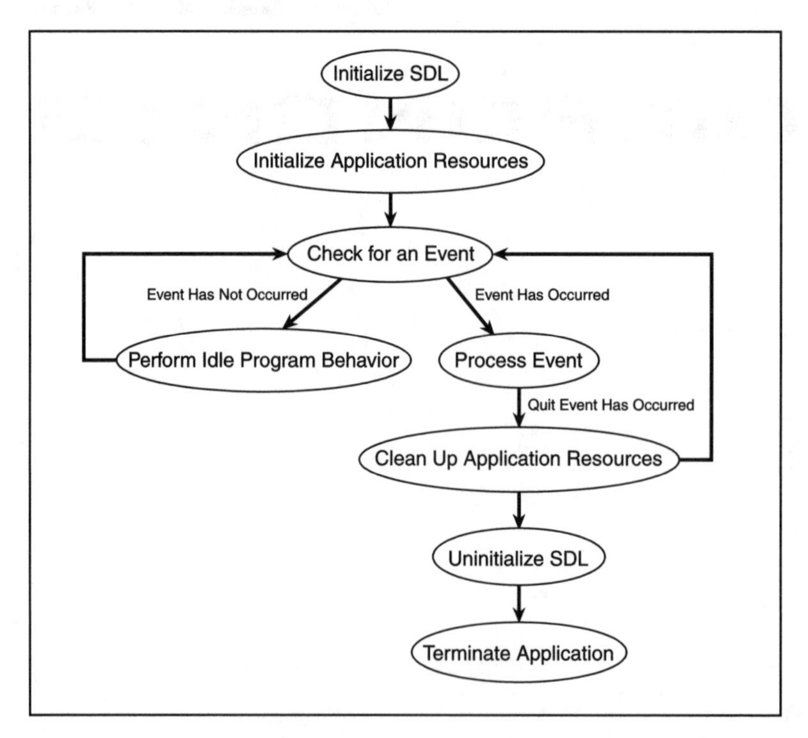

Figure 13.1 *Standard SDL application program flow*

As a developer, you know that all of these events must occur, and if you start from scratch, you will write pretty much the same code each time to accomplish them. One of the purposes of this framework is to get rid of that repetitious code that exists in all applications, freeing you to work with the useful code.

Core Components at a Glance

There are five classes in the core components—CMessageHandler (a message-handling class), CApplication (which directs the application as a whole), CEventHandler (which handles events as they come in), CThread (which manages a thread), and CTimer (which handles timers). Except for CThread and CTimer, these classes manage the basic tasks in all programs. Figure 13.2 shows the basic hierarchy of the core classes.

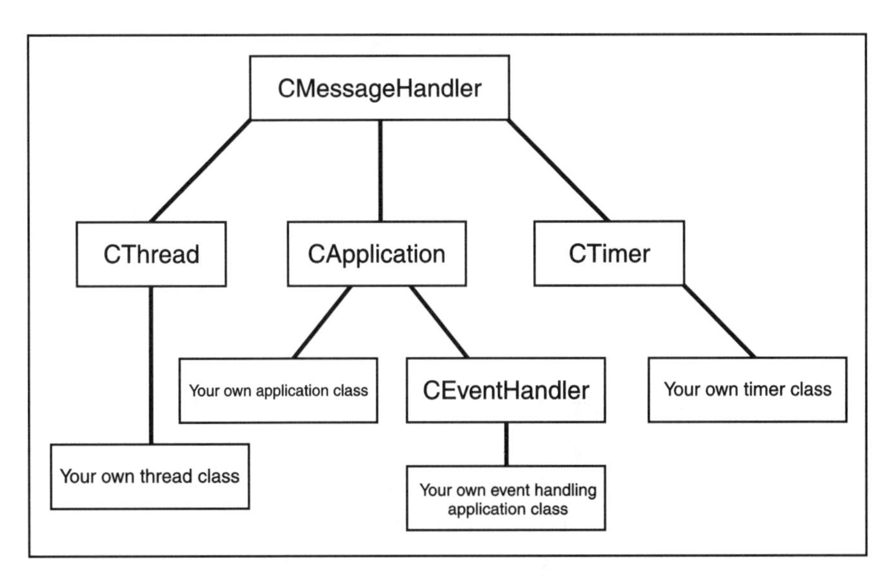

Figure 13.2 *Class hierarchy of the core components*

Message-Handler Class: CMessageHandler

CMessageHandler is a more abstract class than any of the others in the core components. It's the base class of all of the other classes. Its purpose is to provide a mechanism by which classes can communicate with one another through a hierarchy.

Each object of a class in the core components (except a CApplication object) has a parent object and any number of child objects. CMessageHandler allows a child object to send messages to and get information from its parent. This process occurs by sending messages and a number of parameters (up to four) that provide extra information about the message. (Each type of message has its own unique ID number that cannot be shared with any other message.)

Another purpose of `CMessageHandler` is to assign unique message IDs. These are referenced by an identifier, not by the raw number, so the actual value of the identifier is not important to you as a programmer. You just compare the message ID being sent to the identifier to find out what sort of message has been sent. Message IDs are assigned with a static member function call.

Application Class: CApplication

`CApplication` is a class derived from `CMessageHandler`. Its main purpose is to give a definite flow to an application and eliminate the need for a `main` function. `CApplication` is not intended to be instantiated. (The default behavior does practically nothing.) It is an intermediate step between `CMessageHandler` and `CEventHandler`.

`CApplication` also enforces only having a single instance of any `CApplication`-derived class.

Event-Handler Class: CEventHandler

`CEventHandler` is derived from `CApplication` and ultimately from `CMessageHandler`. It adds to `CApplication` by providing event handlers for all of the SDL event types. This makes life easy because to change the behavior of the application, all you have to do is modify a derived class' event-handling member function.

Thread Class: CThread

`CThread` is derived from `CMessageHandler`, so it can have a message handler parent (typically the `CApplication`- or `CEventHandler`-derived object for that application) and it can send messages to that parent. This vastly simplifies communication to and from the main thread.

Timer Class: CTimer

`CTimer` is much like `CThread`. It is based on `CMessageHandler`, so it can easily communicate with the main thread through messages. The only real difference is that it is periodically triggered, rather than running constantly as `CThread` does.

Core Components in Depth

Now that you've taken a look at how the core components of the application framework do their jobs and what roles they play, it is time to take a closer look at how they work. I am not going to go into the implementation of these classes line by line; instead, I'll show you the interface to these classes.

Message Handler Class

`CMessageHandler` is the simplest of the five classes, but it is also the most fundamental because all of the other classes are derived from it. Here is what the class definition for `CMessageHandler` looks like.

```
//message id
typedef Uint32 MSGID;
//message parameters
typedef void* MSGPARM;
/*
	==CMessageHandler==
	Message notification class.
	Base class of all other core components.
	Provides a parent child relationship to derived objects.
	Hungarian: mhX, *pmhX
*/
class CMessageHandler
{
private:
	//parent message handler
	CMessageHandler* m_pmhParent;
	//next message id(static)
	static MSGID s_NextMSGID;
public:
	//constructor
	CMessageHandler(CMessageHandler* pmhParent);
	//destructor
	virtual ~CMessageHandler();
	//set parent
	void SetParent(CMessageHandler* pmhNewParent);
```

```
    //get parent
    CMessageHandler* GetParent();
    //has parent?
    bool HasParent();
    //send message
    bool SendMessage(MSGID MsgID,MSGPARM Parm1=NULL,MSGPARM
Parm2=NULL,MSGPARM Parm3=NULL,MSGPARM Parm4=NULL);
    //process message(pure virtual)
    virtual bool OnMessage(MSGID MsgID,MSGPARM Parm1,MSGPARM
Parm2,MSGPARM Parm3,MSGPARM Parm4);
    //get next message id(static)
    static MSGID GetNextMSGID();
    //msgid: add child(static): Parm1=Parent, Parm2=Child
    static MSGID MSGID_AddChild;
    //msgid: remove child(static): Parm1=Parent, Parm2=Child
    static MSGID MSGID_RemoveChild;
    //add child handler
    virtual void OnAddChild(CMessageHandler* pmhChild);
    //remove child handler
    virtual void OnRemoveChild(CMessageHandler* pmhChild);
};
```

There are essentially three aspects to CMessageHandler—message ID assignment, parent management, and message handling. There are also the constructor and destructor, which I will discuss separately.

Message ID Assignment

Many different APIs and other frameworks use message identifiers. In standard WIN32 programming, all of the various WM_* constants are much like this; in SDL, there are a number of enumerations just like this. The reason for having such a scheme is to make it easy to differentiate one type of message from another.

Unfortunately, this sort of thing generally requires a great deal of bookkeeping on the part of the programmer. You have to lay out certain message IDs and reserve others; when creating new message IDs, you have to ensure that none are duplicated.

I have eliminated that problem by storing the "next" message ID in a global variable (or rather, a static member of CMessageHandler, which amounts to the same thing). The next message ID is assigned to an identifier (another static member), and the following message ID is increased by one. To check whether a particular message ID has been encountered, you simply use an `if` statement. (Since the variables are not constants you cannot use a `switch` statement, but `if...else if...else` blocks are more efficient anyway.)

The static member that stores the next message ID is called `s_NextMSGID`. Initially, its value is 0…not that it really matters. To assign a new message ID, you use `CMessageHandler::GetNextMSGID`.

```
MSGID CMessageHandler::GetNextMSGID();
```

This function takes no parameters and returns the next message ID available. The first message ID to be assigned is 0, and so forth. For an example of how to use this function, take a look at the static members `MSGID_AddChild` and `MSG_RemoveChild`. In MessageHandler.cpp (see FOSDL13_1 on the CD-ROM), the following two lines give values to these static members.

```
MSGID CMessageHandler::MSGID_AddChild=CMessageHandler::GetNextMSGID();
MSGID CMessageHandler::MSGID_RemoveChild=CMessageHandler::GetNextMSGID();
```

If these were the only two message IDs in the program, one would have a value of 0 and the other would have a value of 1. The actual value assigned does not matter. (Did I already say that?) If there were other message IDs assigned in other source files, then these message numbers might or might not be 0 and 1, depending on the compiler.

A minor caveat…. These message IDs are variables, not constants, so you have to be sure not to assign them values. If you really want to be safe, you can make static getter functions, but that's more typing than I typically like to do.

Since pretty much every other class in the core components derives from `CMessageHandler`, using `CMessageHandler::GetNextMSGID` is not a problem—you don't even have to include anything extra.

Parent Management

Another important aspect of `CMessageHandler` concerns the assignment of a parent object to another object. A pointer to this parent is stored in `m_pmhParent`, which is a private member. (In other words, I don't want the user of the class to have access to it for reasons that will become clear in a moment.)

There are three functions concerned with parent management for CMessageHandler: SetParent, GetParent, and HasParent. First, here's SetParent.

```
void CMessageHandler::SetParent(CMessageHandler* pmhNewParent);
```

This function returns no value and takes as its sole parameter a pointer to a new CMessageHandler (or derived class) to assign as the object's parent. The function does more than simply assign a new value for m_pmhParent. First, it checks to see whether the object already has a parent. If it does, the function sends a MSGID_RemoveChild to the old parent. The new value for m_pmhParent is assigned, and then (if the new parent is not NULL), the function sends a MSGID_AddChild message to the new parent.

The second function, GetParent, is rather straightforward.

```
CMessageHandler* CMessageHandler::GetParent();
```

This function simply returns the current value of m_pmhParent. It takes no parameters.

The third and final function is HasParent, which is used by SetParent to determine whether or not an object has a valid parent.

```
bool CMessageHandler::HasParent();
```

This function returns true if m_pmhParent is not NULL and false if it is NULL. I considered calling this function IsOrphan, but I wanted to keep the whole "Parent" theme going.

Message Handling

Perhaps the most important aspect of CMessageHandler is the one for which it was named—message handling. Each object in the hierarchy does a particular job, but there must be a way to communicate with other objects. With the whole parent-child idea, communication has to be two-way. The SendMessage function allows this.

```
bool CMessageHandler::SendMessage(MSGID MsgID,MSGPARM Parm1=NULL,MSGPARM
Parm2=NULL,MSGPARM Parm3=NULL,MSGPARM Parm4=NULL);
```

This function takes five parameters—a MSGID (called MsgID) that specifies which message is being sent and four MSGPARM values (Parm1 through Parm4). The meaning of these values depends on what message is being sent. The function returns true if the message was handled. If you need to return extended information (other than true or false), you can simply put a pointer to something into one of the parameters and have the handler fill it with a return value.

When SendMessage is called, CMessageHandler tries to handle the message itself by calling OnMessage. (You will take a look at this function in a moment.) Failing that, the message is sent along to the parent, if the object has one. If no parent exists, then false is returned.

When a CMessageHandler attempts to handle a message on its own, it uses the OnMessage function (which is virtual and likely to be overridden in derived classes).

```
bool CMessageHandler::OnMessage(MSGID MsgID,MSGPARM Parm1,MSGPARM
Parm2,MSGPARM Parm3,MSGPARM Parm4);
```

As you can see, OnMessage has the same parameter list as SendMessage, as well as the same return type. OnMessage's purpose is to dispatch messages to the appropriate handler. There are already two messages defined for CMessageHandler—MSGID_AddChild and MSGID_RemoveChild. If either of these messages occurs, calls are made to OnAddChild or OnRemoveChild. If neither message occurs, the function simply returns false.

What this means to you is that when you derive classes from CMessageHandler and you override OnMessage, you must call CMessageHandler::OnMessage if you don't find the messages for which you are looking. This is the mechanism that allows default processing of messages.

The two specific message handlers are OnAddChild and OnRemoveChild; both look rather similar.

```
void CMessageHandler::OnAddChild(CMessageHandler* pmhChild);
void CMessageHandler::OnRemoveChild(CMessageHandler* pmhChild);
```

Neither of these functions returns a value, and both take as parameters pointers to a CMessageHandler that is being added or removed as a child (depending on which of the functions is called). The CMessageHandler implementation for these functions does absolutely nothing. Both functions are virtual and are meant to be overridden if a child class needs to keep track of child objects.

Constructor and Destructor

Finally, you have the constructor and destructor. The constructor assigns an initial value to m_pmhParent by calling SetParent. The destructor sets the parent to NULL (allowing for the final sending of MSGID_RemoveChild). Here's what the constructor looks like.

```
CMessagHandler::CMessageHandler(CMessageHandler* pmhParent);
```

The constructor simply takes a pointer to another CMessageHandler to use as the initial value for the parent. The destructor looks just like every other destructor that ever existed, so I won't bother to show it.

As you can see, CMessageHandler has absolutely nothing to do with SDL itself, yet it includes sdl.h at the top of MessageHandler.h. Why? Because somewhere within sdl.h, NULL is given a value. Otherwise, I would've had to use 0. Silly, eh?

Application Class

The second class in the core components is CApplication, which is derived from CMessageHandler. The entire goal of CApplication is to eliminate the need to write a main function. (There will still be a main function, of course, but it will be hidden in the implementation of CApplication.)

```
/*
	==CApplication==
	Singleton.
	Base class for all other application classes.
*/
class CApplication : public CMessageHandler
{
private:
	//singleton pointer
	static CApplication* s_pTheApplication;
	//set singleton pointer
	static void SetApplication(CApplication* pTheApp);
public:
	//constructor
	CApplication();
	//destructor
	virtual ~CApplication();
	//initialization
	virtual bool OnInit(int argc,char* argv[]);
	//event occurrence
	virtual void OnEvent(SDL_Event* pEvent);
```

```
    //idle behavior
    virtual void OnIdle();
    //cleanup
    virtual void OnExit();
    //execution of application
    static int Execute(int argc,char* argv[]);
    //get singleton
    static CApplication* GetApplication();
};
```

The odd thing about CApplication is that it is a singleton. You can naturally only have one application object at a time. This is enforced by the static member s_pTheApplication. The static member functions GetApplication and SetApplication are concerned with setting and retrieving this value. SetApplication is called during CApplication's constructor. If the value has already been set, the program will terminate with an error message in stderr.txt.

The main function, shown below, calls only one function—CApplication::Execute.

```
//main function
int main(int argc,char* argv[])
{
    //run the application
    return(CApplication::Execute(argc,argv));
}
```

CApplication::Execute first checks to see that s_pTheApplication has a value other than NULL. If the value is NULL, then no application has been instantiated, and the program terminates immediately after sending an error message to stderr.txt.

Once the value of s_pTheApplication has been checked, Execute attempts to initialize the application by calling the OnInit member function of whatever s_pTheApplication points to. If OnInit returns false, then the application terminates because it can't be initialized. (It is assumed that any failure to initialize will be reported during the call to OnInit.)

Next, the event/idle loop begins. First, SDL polls for events. If an event other than a quit event occurs, it is sent to OnEvent. If no event occurs, OnIdle is called instead. This keeps occurring until a quit event happens, at which point Execute breaks out of the loop.

After the loop is finished, OnExit is called and any cleanup is done. Finally, the application terminates normally.

CApplication, as you can see, is a pretty small class. Most of the time you will want to override OnInit, OnExit, and OnEvent at the very least, and usually OnIdle as well.

This brings up the question of how you instantiate a CApplication object. Since there is no main function to write, there has to be some manner of instantiating a CApplication object. First, you will never instantiate a CApplication object because CApplication doesn't really do much. Instead, you will derive a class from CApplication, and then instantiate that instead. The instantiation will occur in the global scope. Suppose you derived a class from CApplication called CTestApplication. Somewhere in TestApplication.cpp you would have the following line.

```
CTestApplication TheApp;
```

The constructor will take it from there. Neat, huh?

CApplication, like CMessageHandler, doesn't really do much. However, at least now there is some sort of tie-in with SDL. Mainly this has to do with initialization (CApplication initializes all systems of SDL) and event grabbing.

Event-Handler Class

The event-handler class is derived from CApplication. It includes new member functions that take care of handling events. In CApplication, there is only a single event-handling function—OnEvent (which CEventHandler overrides, of course). CEventHandler takes the information from the event and dispatches it to the appropriate member function. Here's what the class looks like.

```
/*
	==CEventHandler==
	Event dispatching application class
*/
class CEventHandler : public CApplication
{
public:
	//constructor
```

```
        CEventHandler();
        //destructor
        virtual ~CEventHandler();
        //event handling
        virtual void OnEvent(SDL_Event* pEvent);
        //event filtering
        virtual bool FilterEvent(SDL_Event* pEvent);
//active events
        //keyboard(input)
        virtual void OnInputFocus();
        virtual void OnInputBlur();
        //mouse
        virtual void OnMouseFocus();
        virtual void OnMouseBlur();
        //application active
        virtual void OnMinimize();
        virtual void OnRestore();
//keyboard events
        virtual void OnKeyDown(SDLKey sym,SDLMod mod,Uint16 unicode);
        virtual void OnKeyUp(SDLKey sym,SDLMod mod,Uint16 unicode);
//mouse events
        virtual void OnMouseMove(Uint16 x,Uint16 y,Sint16 relx,Sint16
rely,bool bLeft,bool bRight,bool bMiddle);
        virtual void OnLButtonDown(Uint16 x,Uint16 y);
        virtual void OnLButtonUp(Uint16 x,Uint16 y);
        virtual void OnRButtonDown(Uint16 x,Uint16 y);
        virtual void OnRButtonUp(Uint16 x,Uint16 y);
        virtual void OnMButtonDown(Uint16 x,Uint16 y);
        virtual void OnMButtonUp(Uint16 x,Uint16 y);
//joystick events
        virtual void OnJoyAxis(Uint8 which,Uint8 axis,Sint16 value);
        virtual void OnJoyButtonDown(Uint8 which,Uint8 button);
        virtual void OnJoyButtonUp(Uint8 which,Uint8 button);
        virtual void OnJoyHat(Uint8 which,Uint8 hat,Uint8 value);
        virtual void OnJoyBall(Uint8 which,Uint8 ball,Sint16 xrel,Sint16
yrel);
//resize event
        virtual void OnResize(int w,int h);
//expose event
```

```
    virtual void OnExpose();
//user event
    virtual void OnUser(Uint8 type,int code,void* data1,void* data2);
};
```

Other than the constructor, destructor, OnEvent, and FilterEvent, the rest of the member functions are concerned with handling specific types of events. The parameters are the same as the members of the various types of events that you receive in a normal application. Since I have already covered events extensively, I won't go through them all again. Each event handler in CEventHandler's implementation does absolutely nothing. They are just stubs that are meant to be overridden in derived classes.

Two events do not have handlers—SysWM and Quit. CApplication handles Quit events internally, and SysWM events are simply ignored. Certain events (such as mouse button presses and active events) have been split into several different specific events just to make life even easier—one for each button, one for each type of focus, and so on.

The other member functions, specifically OnEvent and FilterEvent, play specific roles. The behavior of OnEvent (which did absolutely nothing in CApplication) has been changed so that the type of event triggers the specific event-handling function. The FilterEvent member function occurs before the event is dispatched. FilterEvent, in CEventHandler's implementation, simply returns false. If true is returned, the event is not dispatched (in other words, it has been filtered). This is meant to assist in event trapping with later components of the application framework.

The constructor and destructor don't actually do anything; they are included for completeness.

Thread Class

The next core component is the CThread class. It is derived from CMessageHandler and it encapsulates a thread. You must be careful with this class because multi-threaded programming can easily be disastrous. CThread is a simplistic class that is meant only for simplistic tasks. To make a more robust class, you would need to put a great deal more thought into it.

```
/*
    ==CThread==
    Base class for all user defined thread classes
*/
class CThread : public CMessageHandler
{
private:
    //pointer to the thread
    SDL_Thread* m_pThread;
    //thread ID
    Uint32 m_ThreadID;
    //running flag
    bool m_bRunning;
    //suspended flag
    bool m_bPaused;
protected:
    //start the thread(should be called by derived classes constructor)
    void Start();
    //thread function
    static int ThreadFunction(void* data);
    //onstart handler
    virtual void OnStart();
    //onstop handler
    virtual void OnStop();
    //onpause handler
    virtual void OnPause();
    //onresume handler
    virtual void OnResume();
public:
    //constructor
    CThread(CMessageHandler* pmhParent);
    //destructor
    virtual ~CThread();
    //get thread pointer
    SDL_Thread* GetThread();
    //get thread id
    Uint32 GetThreadID();
    //stop the thread
    void Stop();
    //set paused state
```

```
    void Pause();
    void Resume();
    //check paused state
    bool IsPaused();
    //check running state
    bool IsRunning();
    //thread procedure
    int OnExecute();
};
```

CThread only adds four data members—m_pThread (a pointer to an SDL_Thread), m_ThreadID (the ID of the running thread), m_bRunning (an indicator of whether or not the thread is running), and m_bPaused (an indicator of whether or not the thread is paused).

You can access the two SDL-related members (m_pThread and m_ThreadID) with GetThread and GetThreadID, respectively.

You can access the status (running or not and paused or not) with IsRunning and IsPaused. To change the paused state, you use Pause or Resume. To change the running state, you use Start or Stop. Only Stop has public access.

There are also event handlers built into CThread, namely OnStart, OnStop, OnPause, and OnResume. These can be called from threads outside of the thread running the CThread object, so you should be careful. In the CThread implementation, these handlers do nothing.

CThread's main work is done through OnExecute (a virtual function), which customizes what a CThread-derived object does. The mechanism that allows this to work is ThreadFunction, a static member function used to create all threads.

CThread itself is not useful if instantiated. The thread terminates almost immediately after it is started, and there is no way to start it. You must create a derived class that calls Start during the constructor.

Timer Class

CTimer, the last of the core components, encapsulates a timer object. It is similar to CThread in many ways, although it is generally much safer to use. Like CThread, using CTimer itself is silly…the class does nothing.

```
/*
	==CTimer==
	Base class for all timer classes.
*/
class CTimer : public CMessageHandler
{
private:
	//timer id
	SDL_TimerID m_TimerID;
	//interval
	Uint32 m_Interval;
	//timer procedure
	static Uint32 TimerProc(Uint32 interval,void* param);
public:
	//constructor
	CTimer(CMessageHandler* pmhParent,Uint32 interval);
	//destructor
	virtual ~CTimer();
	//get interval
	Uint32 GetInterval();
	//set interval
	void SetInterval(Uint32 Interval);
	//get timer id
	SDL_TimerID GetTimerID();
	//start timer
	void Start();
	//stop timer
	void Stop();
	//on timer handler
	virtual void OnTimer();
};
```

The cool thing about `CTimer` is that you can start, stop, and restart it with ease. There are two additional members that give you information about the timer—the interval (`m_Interval`) and the timer ID (`m_TimerID`). If the timer ID is zero, the timer is stopped. (You can call `GetTimerID` to find out the value of the timer ID, and then check it against 0.) Otherwise, the timer is in operation.

You can use `SetInterval` to change the interval at which the timer fires, and you can use `GetInterval` to retrieve the current interval.

Each time the timer pulses, the `OnTimer` member function is called. This function is meant to be overridden in a derived class; in the `CTimer` implementation it does absolutely nothing.

Component Test

Now it is time to put your money where your mouth is and do a test of the core components. You can find this component test in FOSDL13_1 on the CD-ROM.

In the example, all of the core components are used either directly or indirectly to derive three new classes—`CTestEventHandler` (which derives from `CEventHandler` directly and `CApplication` and `CMessageHandler` indirectly), `CTestThread` (which derives from `CThread` directly and `CMessageHandler` indirectly), and `CTestTimer` (which derives from `CTimer` directly and `CMessageHandler` indirectly).

`CTestTimer` and `CTestThread` don't do much. They both simply write strings to stdout.txt. `CTestThread` only writes a single string before it is done, and `CTimer` pulses every 1000 ms and writes to stdout.txt. (In other words, don't let the test application run for days on end.)

`CTestEventHandler` is a simplistic drawing program. I only had to override a few functions—`OnLButtonDown`, `OnMouseMove`, and `OnKeyDown`. With the left mouse button pressed, this application allows you to draw white dots on the screen. To clear the screen, hit any key.

To test the message-handling aspects of the core components, I placed two new `MSGID`s—one for clearing the screen and one for drawing a pixel—so the only function that actually deals with screen drawing is `OnMessage`.

So the core components work, and now you can move on to bigger and better things.

Summary

A thousand-mile journey starts with a single step. Hopefully that step is toward a car or an airplane, because walking a thousand miles seems a bit extreme. Anyway, you've got some fundamental classes to work with now, and you can start adding in more specific classes for dealing with more SDL objects. The book *is* about SDL, after all.

CHAPTER 14

Video Components

Now that you've gotten the core components out of the way, you can start making some components that are actually useful. I am speaking, of course, about video components.

Some people might say that there really is no need to encapsulate SDL's video components into classes. To a certain degree, I agree with them. The SDL video components are already quite object-oriented and well organized. But I truly prefer working with classes to functions.

There is also quite a bit of functionality that was left out of SDL. There is no class to abstract a point on the screen. Also, there are no functions that make dealing with SDL_Rect very easy, and the same thing goes for SDL_Color. In the case of SDL_Color, there isn't even a function that uses this structure unless you are using palettes.

Video Components at a Glance

I have come up with seven classes to use for video components, most of which abstract some structure in SDL. I have divided the components into two broad categories—basic classes (`CPoint`, `CRectangle`, and `CColor`) and graphical classes (`CCanvas`, `CImage`, and `CImageSet`). Although you've already seen this in Chapter 12, Figure 14.1 shows a diagram of the classes in the video components and their relationship to one another.

This list could be rounded out easily with classes for abstract palettes, overlays, and video information, but I'll leave the design of those classes to you since you won't need them for the task at hand. Let's get right to it and talk a bit about the various video components and their roles, starting with the basic classes.

Basic Classes

The three basic classes are `CPoint`, `CRectangle`, and `CColor`. With the exception of `CPoint`, each of these abstract a specific SDL structure,

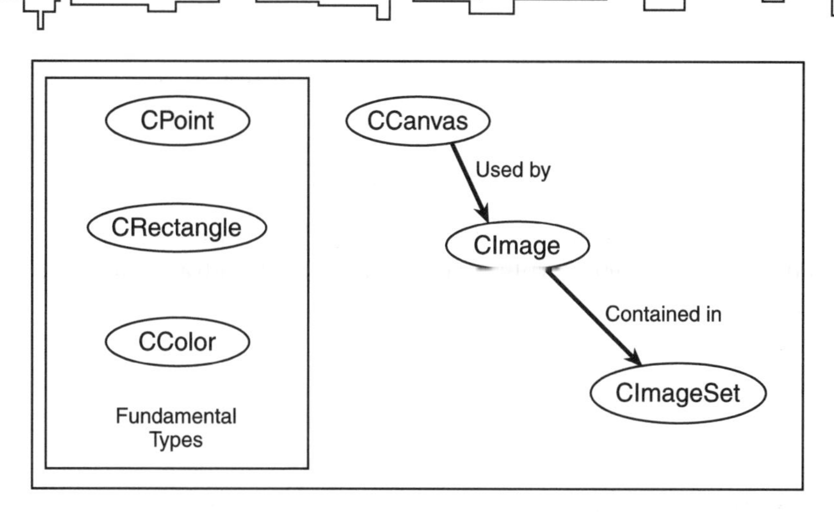

Figure 14.1 *Structure of the video components*

namely SDL_Rect and SDL_Color. I added `CPoint` myself. I like having a class to abstract a 2D coordinate; it just makes life easier.

CPoint

`CPoint` abstracts a 2D coordinate. It has only two parts—x and y and the appropriate setter and getter functions for each. In addition, there are a number of operators defined for `CPoint`—all of the arithmetic operators (+, –, *, and /), as well as the associated assignment operators (+=, –=, *=, and /=). Multiplication and division only take scalar values. There are also comparison operators (== and !=) to make checking points against one another relatively easy. Finally, there are distance calculation functions to tell you the absolute distance of a point from the origin or the distance (or squared distance) between two points.

CRectangle

`CRectangle` abstracts an SDL_Rect. I have added member functions and constructors to `CRectangle` that make setting up a rectangle rather easy. `CRectangle` can be built either by raw coordinate data or from `CPoints`. Additionally, there are conversion operators to convert `CRectangle` into either an SDL_Rect or an SDL_Rect*, so you can use `CRectangle` any place you need one of these types. (This will come in handy when you create `CCanvas` a little later.)

Additionally, there are several operators associated with CRectangle. Moving a rectangle around is as easy as adding or subtracting a CPoint. There are also + and – operators for rectangles (and += and –=), which can be used to find the union (+) or intersection (–) of two rectangles.

Finally, there are getter functions if you want to know the right and bottom coordinates enveloped by a rectangle, as well as functions that will tell you whether a point is within a rectangle. This is a nice, full-featured rectangle class, folks.

CColor

SDL_Color has been somewhat ignored as an SDL structure. No function in SDL itself deals with SDL_Color outside of the palette functions. This makes me think that this little structure is underutilized. CColor intends to fix that.

CColor abstracts SDL_Color and gives you getters, setters, and other accessor functions for the red, green, and blue components. (With the "unused" member, this class easily could be extended to include alpha information if you so desired.) There are also conversion operators to exchange CColor with either SDL_Color or SDL_Color*. In addition, there are numerous arithmetic (+, –, *, and /) and bitwise (|, &, and ^) operators to assist in the creation and modification of colors, as well as the equivalent assignment operators.

Finally, there are a number of static member functions for typical stock colors that you might want to use, such as red, green, blue, yellow, magenta, cyan, black, and white, as well as light and dark versions of these colors.

Graphical Classes

There are three graphical classes—CCanvas, CImage, and CImageSet. This section contains brief descriptions of each. For the relationship between these components, please refer back to Figure 14.1.

CCanvas

CCanvas abstracts an SDL_Surface object. Included among the member functions are the tasks you typically want to accomplish with an SDL_Surface, such as filling rectangles, locking and unlocking, setting pixels, and blitting. There is also a mechanism to add rectangles to a list for dirty rectangle updating (something for which SDL is really good). There are also a few static member "factory" functions for creating the most common type of surfaces.

CImage

CImage assists with blit management. It contains a pointer to a CCanvas object, along with a CRectangle describing an area that will often be used for blitting. In addition, it contains a CPoint for offsetting the destination rectangle, providing something of an anchor point. (There are plenty of images in which you would prefer to use a point of reference other than the upper-left.) Once a CImage has been set up, it can be used many times to blit images onto a canvas using only a single coordinate for reference.

CImageSet

CImageSet is nothing more than a managed collection of CImage objects, so it mainly abstracts a vector of CImage*. There are member functions for adding, finding, and removing images from the set, as well as a function to access an image by its index in the list.

Video Components in Depth

Basic Classes

The basic video classes are CPoint, CRectangle, and CColor. They are used extensively in the other graphical classes.

CPoint

The CPoint class is a very simple abstraction of a coordinate pair x and y. It has most of the operations you would want to do with a 2D point.

```
//point class
class CPoint
{
private:
	//x and y
	int m_x ;
	int m_y ;
```

```
public:
    //constructor
    CPoint ( int x = 0 , int y = 0 ) ;
    CPoint ( CPoint& pt ) ;
    //destructor
    virtual ~CPoint ( ) ;
    //properties
    int& X ( ) ;
    int& Y ( ) ;
    int GetX ( ) const ;
    int GetY ( ) const ;
    void SetX ( int x ) ;
    void SetY ( int y ) ;
    //setter
    CPoint& Set ( int x , int y ) ;
    CPoint& Copy ( CPoint& pt ) ;
    //move
    CPoint& Move ( int dx , int dy ) ;
    CPoint& Add ( CPoint& pt ) ;
    CPoint& Subtract ( CPoint& pt ) ;
    //scale
    CPoint& Scale ( int scalar ) ;
    //distance
    int Distance ( CPoint& pt ) ;
    //operators
    //assignment
    CPoint& operator = ( CPoint& pt ) ;
    CPoint& operator += ( CPoint& pt ) ;
    CPoint& operator -= ( CPoint& pt ) ;
    CPoint& operator *= ( int scalar ) ;
    CPoint& operator /= ( int scalar ) ;
    //unary
    CPoint operator - ( ) ;
    CPoint operator + ( ) ;
    //arithmetic
    CPoint operator + ( CPoint& pt ) ;
    CPoint operator - ( CPoint& pt ) ;
    CPoint operator * ( int scalar ) ;
    CPoint operator / ( int scalar ) ;
    //comparison
```

```
        bool operator == ( CPoint& pt ) ;
        bool operator != ( CPoint& pt ) ;
};
CPoint operator * ( int scalar , CPoint& pt ) ;
```

The constructors create a point based on a pair of x,y values (both parameters are optional and default to 0) or from another `CPoint` object, like this:

```
CPoint pt1(10,10);//create a point with coordinate (10,10)
CPoint pt2(pt1);//copy pt1 into pt2
```

The getters, setters, and accessors (`GetX`, `GetY`, `SetX`, `SetY`, `x`, and `y`), are generally self-explanatory. `x` and `y` return references to the `x` and `y` values of the point, so you can modify it like this:

```
CPoint pt;
pt.X()=10;//set x to 10
pt.Y()=10;//set y to 10
```

Since `x` and `y` return a reference, you can also use them like `GetX` and `GetY`. In fact, this might make you question why you even need to have `SetX` and `GetX` when the `x` function can do both. The reason is, when you are working with a `const CPoint` object (it happens, believe me), you cannot return a modifiable reference to one of the members of that object.

You can also perform operations on the `CPoint` objects using member functions such as `Set`, `Copy`, `Move`, `Add`, `Subtract`, and `Scale`. Brief examples of each of these are shown here.

```
CPoint pt;
pt.Set(10,10);//set point to 10,10
CPoint pt2;
pt2.Copy(pt);//copy pt to pt2
pt.Move(10,10);//move by +10,+10, making pt equal to 20,20
pt.Add(pt2);//add contents of pt2(10,10), to pt(20,20), to come up with
(30,30)
pt.Subtract(pt2);//subtract contents of pt2(10,10) to pt(30,30) to come
up with (20,20)
pt.scale(2);//multiply x and y by 2, to come up with (40,40)
```

There are also operators that you can use instead of these member functions. The operators include =, +=, −=, *=, /=, +, −, *, and /. In the case of *=, *, /, and /=, the second operand is a scalar; in all other cases, it is another CPoint. There is also an external operator * that takes a scalar first and a CPoint second, so you can do either 2*pt or pt*2 and the compiler won't complain.

Additionally, there are unary + and – operators for CPoint. The unary + really doesn't do anything to the point, but the – operator multiplies the point by a scalar –1.

There are only two relational operators, == and !=, so that you can check for equality or lack of equality between points. Two points are equal when both xs and ys are equal.

Finally, there is a Distance member function, which tells you the distance between two points. Since this uses integers, it is rounded off to the next lower integer.

CRectangle

CRectangle does a good job of abstracting an SDL_Rect structure and adds some much-needed functionality to that rather plain, vanilla structure.

```
//CRectangle--abstract an SDL_Rect
class CRectangle
{
private:
	//internal representation of a SDL_Rect
	SDL_Rect m_rect ;
public:
	//constructors--direct member assignment
	CRectangle ( Sint16 x = 0 , Sint16 y = 0 , Uint16 w = 0 , Uint16
h = 0 ) ;
	//copy from SDL_Rect
	CRectangle ( SDL_Rect rc ) ;
	//copy from SDL_Rect*
	CRectangle ( SDL_Rect* prc ) ;
	//copy from another CRectangle
	CRectangle ( CRectangle& rc ) ;
	virtual ~CRectangle ( ) ;
	//accessors for x, y, h, and w
	Sint16& X ( ) ;
	Sint16& Y ( ) ;
	Uint16& W ( ) ;
	Uint16& H ( ) ;
```

```
//getters
Sint16 GetX() const;
Sint16 GetY() const;
Uint16 GetW() const;
Uint16 GetH() const;
//setters
void SetX(Sint16 x);
void SetY(Sint16 y);
void SetW(Uint16 w);
void SetH(Uint16 h);//conversion operators
//convert to SDL_Rect
operator SDL_Rect ( ) ;
//convert to SDL_Rect*
operator SDL_Rect* ( ) ;
//convert to CPoint
operator CPoint ( ) ;
//set values for members
CRectangle& Set ( Sint16 x , Sint16 y , Uint16 w , Uint16 h ) ;
//copy member values from another CRectangle
CRectangle& Copy ( CRectangle& rc ) ;
//set to an empty rectangle
CRectangle& SetEmpty ( ) ;
//check for emptiness
bool IsEmpty ( ) ;
//offset rectangle by coordinates or point
CRectangle& Offset ( Sint16 dx , Sint16 dy ) ;
CRectangle& Offset ( CPoint& pt ) ;
//move to a position, either coordinates or point
CRectangle& Move ( Sint16 x , Sint16 y ) ;
CRectangle& Move ( CPoint& pt ) ;
//intersect with another rectangle
CRectangle& Intersect ( CRectangle& rc ) ;
//create union with another rectangle
CRectangle& Union ( CRectangle& rc ) ;
//check if a point is within the rectangle
bool Contains ( Sint16 x , Sint16 y ) ;
bool Contains ( CPoint& pt ) ;
//assignment operators
CRectangle& operator = ( CRectangle& rc ) ;
CRectangle& operator += ( CPoint& pt ) ;
```

```
    CRectangle& operator -= ( CPoint& pt ) ;
    CRectangle& operator += ( CRectangle& rc ) ;
    CRectangle& operator -= ( CRectangle& rc ) ;
    //arithmetic operators
    CRectangle operator + ( CPoint& pt ) ;
    CRectangle operator - ( CPoint& pt ) ;
    CRectangle operator + ( CRectangle& rc ) ;
    CRectangle operator - ( CRectangle& rc ) ;
    //comparisons
    bool operator == ( CRectangle& rc ) ;
    bool operator != ( CRectangle& rc ) ;
    //clip or wrap points
    CPoint Clip ( CPoint pt ) ;
    CPoint Wrap ( CPoint pt ) ;
};
//add/subtract point and rectangle
CRectangle operator + ( CPoint& pt , CRectangle& rc ) ;
CRectangle operator - ( CPoint& pt , CRectangle& rc ) ;
```

There are four separate constructors—plenty of ways to make a CRectangle object. Two constructors are ones you would expect—one that takes each of the member variables and one that copies from another CRectangle object. The other two copy from either an SDL_Rect or an SDL_Rect*, so you have plenty of options for constructing a CRectangle.

```
SDL_Rect rc;//standard SDL_Rect
rc.x=rc.y=0;//x and y at (0,0)
rc.w=rc.h=10;//width and height at 10
CRectangle rc1(0,0,10,10);//construct by members
CRectangle rc2(rc1);//copy from another CRectangle
CRectangle rc3(rc);//copy from SDL_Rect
CRectangle rc4(&rc);//copy from SDL_Rect*
```

Also, there are the standard setters, getters, and accessors—SetX, SetY, SetW, SetH, GetX, GetY, GetW, GetH, X, Y, W, and H. These all play essentially the same roles as they do in CPoint.

Because CRectangle abstracts an SDL_Rect object, there are conversion operators so you can use a CRectangle wherever you need an SDL_Rect or SDL_Rect*. Also, you can use a CRectangle any place you need a CPoint. (It only uses the x and y components of the rectangle.) No, you cannot use CRectangle in CPoint math.

Set, Copy, Move, Offset, SetEmpty, IsEmpty, Intersect, and Union round out the CRectangle member functions. Set behaves much like the memberwise constructor. SetEmpty sets a CRectangle's members to 0. IsEmpty tests for emptiness. Move changes the x and y positions to new positions. (You can either specify coordinates or a CPoint.) Offset moves the rectangle relative to its old position. (Again, you can use coordinates or a CPoint.) Intersect takes another rectangle and determines the largest rectangle contained within both of the rectangles, and Union takes another rectangle and determines the smallest rectangle that will fit both of the rectangles.

You can also use Contains (with either a coordinate or a CPoint—your choice) to check whether a point is within a rectangle. Another set of functions dealing with CPoint includes Clip (which brings a point to the closest point inside a rectangle if it is not already inside) and Wrap (which makes the CRectangle something like a torus and brings the CPoint into the CRectangle by subtracting or adding height and width to the position of the point until it is within the rectangle).

There are also several operators that deal with rectangles. The =, ==, and != operators are essentially self-explanatory; they are used for assignment and a check for equality (all members must be the same) or inequality. The +, −, +=, and −= operators are a little more strange. You can add to or subtract from a CRectangle either a CPoint (in which case you move the rectangle by the coordinates stored in the CPoint) or another CRectangle. When you add two CRectangles, it results in a union of those two rectangles. When you subtract, it results in the intersection.

CColor

CColor, as a class, is rather large for something as simplistic as color representation. Nevertheless, in the quest to make life easier for everyone, I made it as full-featured as I know how without going too far overboard. Here's what the class definition looks like.

```
/*
	==CColor==
	Abstracts SDL_Color
*/
class CColor
{
private:
```

```
    //actual color representation
    SDL_Color m_Color;
public:
    //standard constructor
    CColor(Uint8 r=0,Uint8 g=0,Uint8 b=0);
    //copy constructor
    CColor(const CColor& Color);
    //destructor
    virtual ~CColor();
    //get rgb
    Uint8 GetR() const;
    Uint8 GetG() const;
    Uint8 GetB() const;
    //set rgb
    void SetR(Uint8 r);
    void SetG(Uint8 g);
    void SetB(Uint8 b);
    //rgb accessors
    Uint8& R();
    Uint8& G();
    Uint8& B();
    //conversion operators
    operator SDL_Color();
    operator SDL_Color*();
    //assignment operators
    CColor& operator=(CColor& Color);
    CColor& operator+=(CColor& Color);
    CColor& operator-=(CColor& Color);
    CColor& operator*=(CColor& Color);
    CColor& operator*=(int Multiplier);
    CColor& operator/=(int Divisor);
    CColor& operator|=(CColor& Color);
    CColor& operator&=(CColor& Color);
    CColor& operator^=(CColor& Color);
    //primary colors
    static CColor Red(Uint8 shade=255);
    static CColor Green(Uint8 shade=255);
    static CColor Blue(Uint8 shade=255);
    //secondary colors
    static CColor Yellow(Uint8 shade=255);
```

```
        static CColor Cyan(Uint8 shade=255);
        static CColor Magenta(Uint8 shade=255);
        //dark colors
        static CColor DarkRed(Uint8 shade=128);
        static CColor DarkGreen(Uint8 shade=128);
        static CColor DarkBlue(Uint8 shade=128);
        static CColor DarkYellow(Uint8 shade=128);
        static CColor DarkCyan(Uint8 shade=128);
        static CColor DarkMagenta(Uint8 shade=128);
        //light colors
        static CColor LightRed(Uint8 gray=128,Uint8 shade=255);
        static CColor LightGreen(Uint8 gray=128,Uint8 shade=255);
        static CColor LightBlue(Uint8 gray=128,Uint8 shade=255);
        static CColor LightYellow(Uint8 gray=128,Uint8 shade=255);
        static CColor LightCyan(Uint8 gray=128,Uint8 shade=255);
        static CColor LightMagenta(Uint8 gray=128,Uint8 shade=255);
        //grayscale
        static CColor White(Uint8 shade=255);
        static CColor LightGray(Uint8 shade=192);
        static CColor DarkGray(Uint8 shade=128);
        static CColor Black(Uint8 shade=0);
};
//arithmetic operators
CColor operator+(CColor& Color1,CColor& Color2);
CColor operator-(CColor& Color1,CColor& Color2);
CColor operator*(CColor& Color1,CColor& Color2);
CColor operator*(CColor& Color,int Multiplier);
CColor operator/(CColor& Color,int Divisor);
//bitwise operators
CColor operator|(CColor& Color1,CColor& Color2);
CColor operator&(CColor& Color1,CColor& Color2);
CColor operator^(CColor& Color1,CColor& Color2);
CColor operator~(CColor& Color);
//comparison operators
bool operator==(CColor& Color1,CColor& Color2);
bool operator!=(CColor& Color1,CColor& Color2);
```

I divide the members of `CColor` into three categories—accessor functions, operators, and stock color functions.

The accessor functions—GetR, GetG, GetB, SetR, SetG, SetB, R, G, and B—are mostly self-explanatory. The Get functions retrieve the values of red, green, and blue, and the Set functions assign new values. The remaining member functions (without either Set or Get) directly access the component of the color, so you can assign it without a Set function, like this:

```
CColor color;
Color.R()=255;
```

I typically refer to this sort of member function as a *property*; I sort of stole the idea from the Visual Basic property mechanism.

The operators are likewise relatively self-explanatory. When you use them, the various components are added, subtracted, bitwise ORed, bitwise ANDed, or bitwise XORed to create a new value for that color component. The only oddballs are multiplication and division. One form of multiplication causes all values to be multiplied by a single scalar value. The sole version of division also works this way. The second form of multiplication takes two colors, multiplies their color components together, and then divides the result by 255. As far as colors are concerned, 255*255 is equal to 255. In a way, this is like treating a color component of 0 as 0.0 and a color component of 255 as 1.0, and then doing the floating-point multiplication—treating colors sort of like a 3D vector and doing a dot product. There are uses for this, believe me.

The stock color functions, such as Red, Green, Blue, Yellow, Cyan, Magenta, Black, and White, allow you to assign stock colors, so creating colors can be quite easy. Each of the primary and secondary colors (as well as white) takes a shade parameter that defaults to 255, so the following code creates the exact same color twice.

```
CColor Color1, Color2;
Color1=CColor::White();
Color2=CColor::White(255);
```

The stock colors that create light versions of the standard colors, such as LightRed and LightGreen, take two parameters, both of which are optional. The first parameter is a gray shade upon which to base the light color, and the second is the shade of the primary color to use. The following code creates the same color twice.

```
CColor Color1,Color2;
```

```
Color1=CColor::LightRed();
Color1=CColor::White(128)|CColor::Red(255);
```

Both statements will create a color that has a red component of 255 and green and blue components of 128. I think you get the idea, so I'll move on.

Of particular importance are the constructors. There are two of these—one that takes each of the red, green, and blue components and one that will copy another color. Typically you will use the former more often than the latter. The latter is primarily intended for use with STL containers.

Specifying a particular RGB color is as easy as this:

```
CColor Color;
Color=CColor(255,0,0);//red
```

This might not seem terribly significant at the moment, but it will be when you get to `CCanvas` and you are passing `CColor` values but you don't want to actually create a variable for one.

Graphical Classes

The graphical classes are `CCanvas`, `CImage`, and `CImageSet`. You're going to take a look at the full class definitions for these classes, but as with the basic classes you won't look too much into the actual implementation.

CCanvas

`CCanvas` abstracts an SDL_Surface*—it's as simple as that. Much of the functionality of SDL_Surface objects has been built into `CCanvas`, including a pixel-setting and pixel-getting set of functions, which SDL does not have.

```
//CCanvas class
class CCanvas
{
private:
	//a list of update rectangles
	list < SDL_Rect* > m_lstUpdateRects ;
protected:
	//pointer to an SDL_Surface
	SDL_Surface* m_pSurface ;
```

```
public:
     //constructor
     CCanvas ( SDL_Surface* pSurface = NULL ) ;
     //destructor
     virtual ~CCanvas ( ) ;
     //getter/setter for the SDL_Surface*
     SDL_Surface* GetSurface ( ) ;
     void SetSurface ( SDL_Surface* pSurface ) ;
     //lock and unlock ( for direct pixel access )
     bool Lock ( ) ;
     void Unlock ( ) ;
     //get/set pixel (canvas should be locked)
     CColor GetPixel ( int x , int y ) ;
     void SetPixel ( int x , int y , CColor& color ) ;
     //match color with closest
     CColor MatchColor ( CColor color ) ;
     //width and height retrieval
     int GetWidth ( ) ;
     int GetHeight ( ) ;
     //add an update rectangle
     void AddUpdateRect ( CRectangle& pUpdateRect ) ;
     //clear all update rectangles
     void ClearUpdateRects ( ) ;
     //update any rectangles in the queue
     void UpdateRects ( ) ;
     //flip surface. normally, this just updates the entire surface
     bool Flip ( ) ;
     //set a color key
     bool SetColorKey ( CColor& color ) ;
     //retrieve the color key
     CColor GetColorKey ( ) ;
     //clear the color key
     bool ClearColorKey ( ) ;
     //set the clipping rectangle
     void SetClipRect ( CRectangle* pRect ) ;
     //get the clipping rectangle
     CRectangle GetClipRect ( ) ;
     //solid color fill a rectangle
     bool FillRect ( CRectangle& rect , CColor& color ) ;
     //clear entire surface to a color
```

```
    bool Clear ( CColor& color ) ;
    //blit to this surface from another surface
    bool Blit ( CRectangle& rectDst , CCanvas& cnvSrc , CRectangle&
rectSrc ) ;
    //factory methods
    //create an rgb surface of a particular format
    static CCanvas* CreateRGB ( Uint32 flags , int width , int
height, int depth, Uint32 Rmask, Uint32 Gmask, Uint32 Bmask, Uint32
Amask) ;
    //create an rgb surface of the display format
    static CCanvas* CreateRGBCompatible ( Uint32 flags , int width ,
int height ) ;
    //load a bitmap
    static CCanvas* LoadBMP ( string sFileName ) ;
    //load a bitmap, convert it to the display format
    static CCanvas* LoadBMPCompatible ( string sFileName ) ;
} ;
```

CCanvas has only two data members. One is a list of update rectangles (contained by a linked list of SDL_Rect*), and the other is an SDL_Surface* variable, which is used for all calls to SDL functions.

There is only one constructor to CCanvas, and it takes a pointer to an SDL_Surface. This is an optional parameter that defaults to NULL. You can have a CCanvas with a NULL surface, although this makes the CCanvas less useful than it could be. You can also have two CCanvas objects with the same pointer, because there are the GetSurface and SetSurface functions to access this member.

You can retrieve the width and height of the surface using GetWidth and GetHeight. This retrieves the values straight from the SDL_Surface so you don't have to store them anywhere.

As far as graphics primitives go, the only one I bothered to include was the pixel. If you really want to, you can add other primitives such as lines, ellipses, and polygons. The pixel is the atomic unit of each of these anyway. Before you set pixels, you must call Lock. After you are done setting pixels, you call Unlock. You use SetPixel and GetPixel to set or get pixels, respectively.

```
//pCanvas is assumed to be a CCanvas* that has been properly initialized
if(pCanvas->Lock())
{
```

```
        //successful lock
        //set pixel
        pCanvas->SetPixel(100,100,CColor(255,255,255));
        //unlock
        pCanvas->Unlock();
}
else
{
        //canvas could not lock
}
```

Notice I have used a `CColor` rather than mapping the RGB color manually.

Surfaces are used mostly for blits, and that functionality has been built into `CCanvas` with the `Blit` member function. The `CCanvas` object on which you call this member function is the destination canvas.

```
//pCanvas1 and pCanvas2 is a valid pointer to CCanvas object
pCanvas1->Blit(CRectangle(0,0,100,100),pCanvas2,CRectangle(0,0,100,100));
```

Notice the use of `CRectangle` objects, rather than SDL_Rects.

If you want transparency, look no farther than `SetColorKey`, along with its kindred functions `GetColorKey` and `ClearColorKey`. These functions deal with `CColor` objects.

You can also change the clipping area using `SetClipRect` and retrieve it using `GetClipRect`. These functions deal with `CRectangle` objects.

To update dirty rectangles, you use `AddUpdateRect` to add a rectangle to the update list, `ClearUpdateRects` to clear out the update rectangle list, and `UpdateRects` to update all of the rectangles on the list. If you don't want to use dirty rectangle updating, you can use `Flip` instead, which updates the entire surface or flips to the back buffer, depending on the configuration of the surface.

To clear the surface, you use the `Clear` member function with a color, and the entire surface is cleared to be that color. If you just want a filled rectangle somewhere, you call `FillRect`, which takes a `CRectangle` and a `CColor` and does its job.

Finally, the factory methods (`CreateRGB`, `CreateRGBCompatible`, `LoadBMP`, and `LoadBMPCompatible`) are static member functions that create new `CCanvas` objects. If the term `Compatible` is used in the call, the function will first make the requested canvas and then convert it to the display pixel format. Each of these functions takes parameters similar to the calls to SDL that create these types of surfaces.

CImage

A CImage abstracts a portion of a CCanvas. There is not much data contained within CImage itself. Mostly it relies on CCanvas functionality to do its job.

```
//CImage--abstracts a blittable portion of a canvas
class CImage
{
private:
	//pointer to canvas
	CCanvas* m_pcnvSrc ;
	//source rectangle
	CRectangle m_rcSrc ;
	//destination rectangle
	CRectangle m_rcDst ;
public:
	//construct from source canvas, source rectangle,and offset point
	CImage ( CCanvas* pcnvSource , CRectangle rcSource , CPoint
ptOffset ) ;
	//destroy image
	virtual ~CImage ( ) ;
	//retrieve pointer to canvas
	CCanvas* GetCanvas ( ) ;
	//set new canvas
	void SetCanvas ( CCanvas* pcnvSource ) ;
	//access source rectangle
	CRectangle& SrcRect ( ) ;
	//access destination rectangle
	CRectangle& DstRect ( ) ;
	//blit image onto a canvas
	void Put ( CCanvas* pcnvDest , CPoint ptDst ) ;
};
```

CImage has three member functions—a pointer to a CCanvas and two CRectangles, one for the source rectangle and one for the destination rectangle if the image were being blitted at (0,0). The destination rectangle will often have a negative x and y.

To construct a CImage object, you supply a pointer to a canvas, a source rectangle, and an anchor point. Typically, the anchor point will be (0,0), but if you want the image to be referenced based on any point other than the upper-left corner, you will likely want to use a different value.

```
//create image that centers a 100x100 image at position (50,50)
CImage* pimg=new CImage(pCanvas,CRectangle(0,0,100,100),CPoint(50,50));
```

There are standard setter and getter functions for the CCanvas pointer—SetCanvas and GetCanvas, respectively. For the source and destination rectangles, there are simply accessors—SrcRect and DstRect.

The real work of CImage is done by the Put member function. It takes a pointer to a destination canvas and a CPoint that specifies where to put the image.

CImageSet

A CImageSet is nothing but a container for your images. You can add and remove images as you see fit. You can also look for images and reference them by index. The purpose of CImageSet is to make it easier to deal with large numbers of images.

```
//CImageSet--controls any number of images
class CImageSet
{
private :
	//container for images
	vector < CImage* > m_vecImages ;
public:
	//construct empty image set
	CImageSet();
	virtual ~CImageSet();
	//add an image
	void AddImage ( CImage* pimg ) ;
	//check for an image in the list
	bool HasImage ( CImage* pimg ) ;
	//find an image
	int FindImage ( CImage* pimg ) ;
	//remove an image
	void RemoveImage ( CImage* pimg ) ;
	//retrieve an image from the list by index
```

```
	CImage* GetImage ( int index ) ;
	//access image list directly
	vector < CImage* >& ImageList ( ) ;
	//retrieve number of images in the set
	int ImageCount ( ) ;
};
```

A `CImageSet` only has one member—a vector of `CImage*` variables. A `CImageSet` contains no images when it is initially constructed. You can always get the number of images in the set by calling `ImageCount`. You can also manually reference the image list by calling `ImageList`.

`AddImage` will add a new image to the end of the list. `RemoveImage` will take an image out of the list. (Be careful—`RemoveImage` changes the indices of all images after the image that is being removed.)

You can use `HasImage` to see whether a particular image is in the list. Also, you can call `FindImage` to find the index for a particular image. It returns -1 if the image is not found.

If you have the index of an image, you use `GetImage` to retrieve a pointer to it. From there you can use the `Put` member function to put the image onto a canvas somewhere.

Component Test

For the component test, I also added an additional class, `CMainCanvas`, to the set of graphical classes to make construction of the main window easier. Since the SDL_Surface is freed during `CCanvas`'s destructor, I did not want the same thing to happen for the main window (since it should not happen for the main surface), but I also didn't want to put special case code into the program itself.

The component test for this chapter is a simple program based mostly on the component test for Chapter 13. Instead of allowing pixel drawing with the mouse, however, it places on the screen a small circular image that follows the mouse. You can find the program in FOSDL 14_1 and see a quick snapshot of it in Figure 14.2.

Since we are already getting quite a few files into our little application framework, it's not a bad idea to take a look at all of the files and objects with which we are concerned. Table 14.1 lists all of the files required to compile FOSDL14_1.

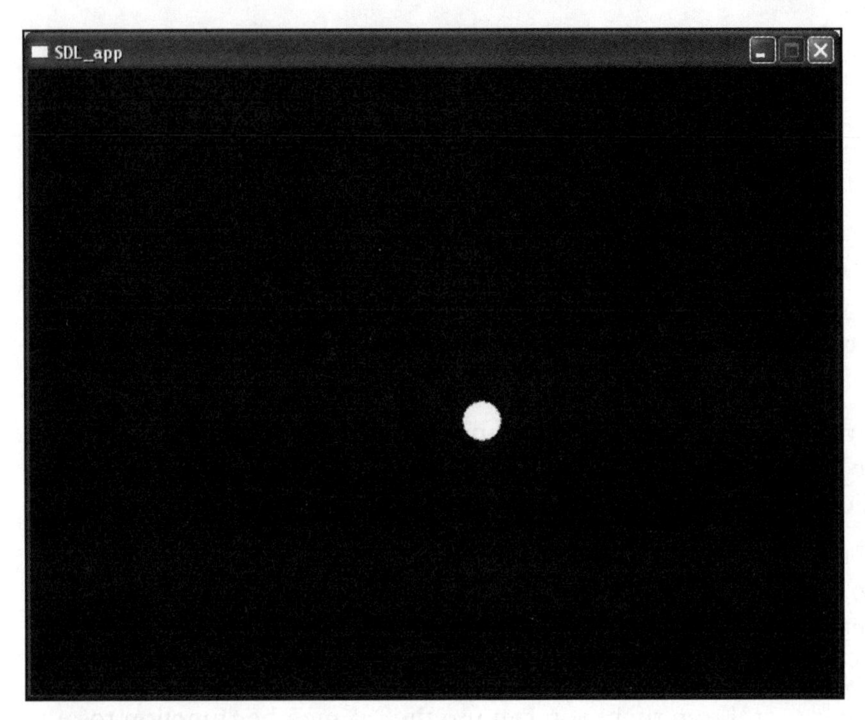

Figure 14.2 *The output of FOSDL14_1*

Table 14.1 File List

Class	Header	Source	Purpose
`CApplication`	Application.h	Application.cpp	Base class for application-type objects
`CCanvas`	Canvas.h	Canvas.cpp	Abstracts an SDL_Surface structure
`CColor`	Color.h	Color.cpp	Abstracts an SDL_Color structure
`CCursor`	Cursor.h	Cursor.cpp	Abstracts an SDL_Cursor structure
`CEventHandler`	EventHandler.h	EventHandler.cpp	Base class for event-handling applications

Table 14.1 File List *(continued)*

Class	Header	Source	Purpose
`CImage`	Image.h	Image.cpp	Abstracts a rectangular area of a `CCanvas` object
`CImageSet`	ImageSet.h	ImageSet.cpp	Abstracts a collection of `CImage` objects
`CMainCanvas`	MainCanvas.h	MainCanvas.cpp	Abstracts the main display surface
`CMessageHandler`	MessageHandler.h	MessageHandler.cpp	Base class for `CApplication`, `CThread`, and `CTimer`
`CPoint`	Point.h	Point.cpp	Abstracts a two-dimensional coordinate
`CRectangle`	Rectangle.h	Rectangle.cpp	Abstracts an SDL_Rect
`CTestEventHandler`	TestEventHandler.h	TestEventHandler.cpp	Test case for application class
`CThread`	Thread.h	Thread.cpp	Abstracts a thread
`CTimer`	Timer.h	Timer.cpp	Abstracts a timer

Summary

You will use all of the video components you saw in this chapter in Chapter 17, "User Interface Components," when you start creating the user interface components. They are quite useful and are even easier to use than the SDL functions, if such a thing is possible. Or maybe I just like being object-oriented....

CHAPTER 15

Audio Components

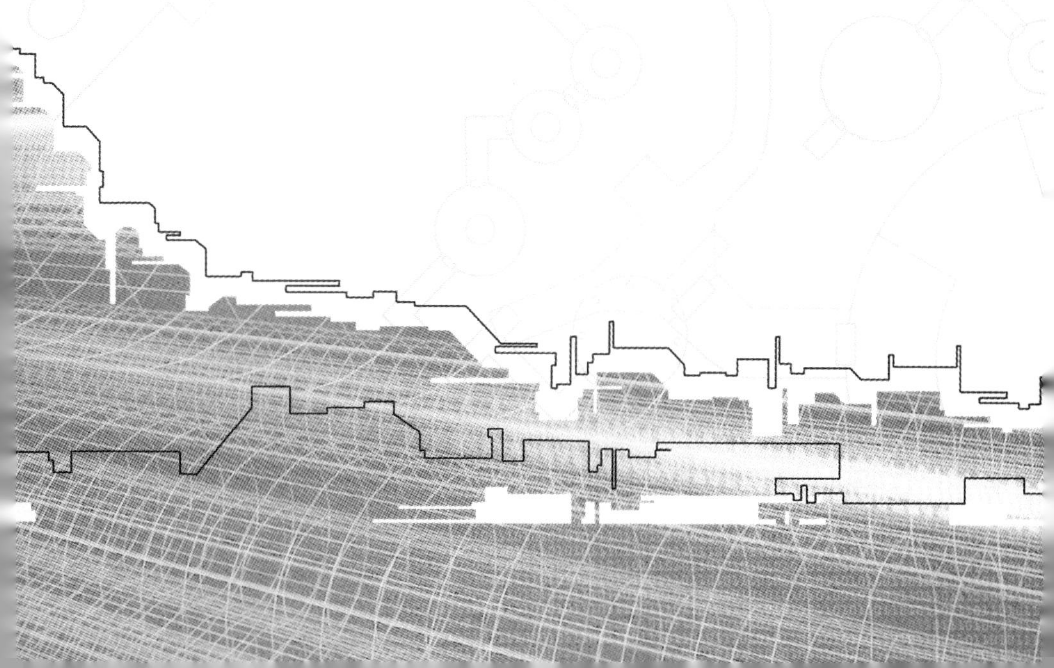

So far, you've got your core components and video components, but if you want to create a rich application, you also need audio. I will not be using SDL's audio subsystem; instead, I will use SDL_mixer because it has better features.

Audio Components at a Glance

To effectively use audio, you need a number of components. First you need a controlling component called `CAudio`, a singleton that allows you to open and close the audio device. Next you need components to abstract `Mix_Chunk` and `Mix_Music`. You can call these components `CSound` and `CAudio`. They will allow you to load and manipulate sound files. Additionally, you need to abstract channels (using `CChannel`). I will not bother with abstracting channel groups, but you could easily do so. Figure 15.1 presents a diagram of the audio components.

CAudio

`CAudio` has one task—to open and close the audio device. This makes `CAudio` a singleton, and there are simply static member functions set up to make this task easy.

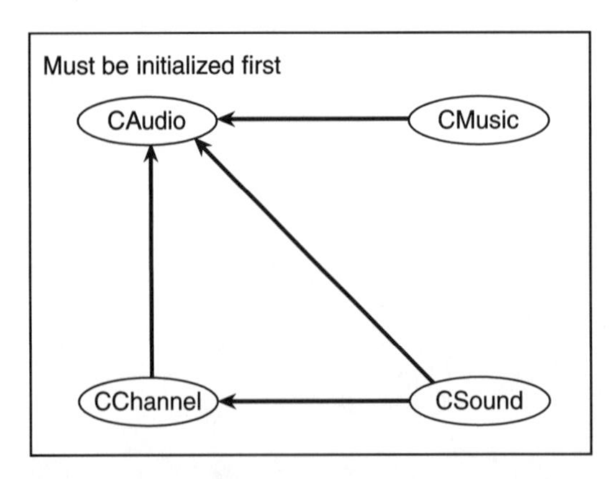

Figure 15.1 *Block diagram of audio components*

CSound

CSound abstracts Mix_Chunk, and that's pretty much all it does. It allows for the loading of WAV or VOC files and the ability to change the volume for the chunk. CChannel contains the rest of the behavior for playing the chunks.

CMusic

CMusic abstracts a Mix_Music. Since music in SDL_mixer essentially only has one channel, all of the other functions for playing, halting, pausing, and resuming the music exist as static member functions of CMusic.

CChannel

The CChannel class abstracts a channel, which means that the entire class only represents a single number. Everything you would want to do with a channel is abstracted in this class. In addition, the ability to allocate a new number of channels is built into CChannel in the form of a static member function.

Audio Components in Depth

There are only four audio components, and they are very easy to use. Whether they are actually easier to use than the SDL_mixer functions remains to be proven, but since the entire framework is in a nice object-oriented form, I figured I might as well make the audio components that way too.

CAudio

The CAudio class is a singleton, so it should not be instantiated. All of the member functions for this class are static, and there aren't many anyway.

```
/*
	==CAudio==
	Allows opening and closing of audio device
*/
class CAudio
		{
		public:
```

```
	//open audio device
	static bool Open(int chunksize,int frequency=MIX_DEFAULT_FREQUENCY,
Uint16 format=MIX_DEFAULT_FORMAT,int channels=MIX_DEFAULT_CHANNELS);
	//close audio device
	static void Close();
	//get frequency
	static int GetFrequency();
	//get format
	static Uint16 GetFormat();
	//get channels
	static int GetChannels();
};
```

To open the audio device, you call `Open`. All of the parameters are optional except for the chunk size, which comes first (rather than last, as it did in `Mix_OpenAudio`). The `frequency`, `format`, and `channels` all have their default values—22050 for `frequency`, a system-dependent 16-bit format for `format`, and 2 for `channels`. This member function returns true if everything went well.

When you are done with the audio subsystem, you call `Close`, which takes no parameters.

The other three member functions, `GetFrequency`, `GetFormat`, and `GetChannels`, do what you would expect—they retrieve the current values for the audio device. `CAudio` is not exactly a difficult class to use. Most of the time, you'll simply call `CAudio::Open` at the beginning of the program (during the application's `OnInit` member function) and `CAudio::Close` (during the application's `OnExit` member function), like this:

```
//sample CAudio code
//during OnInit
CAudio::Open(4096);//open with a chunk size of 4096, and default
frequency, format, and channels
//during OnExit
CAudio::Close();
```

Much of the time, you probably won't care what actual frequency the audio device has. I know I don't, but somebody somewhere might find those functions useful.

CSound

SDL_mixer's stock in trade is sound effects, which are represented by Mix_Chunk. One of the audio components, CSound, further abstracts this type in an object-oriented manner.

```
/*
	==CSound==
	abstracts Mix_Chunk
*/
class CSound
{
private:
	//chunk pointer
	Mix_Chunk* m_pChunk;
public:
	//constructor
	CSound(char* filename);
	//destructor
	virtual ~CSound();
	//get chunk
	Mix_Chunk* GetChunk();
	//check for a valid chunk
	bool IsValid();
	//set volume
	void SetVolume(int volume);
	//get volume
	int GetVolume();
};
```

The constructor is the most important part of this class. CSound is meant to be dynamically allocated and used through pointers, but you don't have to use it that way if you don't want. You can access the Mix_Chunk pointer (m_pChunk) through the GetChunk member function. (CChannel typically does this, but you never know.) Also, you can use the IsValid member function to see whether a chunk is valid. (It will return false if the chunk was loaded incorrectly.) Also, you can set or get the volume using SetVolume or GetVolume, respectively.

```
//sample code with CSound
//make new sound
CSound* pSound=new CSound("sound.wav");
```

```
//check for validity
if(!pSound->IsValid())
{
	//error! sound is not valid
}
//set the volume
pSound->SetVolume(64);
//destroy the sound
delete pSound;
```

Most of the time you won't need to use `GetChunk` yourself, but it is provided for convenience and use with `CChannel`.

CMusic

`CMusic` is a lot like `CSound`, but it is also a lot like `CChannel`. Since there is only one music channel, all of the music-playing functions are supplied as static member functions that are a part of `CMusic`. `CMusic` objects abstract a `Mix_Music` pointer.

```
/*
	==CMusic==
	Abstracts Mix_Music
*/
class CMusic
{
private:
	//pointer to music
	Mix_Music* m_pMusic;
public:
	//constructor
	CMusic(const char* filename);
	//destructor
	virtual ~CMusic();
	//get music pointer
	Mix_Music* GetMusic();
	//check for validity
	bool IsValid();
	//get music type
	Mix_MusicType GetType();
	//set volume
```

```
    static void SetVolume(int volume);
    //get volume
    static int GetVolume();
    //play music
    static void Play(CMusic* pMusic,int loops=-1);
    //fade in
    static void FadeIn(CMusic* pMusic,int ms,int loops=-1);
    //pause
    static void Pause();
    //resume
    static void Resume();
    //rewind
    static void Rewind();
    //stop
    static void Stop();
    //fade out
    static void FadeOut(int ms);
    //is playing?
    static bool IsPlaying();
    //is paused?
    static bool IsPaused();
    //is fading?
    static bool IsFading();
    //is fading out?
    static bool IsFadingOut();
    //is fading in?
    static bool IsFadingIn();
};
```

Like `CSound`, `CMusic`'s most important member function is its constructor. You supply a file name to the constructor, and it loads the music, if possible. You can access this pointer using the `GetMusic` member function. Since there can be loading errors, the `IsValid` function ensures that the music loaded correctly.

The rest of the member functions are static and allow you to play, pause, resume, stop, fade in or fade out, and set the volume for the music, along with pretty much any other music-related task you can imagine.

```
//sample code using CMusic
//new music
CMusic* pMusic=new CMusic("song.xm");
```

```
//check for validity
if(!pMusic->IsValid())
{
	//error! music invalid!
}
//play the music
CMusic::Play(pMusic);
//halt the music
CMusic::Stop();
//destroy the music
delete pMusic;
```

Alternatively, you can use `pMusic->Play(pMusic)` rather than `CMusic::Play(pMusic)`, but in my opinion that just gets confusing.

CChannel

`CChannel` is a bit like `CMusic`'s static functions, except that each `CChannel` object represents a single channel and `CChannel`'s static member functions manage the number of channels available. You will never need to construct a `CChannel` object on your own.

```
/*
	==CChannel==
	Abstracts an SDL_mixer channel
*/
class CChannel
{
private:
	//channel number
	int m_Channel;
	//vector of channels
	static std::vector<CChannel*> s_ChannelList;
public:
	//construct a channel
	CChannel(int channel);
	//destroy a channel
	virtual ~CChannel();
	//play
	bool Play(CSound* pSound,int loops=0,int ticks=-1);
	//fade in
```

```
    bool FadeIn(CSound* pSound,int ms,int loops=0,int ticks=-1);
    //pause
    bool Pause();
    //resume
    bool Resume();
    //stop
    bool Stop();
    //fade out
    bool FadeOut(int ms);
    //expire
    bool Expire(int ms);
    //is playing
    bool IsPlaying();
    //is paused
    bool IsPaused();
    //is fading
    bool IsFading();
    //is fading in
    bool IsFadingIn();
    //is fading out
    bool IsFadingOut();
    //allocate channels
    static bool Allocate(int channelcount);
    //determine number of channels
    static int ChannelCount();
    //get a channel
    static CChannel* GetChannel(int channel=-1);
};
```

The list of `CChannel` objects is kept in an STL vector container. When you call `Allocate`, the number of channels in this list is increased or decreased as needed. You can use `ChannelCount` to retrieve the number of channels. You can use `GetChannel` to get a particular channel number. If you place -1 into `GetChannel` (or no value, since it defaults to -1), `GetChannel` attempts to find a channel that is not currently playing. If it cannot find one, it returns `NULL`. You can then use functions such as `Play`, `Stop`, and `FadeIn` to play sounds. Even if it returns `NULL`, you can still safely try to play a sound because each of these member functions validates this pointer.

```
//sample code using CChannel
//allocate the number of channels
CChannel::Allocate(10);
//play a sound on a specific channel
CChannel::GetChannel(3)->Play(pSound);
//play a sound on any available channel
CChannel::GetChannel()->Play(pSound);
//deallocate all channels
CChannel::Allocate(0);
```

The neat thing about `CChannel` is that it is pretty robust. If you specify an invalid channel number, the functions will still be called but nothing bad will happen. Cool, huh?

Component Test

FOSDL15_1 is the component test for the audio components. This application (derived from FOSDL14_1) adds the audio components to the framework. (We seem to be accumulating components rather quickly now.) When you run the application, it plays music in the background (courtesy of `CMusic`); a sound is played when you strike a key. You can tap keys quickly, and up to four copies of the sound will play simultaneously. This is done through `CSound` and `CChannel`. `CAudio` is, of course, used to open and close the audio device.

Since I've added a few files in this chapter, Table 15.1 shows the full list of files and brief descriptions of each. All of the listed files are required for FOSDL15_1. Also, when compiling, you need to link to both the standard SDL libraries (sdlmain.lib and sdl.lib) as well as the mixer library (sdl_mixer.lib).

Table 15.1 Updated File List

Class	Header	Source	Purpose
`CApplication`	Application.h	Application.cpp	Base class for application-type objects

Table 15.1 Updated File List ***(continued)***

Class	Header	Source	Purpose
CAudio	Audio.h	Audio.cpp	Initializer/ manager for audio usage
CCanvas	Canvas.h	Canvas.cpp	Abstracts an SDL_Surface structure
CChannel	Channel.h	Channel.cpp	Abstracts a sound channel
CColor	Color.h	Color.cpp	Abstracts an SDL_Color structure
CCursor	Cursor.h	Cursor.cpp	Abstracts an SDL_Cursor structure
CEventHandler	EventHandler.h	EventHandler.cpp	Base class for event-handling applications
CImage	Image.h	Image.cpp	Abstracts a rectangular area of a CCanvas object
CImageSet	ImageSet.h	ImageSet.cpp	Abstracts a collection of CImage objects
CMainCanvas	MainCanvas.h	MainCanvas.cpp	Abstracts the main display surface
CMessageHandler	MessageHandler.h	MessageHandler.cpp	Base class for CApplication, CThread, and CTimer

Table 15.1 Updated File List *(continued)*

Class	Header	Source	Purpose
CApplication	Application.h	Application.cpp	Base class for application-type objects
CMusic	Music.h	Music.cpp	Abstracts a piece of music
CPoint	Point.h	Point.cpp	Abstracts a two-dimensional coordinate
CRectangle	Rectangle.h	Rectangle.cpp	Abstracts an SDL_Rect
CSound	Sound.h	Sound.cpp	Abstracts a sound chunk
CTestEventHandler	TestEventHandler.h	TestEventHandler.cpp	Test case for application class
CThread	Thread.h	Thread.cpp	Abstracts a thread
CTimer	Timer.h	Timer.cpp	Abstracts a timer

Summary

Now consider what sort of hula hoops you would've had to go through to create the audio components using the SDL audio subsystem. I shudder to think of it. The audio components, while relatively simplistic, will still give you the functionality you need to create framework applications using sound.

CHAPTER 16

Networking Components

You might have been disappointed back in Chapter 10 because it didn't include any examples of using SDL_net. Prepare for your disappointment to end because once you have built the networking components of the framework, there will indeed be an example of how to use them. In this chapter, I will show you some networking classes, which will make it very simple to create an application that communicates with TCP/IP.

Networking Components at a Glance

There are five networking components in the framework. These are `CNet`, `CIPAddress`, `CTCPSocket`, `CHostSocket`, and `CClientSocket`.

CNet

`CNet` is a simple wrapper that calls `SDLnet_Init` and `SDLnet_Quit`. That is the entire purpose of this class—to initialize and uninitialize SDL_net for you.

CIPAddress

`CIPAddress` abstracts the `IPaddress` type of SDL_net. It is a rather simple class with very few member functions. (Heck, there are only two members of `IPaddress`, so how complicated could such a class be?) `CIPAddress` is used to keep track of the IP addresses of computers in the network, hence the name.

CTCPSocket

`CTCPSocket` abstracts SDL_net's `TCPSocket` pointer type. It works equally well for both client sockets and server sockets, which is why the `CHostSocket` and `CClientSocket` exist as child classes of this class. This class contains all the functionality you need to write and read data to and from other machines.

CHostSocket

CHostSocket is a child class of CTCPSocket. It is intended to be used as a server socket, and it contains a collection of CChildSockets to represent other computers in the network. This makes it very easy to broadcast messages to all of the clients of a particular host socket.

CClientSocket

CClientSocket is a child class of CTCPSocket; it abstracts a connection to another computer. A CHostSocket contains a number of these types of sockets to represent their connections to client computers. All of the real work of a networking application is done through client sockets.

Networking Components in Depth

Now take a look at each of the networking components in depth to see how to use them.

CNet

CNet is by and large the simplest class of all of the networking components. For one thing, it doesn't need instantiation because all of its member functions are static. Also, there are only two member functions in the first place.

```
//CNet class
//initializes and quits SDL_net
//singleton
class CNet
{
public:
	//initialize SDL_net
	static void Init();
	//quit SDL_net
	static void Quit();
};
```

Using CNet is rather simple. You call CNet::Init() when you want to initialize SDL_net and CNet::Quit() when you are done using SDL_net. Couldn't be simpler.

CIPAddress

CIPAddress is the first of the networking components that is meant to be instantiated. It encapsulates the IPaddress structure.

```
//CIPAddress class
//encapsulates IPaddress structure
class CIPAddress
{
private:
	//internal representation
	IPaddress m_IP;
public:
	//constructor
	CIPAddress(char* host,Uint16 port);
	//construct from an IPaddress
	CIPAddress(IPaddress* pipaddress);
	//destructor
	virtual ~CIPAddress();
	//get host
	Uint32 GetHost();
	//get port
	Uint16 GetPort();
	//resolve the IP address
	char* Resolve();
	//conversion operator
	operator IPaddress*();
};
```

There are two ways to construct a CIPAddress object. One is by supplying a host name (such as 192.168.0.1 or www.gamedev.net) and a port number and allowing SDL_net to resolve the host. Placing a NULL in the host parameter will create an IP suitable for making a server socket.

The other method of constructing a CIPAddress object is to pass a pointer to an IPaddress structure. CIPAddress will copy the members from this pointer into its internal representation.

You can get the host (a Uint32 value) by calling GetHost, and you can get the port (a Uint16 value) by calling GetPort. There is also a conversion operator that allows you to use a CIPAddress object any place you would use an IPaddress*.

Finally, you can resolve the host of a CIPAddress object by calling Resolve. It returns a string that should not be freed.

CTCPSocket

CTCPSocket is actually pretty neat. It encapsulates a TCPsocket and does all of the operations you would want to do with a socket. Since there are a billion ways to format and read or write data to and from a socket, I decided to stick with a simple standard—strings. Sure, this gives the application more work to do because it has to parse the string data into some readable form, but it is pretty flexible at the same time.

CTCPSocket is designed primarily as a base class for the other socket classes and is really not meant to be instantiated, although it can still be useful if you do instantiate it.

```
//CTCPSocket class
//encapsulates TCPsocket
class CTCPSocket
{
private :
	//internal representation
	TCPsocket m_Socket ;
	//static list of all sockets
	static list < CTCPSocket* > s_lstSockets ;
public:
	//uses SDLNet_TCP_Open
	CTCPSocket ( CIPAddress* pIPAddress ) ;
	//create from an already existing TCPSocket
	CTCPSocket ( TCPsocket socket ) ;
	//uses SDLNet_TCP_Accept
	CTCPSocket ( CTCPSocket* pSocket ) ;
	//close socket
	virtual ~CTCPSocket();
	//retrieve master socket list
	static list < CTCPSocket* >& SocketList ( ) ;
	//accessors
	TCPsocket& Socket ( ) ;
	//conversion operator
	operator TCPsocket ( ) ;
	//get the IP address
```

```
    CIPAddress GetIP ( ) ;
    //get the status of the socket
    bool GetStatus ( ) ;
    //send a string
    bool Send ( string sData ) ;
    //receive a string
    string Receive ( ) ;
    //is there data to be read?
    bool Ready ( ) ;
    //check this socket
    void Check ( ) ;
    //when a check proves that a socket is ready, call this function
    virtual void OnReady ( ) ;
    //check all sockets
    static void CheckAll ( ) ;
};
```

The internal representation of CTCPSocket is, of course, nothing more than a TCPsocket held in the member m_Socket. You can use CTCPSocket to create either a client socket (from an already existing server socket) or a server socket; it has constructors for both. In addition, you can create a CTCPSocket object from an already existing TCPsocket pointer.

```
//open a socket
socket=new CTCPSocket(&ip);//ip is a CIPAddress
//use existing socket
socket=new CTCPSocket(sock);//sock is a TCPsocket
//accept new socket from a server socket
socket=new CTCPSocket(hostsock);//hostsock is a server socket
```

In addition, CTCPSocket keeps track of all existing sockets in a static list called s_lstSockets. This is incredibly handy because then the program doesn't have to keep track of all of the sockets (although you will still want to keep track of the more important sockets). You can access the list of all sockets with a call to SocketList(). This member function returns a reference to the list of sockets, so you can manipulate it as you like.

You can also get direct access to the TCPsocket underneath the CTCPSocket by calling Socket(). A CTCPSocket has a conversion operator for this as well.

You can get the IP address associated with a socket by calling `GetIP()`. Since the IP address acts as a unique ID number within the network, you will often store data associated with a particular IP address to keep things nice and organized.

The `GetStatus()` member function will let you know whether the socket is `NULL`. This is a check you can use to see whether the socket could be opened. It returns true if the socket is not `NULL`.

You can send or receive information with a `CTCPSocket` object by using `Send` and `Receive`. For simplicity's sake, I have used strings as the data to be sent or received. If you want to use this sort of scheme for passing data back and forth between computers, you will probably want to set aside some special characters to delimit commands.

To check sockets to see whether data has come in on one or more of them, you use the `Check` member function, which checks an individual socket to see if data is pending. Also, there is a `CheckAll` static member function, which goes through the list of all sockets and checks each one.

To see whether a socket has data ready, use the `Ready` member function. It returns true if data is pending and false if it is not. Of course, you'll never have to do this yourself because it is all done for you in a call to `Check`.

If, during a call to `Check`, it turns out that the socket is ready, then a call to `OnReady` occurs. This is a virtual function that acts somewhat like an event handler, the event being that the socket now has data waiting to be read and processed.

CHostSocket

While `CTCPSocket` is great at abstracting sockets in general, `CHostSocket` is better at abstracting server sockets. This class is derived from `CTCPSocket` and looks like this:

```
//CHostSocket class
//abstracts a server socket
class CHostSocket : public CTCPSocket
{
public:
	//constructor
	CHostSocket(CIPAddress* pip);
```

```
    //destructor
    virtual ~CHostSocket();
    //when ready with data
    void OnReady();
    //creation
    static CHostSocket* Create(Uint16 port);
    //message ids
    static MSGID MSGID_NewClient;//parm1=CHostSocket*
};
```

As you can see, it is not nearly as long-winded as the declaration for CTCPSocket. Ah, the beauty of inheritance. The constructor used takes a pointer to a CIPAddress, but you don't have to use it directly. Instead, you call the static member function Create and supply a port number, and Create puts together an IP address and creates the socket for you.

Other than Create and the destructor, the only other member function is an override of OnReady. Since there might be a dozen different things you want to do when a host socket is ready (meaning that a new connection is being made), the implementation of CHostSocket's OnReady member function simply sends a message (MSGID_NewClient) to the application. You then deal with the message in the main application's OnMessage handler. The message ID will be MSGID_NewClient, and the first parameter will be a pointer to the host socket.

CClientSocket

CClientSocket is even simpler than CHostSocket because most of the functionality is already present. CClientSocket is also derived from CTCPSocket.

```
//CClientSocket
//abstracts a client socket
class CClientSocket : public CTCPSocket
{
public:
    //constructor
    CClientSocket(CTCPSocket* pSocket);
    //destructor
    virtual ~CClientSocket();
    //on ready handler
    void OnReady();
    //message id
```

```
    static MSGID MSGID_SocketData;//parm1=CTCPSocket*;parm2=char*
};
```

As you can see, there isn't much to this class. The constructor takes a pointer to a `CTCPSocket` (one that is the host socket, presumably), and a new connection is formed with a new machine. The destructor doesn't even do anything.

When the `OnReady` member function of `CClientSocket` is called, it sends a message (`MSGID_SocketData`) to the application. The first parameter is a pointer to the socket, and the second parameter is a string containing the data.

Of course, this is not the only way you could do this, but it's nice and simple.

Component Test

The component test for the networking components is rather plain and simple. It consists of two applications—FOSDL16_1 and FOSDL16_2. FOSDL16_1 is the server application, and FOSDL16_2 is the client application. Naturally, you will need two networked computers to check it out.

FOSDL16_1 initializes the application, sets up networking, and creates a host socket. Then it just sits there and waits for a connection. When one occurs, it sends a `MSGID_NewClient` message, which is handled by creating a new client socket. If a client socket receives a message, the message is written to stdout.txt. It's not particularly feature-packed, but it does work over a network.

In FOSDL16_2, there is simply a `CTCPSocket` that connects to a server socket. (Depending on what kind of network you run the example on, you might want to change the IP in the source of FOSDL16_2 to something more valid. It is currently hard-coded to 192.168.0.1, which is normal for most LANs.) After the socket is created, it sends a single message to the server. If you have a need to change the IP address in the program, you can find the line that does it in CTestEventHandler.cpp, in the body of the `CTestEventHandler::OnInit` function.

These programs don't do much, but they do demonstrate just how easy it truly is to send data from one machine to another. Remember, if you can send a single simple text message, you can send anything. This is the networking equivalent of pixel plotting.

If you want to check out FOSDL16_1 and FOSDL16_2, they are on the CD. You will want to run FOSDL16_1 first on the computer acting as the server, and FOSDL16_2 on the computer you are using as a client. Without FOSDL16_1 running somewhere, FOSDL16_2 has nothing to which to connect. Figure 16.1 shows the basic idea behind what these two programs do.

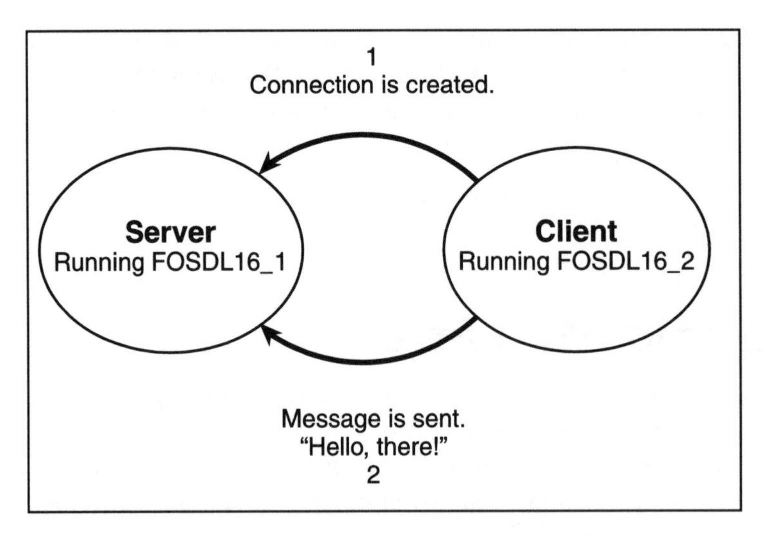

Figure 16.1 *Block diagram of how FOSDL16_1 and FOSDL16_2 work*

Now for an updated file list, which applies equally to FOSDL16_1 and FOSDL16_2.

Table 16.1 Updated File List

Class	Header	Source	Purpose
CApplication	Application.h	Application.cpp	Base class for application-type objects
CAudio	Audio.h	Audio.cpp	Initializer/manager for audio usage
CCanvas	Canvas.h	Canvas.cpp	Abstracts an SDL_Surface structure

Table 16.1 Updated File List ***(continued)***

Class	Header	Source	Purpose
`CChannel`	Channel.h	Channel.cpp	Abstracts a sound channel
`CClientSocket`	ClientSocket.h	ClientSocket.cpp	Abstracts a client socket
`CColor`	Color.h	Color.cpp	Abstracts an SDL_Color structure
`CCursor`	Cursor.h	Cursor.cpp	Abstracts an SDL_Cursor structure
`CEventHandler`	EventHandler.h	EventHandler.cpp	Base class for event-handling applications
`CHostSocket`	HostSocket.h	HostSocket.cpp	Abstracts a host socket
`CImage`	Image.h	Image.cpp	Abstracts a rectangular area of a `CCanvas` object
`CImageSet`	ImageSet.h	ImageSet.cpp	Abstracts a collection of `CImage` objects
`CIPAddress`	IPAddress.h	IPAddress.cpp	Abstracts an IP address
`CMainCanvas`	MainCanvas.h	MainCanvas.cpp	Abstracts the main display surface
`CMessageHandler`	MessageHandler.h	MessageHandler.cpp	Base class for `CApplication`, `CThread`, and `CTimer`
`CMusic`	Music.h	Music.cpp	Abstracts a piece of music
`CNet`	Net.h	Net.cpp	Initializer for networking components
`CPoint`	Point.h	Point.cpp	Abstracts a two-dimensional coordinate
`CRectangle`	Rectangle.h	Rectangle.cpp	Abstracts an SDL_Rect
`CSound`	Sound.h	Sound.cpp	Abstracts a sound chunk
`CTCPSocket`	TCPSocket.h	TCPSocket.cpp	Abstracts a TCP socket
`CTestEventHandler`	TestEventHandler.h	TestEventHandler.cpp	Test case for application class
`CThread`	Thread.h	Thread.cpp	Abstracts a thread
`CTimer`	Timer.h	Timer.cpp	Abstracts a timer

Summary

This has been a simple little trip into the wild and woolly world of network programming. With SDL_net and components built from it, it is not terribly difficult to get something up and running. Of course, this is not the end of the story. Lots of books have been written on networking and programming networked applications, and you should probably get one if you are serious about doing this kind of programming. This is *Focus on SDL,* not *Focus on Network Programming,* so I naturally cannot give this topic the depth of study that it deserves, but at least you've got a small amount of leg-up.

For further reading on network and multiplayer game programming, please refer to *Multiplayer Game Programming* (Premier Press, Inc., 2001). I hear it's one of the best-edited books ever.

CHAPTER 17

User Interface Components

You simply cannot underestimate the value of a good user interface system. A game is, after all, something with which a player interacts. Unfortunately, many people don't give much thought to how their user interface works, so it detracts from the player's experience because they are constantly wrestling with the controls.

Don't do that. Instead, you should come up with a user interface of which the player is hardly (if at all) aware. This is not an easy thing to do. Therefore, this chapter (the last of the chapters detailing the components of the application framework) concerns itself with the classes that deal with user interfaces. A user interface seems to be a very simple thing on the surface, but you will see that it is rich with complexity.

UI Components at a Glance and Hierarchy

The basic component of user interface is called a *control.* A control can be anything from a button to a text box to a label to an option button to a window. For the sake of this discussion, a control is a small portion of the screen (usually), which is rectangular in shape and with which the user interacts through an input device such as a mouse or keyboard. Most times, the controls are the only way the user can interact with the application, and vice versa.

The communication is two-way. The application displays the controls on the screen, the user manipulates them with an input device, and the application then gives feedback so the user knows that he has actually done something. The method of communication from application to user is primarily visual (in other words, the appearance of the control changes), but it can also include other feedback, such as a sound being played when a button is pressed. Figure 17.1 shows an example of communication between an application and a user. Ideally, the cycle is as short as possible from the moment the user generates some sort of input until the time he gets feedback. Figure 17.2 shows an example of a UI.

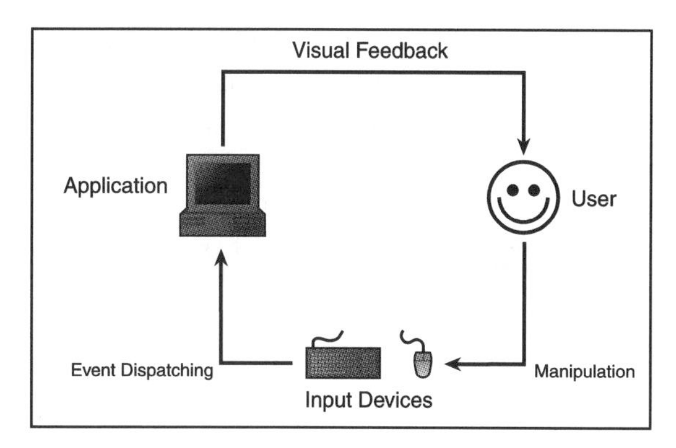

Figure 17.1 *User interface for an application*

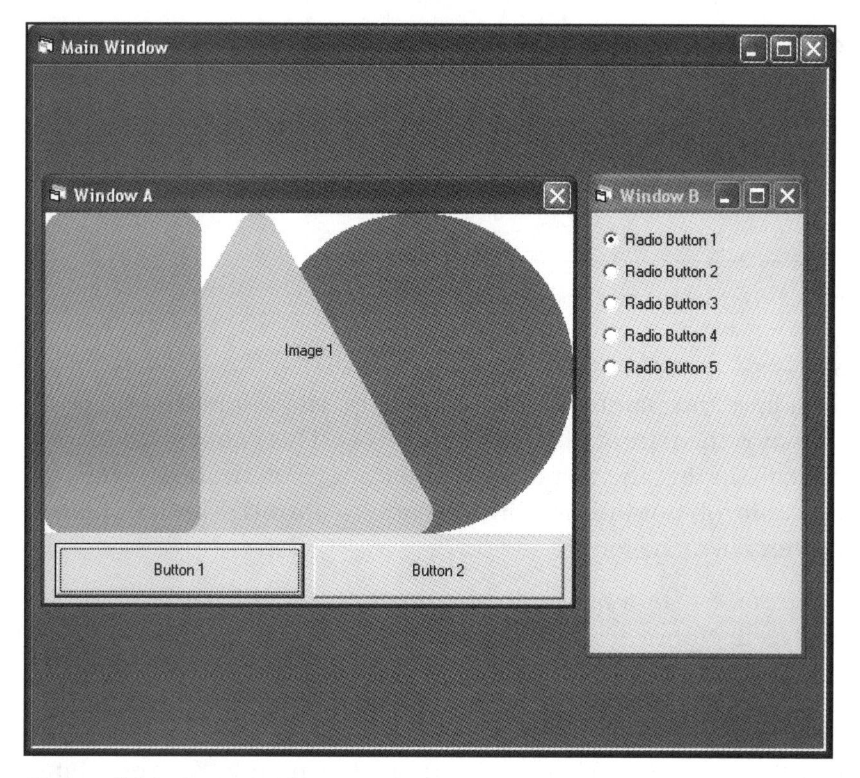

Figure 17.2 *A sample UI system*

Also, a user interface system is necessarily hierarchical in nature. A control (such as a window) can contain other controls, and those controls can contain other controls, ad nauseam. This is best represented as a parent/child relationship, so you will need to implement this sort of relationship when it comes time to create the control classes. Typically, there will only be two or three levels of parent/child relationships, but there are times when more are needed. It is always a good idea to design things to be as flexible as possible. Using the image in Figure 17.2, I created the hierarchical block diagram of parent/child relationships for that particular UI system (see Figure 17.3).

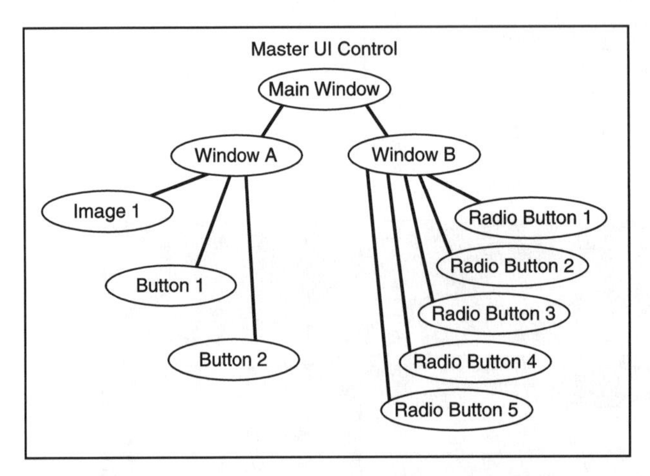

Figure 17.3 *Parent/child relationship between UI controls*

Since you have this parent/child relationship, you will need a single control that is the parent of all other controls. This control will serve a special role in that the rest of your application will deal only with the main control, not individually with other controls. Think of it as a user interface manager.

A user interface system has to do a number of things in order to be effective; I will cover each task separately.

Displaying

User interface elements are visually oriented by nature. You see a button, you move the mouse cursor to it, you click the left mouse button, and you see the illusion of the button being pressed. In reality the screen remains two dimensional, but your eyes are fooled.

Displaying an individual control is no big deal. You only need an image to display (stored within the control as a canvas) and a position

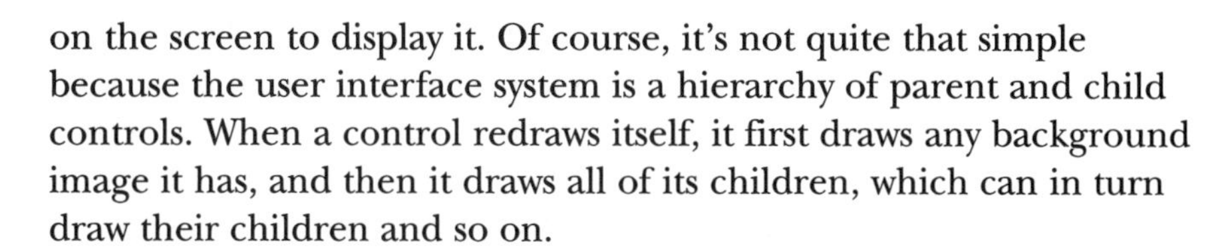

on the screen to display it. Of course, it's not quite that simple because the user interface system is a hierarchy of parent and child controls. When a control redraws itself, it first draws any background image it has, and then it draws all of its children, which can in turn draw their children and so on.

Typically, the main control's canvas is the main display canvas, although it doesn't absolutely need to be this way. After everything else in the game has been drawn, you tell the main control to draw itself, which refreshes all of the controls.

This introduces the concept of layering, because controls can quite possibly overlap. When a control is drawing its child controls, it will start with one, and then draw the next one, and so on until all controls are drawn. The master control typically will not do any drawing of its own.

This also introduces the idea of coordinate systems. Each control is positioned somewhere on its parent (with the main control simply using the coordinate system of the surface to which it is attached). The upper-left corner of any control is treated as the origin (0,0) for all of its children. A child control only knows about its parent's coordinate system and cares nothing for the global coordinate system that encompasses the entire screen. However, by starting with a child and adding all of the coordinates of its chain of parents, you can derive the global coordinates of each of its edges.

Event Filtering

Another important task of any user interface system is to detect when user input should be processed. If the user is not interacting with a control, then the data from the event should follow the usual course of event handling in the application.

Before the application attempts to handle an event, you first send the event to the user interface system and see whether any of the controls handle it. You only send the event to the application itself if it is not handled by any of the controls.

However, you have to check for controls handling events in the reverse order of the way they are drawn because the control that you perceive to be "in front" of all other controls must be the one with which you are interacting.

Also, there are times when you need to direct mouse or keyboard events to one particular control. This is the concept of *input capturing*, or *input focus*. For example, if you have two text boxes on the screen and you are typing from the keyboard, you expect only one box to contain text, not both. You can then say that an individual text box has *keyboard focus*. The same idea applies for the mouse.

Upkeep

As you are handling events within the user interface system, if one of the controls in a list were to cease to exist because it was deleted, that would be a Bad Thing. The system works iteratively and recursively, so input might be lost to a control because it got skipped in the list.

Similarly, if you were to change the order of the controls in their various child lists during this time, a control might miss its opportunity to get input or it might get input twice.

To combat this problem, you keep a list of controls that need to be destroyed and controls that need to be moved to the end of the display list all at one time; this upkeep to the system is done just prior to attempting to handle events. It keeps things running smoothly and eliminates many problems.

Notification

Finally, a user interface system needs a way to notify its parent and/or the application of what happened. This is very similar to what is done with `CMessageHandler`, just in a separate system. When a button is pressed, it sends information down the line to be handled eventually by the application, which knows what to do when a particular button is pressed. Or, a message from a button might trigger a response and another notification message from its parent control, in which case the message is used to eventually notify the application with another message and becomes meaningful.

Typically, something as simple as a button doesn't know what it does or how it affects things. That is not the button's job—it is simply there to be pressed. It is up to the button's parent to decide what to do.

Base Control Class in Depth

Now you can take a look at a rather simple and straightforward base class for the user interface system called CControl. Not a very creative name, I admit, but you get the idea.

```
class CControl
{
private:
	//parent
	CControl* m_pParent;
	//list of child controls
	std::list<CControl*> m_lstChildren;
	//list of windows to bring to front
	static std::list<CControl*> s_lstUpdate;
	//list of windows to close
	static std::list<CControl*> s_lstClose;
	//canvas used by window
	CCanvas* m_pCanvas;
	//position
	CPoint m_ptPosition;
	//id
	Uint32 m_ID;
	//static pointer to main control
	static CControl* s_pMainControl;
	//keyboard focus
	static CControl* s_pKeyboardFocus;
	//mouse focus
	static CControl* s_pMouseFocus;
	//mouse hovering
	static CControl* s_pMouseHover;
public:
	//master control constructor
	CControl(CCanvas* pCanvas);
	//child control constructor
	CControl(CControl* pParent,CRectangle rcDimensions,Uint32 id);
	//destructor
	virtual ~CControl();
	//set parent
	void SetParent(CControl* pmhNewParent);
```

```
	//get parent
	CControl* GetParent();
	//has parent?
	bool HasParent();
	//set ID
	void SetID(Uint32 id);
	//get id
	Uint32 GetID();
	//send message
	bool SendMessage(MSGID MsgID,MSGPARM Parm1=NULL,MSGPARM
Parm2=NULL,MSGPARM Parm3=NULL,MSGPARM Parm4=NULL);
	//process message(virtual)
	virtual bool OnMessage(MSGID MsgID,MSGPARM Parm1,MSGPARM
Parm2,MSGPARM Parm3,MSGPARM Parm4);
	//add child handler
	void AddChild(CControl* pControl);
	//remove child handler
	void RemoveChild(CControl* pControl);
	//bring to front
	void BringToFront();
	//close
	void Close();
	//update all
	static void Update();
	//redraw entire system
	static void Redraw();
	//draw control
	void Draw();
	//customize redrawing
	virtual void OnDraw();
	//event handling
	virtual bool OnEvent(SDL_Event* pEvent);
	//keyboard events
	virtual bool OnKeyDown(SDLKey sym,SDLMod mod,Uint16 unicode);
	virtual bool OnKeyUp(SDLKey sym,SDLMod mod,Uint16 unicode);
	//mouse events
	virtual bool OnMouseMove(Uint16 x,Uint16 y,Sint16 relx,Sint16
rely,bool bLeft,bool bRight,bool bMiddle);
	virtual bool OnLButtonDown(Uint16 x,Uint16 y);
	virtual bool OnLButtonUp(Uint16 x,Uint16 y);
```

```
        virtual bool OnRButtonDown(Uint16 x,Uint16 y);
        virtual bool OnRButtonUp(Uint16 x,Uint16 y);
        virtual bool OnMButtonDown(Uint16 x,Uint16 y);
        virtual bool OnMButtonUp(Uint16 x,Uint16 y);
        //static event filter
        static bool FilterEvent(SDL_Event* pEvent);
        //get position
        CPoint GetPosition();
        //get width and height
        Uint16 GetWidth();
        Uint16 GetHeight();
        //get edges in global coords
        Uint16 GetLeft();
        Uint16 GetRight();
        Uint16 GetTop();
        Uint16 GetBottom();
        //set position
        void SetPosition(CPoint ptPosition);
        //get canvas
        CCanvas* GetCanvas();
        //get main control
        static CControl* GetMainControl();
        //get keyboard focus control
        static CControl* GetKeyboardFocus();
        //set keyboard focus control
        static void SetKeyboardFocus(CControl* pControl);
        //get mouse focus control
        static CControl* GetMouseFocus();
        //set mouse focus control
        static void SetMouseFocus(CControl* pControl);
        //get mouse hover control
        static CControl* GetMouseHover();
        //set mouse focus control
        static void SetMouseHover(CControl* pControl);
        //check for focuses
        bool IsMainControl();
        bool HasKeyboardFocus();
        bool HasMouseFocus();
        bool HasMouseHover();
};
```

As you can see, `CControl` seems to borrow from a number of other classes, such as the message-handling aspects of `CMessageHandler`, the event-handling capabilities of `CEventHandler`, and so on. This is because `CControl` does so many different things.

The `CControl` class is not particularly useful; all it does is return defaults. To have a control that actually does something, you need to derive a new class from `CControl`. So, really, `CControl` is a foundational base class for all other controls.

As far as members of `CControl` go, I divide them into two parts—those that have values for each control and those that simply keep track of the system. The members concerned with an individual control's data include a pointer to its parent (`m_pParent`), a list of its children (`m_lstChildren`), a pointer to a `CCanvas` (`m_pCanvas`), the control's position in parent coordinates (`m_ptPosition`), and a numeric ID number (`m_ID`). The ID number helps differentiate controls from the same class.

As far as the static members are concerned, there is a list of controls that need to be moved to the end of the display list (`s_lstUpdate`), as well as a list of controls that need to be destroyed (`s_lstClose`). Additionally, there are static members for each of the types of focus (`s_pKeyboardFocus` and `s_pMouseFocus`) and a static member for the main control (`s_pMainControl`). Finally, there is a special static member for seeing which control the mouse is currently hovering over (`s_pMouseHover`). This is quite handy for making controls that light up when you hover over them.

Constructors

You can construct a `CControl` in one of two ways. The first method creates the main control, as shown here.

```
CControl::CControl(CCanvas* pCanvas);
```

This constructor takes only a pointer to a canvas. Since the main control has no parent, always has an ID of 0, and ends up being the same size as the canvas, there is no need to supply additional information.

The second way to construct `CControl` is to make a child control, as shown here.

```
CControl::CControl(CControl* pParent,CRectangle rcDimensions,Uint32 id);
```

This constructor takes not only a pointer to a parent, but also the dimensions of the control (in parent coordinates, of course), as well as an ID number that you can use for whatever you need.

Member Access

Naturally, a number of CControl's member functions are concerned with accessing the various members of CControlU, either directly or indirectly. Of particular importance is the manipulation of a control's parent and children. To set a parent for a CControl, you use SetParent.

```
void CControl::SetParent(CControl* pParent);
```

Of course, if you want to retrieve a control's parent, you use GetParent.

```
CControl* CControl::GetParent();
```

Not all controls will have parents; such controls are called orphans. There are several uses for orphan controls. First and foremost, the main control has no parent, so it is an orphan. Second, you might want to create and keep track of commonly used groupings of controls and add and remove them from the user interface system as appropriate.

To see whether something has a parent, use the HasParent member function.

```
bool CControl::HasParent();
```

This function will return true if the parent is not NULL. (Another name I considered for this member function was IsOrphan, but that was a little too esoteric.)

There is also a child list of controls that needs updating from time to time. The member functions to accomplish this are AddChild and RemoveChild, as shown here.

```
void CControl::AddChild(CControl* pControl);
void CControl::RemoveChild(CControl* pControl);
```

You should not call these member functions yourself because they are called whenever SetParent is called, and everything is updated properly. As you might expect, these member functions add or remove a control from a child list, as appropriate.

The remaining member accessor functions don't really need much explanation because they directly set or get a particular attribute about a control, so here they are.

```
void CControl::SetID(Uint32 id);
Uint32 CControl::GetID();
CPoint CControl::GetPosition();
void CControl:: SetPosition(CPoint ptPosition);
Uint16 CControl::GetWidth();
Uint16 CControl::GetHeight();
Uint16 CControl::GetLeft();
Uint16 CControl::GetRight();
Uint16 CControl::GetTop();
Uint16 CControl::GetBottom();
CCanvas* CControl::GetCanvas();
```

Using these functions, you can retrieve or set the ID of the control; set or get the position of the control; determine the width, height, left, right, top, or bottom of a control; or gain access to the canvas used by the control.

Displaying

The display of all user interface controls depends on three functions—Draw, OnDraw, and Redraw.

The Draw function is a non-static, non-virtual function that is called for each control in the hierarchy.

```
void CControl::Draw();
```

Draw calls OnDraw (which you will look at in a minute), and then loops through all of the child controls owned by this control. Finally, after drawing all of the children, Draw updates the parent's canvas. The OnDraw function is a non-static virtual function. You will use it to customize a control's appearance.

> **NOTE**
> Virtual functions help out quite a bit when you are developing a hierarchical system like this one because they allow you to customize the behavior of the various control classes.

```
void CControl::OnDraw();
```

During this function, you do whatever drawing is needed to update the appearance of the control. In theory, the only thing you need to do to draw the entire hierarchy of controls is call the Draw member function of the main control, right? Most certainly. For convenience, the Redraw static member function does just that.

```
void CControl::Redraw();
```

This function simply calls the main control's Draw member function and does a few other things to keep up the control system.

Event Filtering

The event-handling system is rather like the one in CEventHandler. In fact, most of the event-handling functions were stolen from CEventHandler directly, with a slight modification of the return type.

First and foremost is OnEvent, which is called for every control in the hierarchy until one finally handles the event.

```
bool CControl::OnEvent(SDL_Event* pEvent);
```

When this member function is called, the control goes from the end of the child list to the beginning, calling the children's OnEvent function along the way. If the event doesn't get handled along that route, the function will attempt to dispatch the event to one of the event handlers shown in the following code. These are identical, for the most part, to the equivalent handlers in CEventHandler.

```
bool CControl::OnKeyDown(SDLKey sym,SDLMod mod,Uint16 unicode);
bool CControl::OnKeyUp(SDLKey sym,SDLMod mod,Uint16 unicode);
bool CControl::OnMouseMove(Uint16 x,Uint16 y,Sint16 relx,Sint16
rely,bool bLeft,bool bRight,bool bMiddle);
bool CControl::OnLButtonDown(Uint16 x,Uint16 y);
bool CControl::OnLButtonUp(Uint16 x,Uint16 y);
bool CControl::OnRButtonDown(Uint16 x,Uint16 y);
bool CControl::OnRButtonUp(Uint16 x,Uint16 y);
bool CControl::OnMButtonDown(Uint16 x,Uint16 y);
bool CControl::OnMButtonUp(Uint16 x,Uint16 y);
```

The user interface system is only concerned with keyboard and mouse events, as you can see. The default implementation doesn't really do much. The mouse handlers, however, attempt to detect whether the mouse is physically within the control.

To tie the user interface system into an application, you simply use the `FilterEvent` member function. This function is static and does some pre-processing of the event (such as direct routing whenever there is a mouse or keyboard focus in effect), and then simply sends it to the main control's `OnEvent` function.

```
bool CControl::FilterEvent(SDL_Event* pEvent);
```

If this function returns true, then the event has been intercepted by the user interface system, so it should not be processed by the application itself.

The class also needs a way to access the special controls, such as the main control, the various input focus controls, and the control over which the mouse was hovering.

```
CControl* CControl::GetMainControl();
CControl* CControl::GetKeyboardFocus();
CControl* CControl::GetMouseFocus();
CControl* CControl::GetMouseHover();
```

During the course of a program, there needs to be a way to change the focus controls and the mouse hover control. The following functions fulfill that task.

```
void CControl::SetKeyboardFocus(CControl* pControl);
void CControl::SetMouseFocus(CControl* pControl);
void CControl::SetMouseHover(CControl* pControl);
```

Finally, it would be really convenient if a control could tell you whether it is the main control, one of the focus controls, or the mouse hover control.

```
bool CControl::IsMainControl();
bool CControl::HasKeyboardFocus();
bool CControl::HasMouseFocus();
bool CControl::HasMouseHover();
```

The event-handling section of `CControl` is the largest because it has to do a lot.

Upkeep

The upkeep portions of `CControl` are much simpler. The two static lists—one for closing and destroying controls and the other for bringing controls from the beginning of the display list to the end—are manageable with only three functions, and the implementation is completely hidden from the user of the class.

The first of these functions is `BringToFront`; its task is to add the control to the update list, which eventually results in the control being brought to the top of the Z order.

```
void CControl::BringToFront();
```

The second of these functions is simply called `Close`; it adds the control to the close list, which eventually results in the control being destroyed.

```
void CControl::Close();
```

Finally, the `Update` function, a static member function, goes through the update and close lists and updates or closes the controls, clearing out the list for reuse as it proceeds.

```
void CControl::Update();
```

As you can see, managing the UI system is not that complicated once you've got a decently laid out design.

Notification

The notification portion of `CControl` is identical to the mechanism used in `CMessageHandler`, so I won't spend any time describing how it works. Instead, I'll just list the functions.

```
bool CControl::SendMessage(MSGID MsgID,MSGPARM Parm1,MSGPARM Parm2,
MSGPARM Parm3,MSGPARM Parm4);
bool CControl::OnMessage(MSGID MsgID,MSGPARM Parm1,MSGPARM Parm2,
MSGPARM Parm3,MSGPARM Parm4);
```

An Example Control

For the sake of discussion, I will create an example program (FOSDL17_1, if you are interested) that makes an example control—a push button, which is perhaps the most common type of UI control in existence.

For the declaration of `CControl`, `CButton` is a great deal shorter, although it is hardly tiny simply due to the sheer number of necessary members and member functions.

```
class CButton : public CControl
{
private:
	//caption for button
	std::string m_sCaption;
	//colors for button
	CColor m_colFace;
	CColor m_colText;
	CColor m_colHilite;
	CColor m_colShadow;
	//canvas for text
	CCanvas* m_pcnvText;
	//pressed state
	bool m_bPressed;
	//button font
	static TTF_Font* s_ButtonFont;
public:
	//construction
	CButton(CControl* pParent,CRectangle rcDimensions,Uint32
id,std::string sCaption,CColor colFace=CColor(192,192,192),CColor
colText=CColor(0,0,0),CColor colHilite=CColor(255,255,255),CColor
colShadow=CColor(128,128,128));
	//destruction
	virtual ~CButton();
	//customize redrawing
	virtual void OnDraw();
	//left button handlers
	virtual bool OnLButtonDown(Uint16 x,Uint16 y);
	virtual bool OnLButtonUp(Uint16 x,Uint16 y);
	//set caption
	void SetCaption(std::string sCaption);
	//get caption
	std::string GetCaption();
	//set button font
	static void SetButtonFont(TTF_Font* pFont);
	static TTF_Font* GetButtonFont();
	//message for clicking button
	static MSGID MSGID_ButtonClick;//parm1=id
};
```

By far the largest function in CButton is the constructor because you have to supply so much information about a button before you can create it. There are a caption and four different colors so that you can completely customize the appearance of the button. The four colors do have default grayscale values.

Since you need text to render a button, there is a static member called s_ButtonFont, which you can set and retrieve using SetButtonFont and GetButtonFont, respectively. You can set and retrieve the caption, which creates a surface with the text on it, using SetCaption and GetCaption, respectively.

To override the behavior of CControl to make it into a CButton, you need only OnDraw, OnLButtonDown, and OnLButtonUp. Simplicity itself, since CControl does all of the major work.

Finally, when a button is pressed and then released, a notification message (MSGID_ButtonClick) is sent through the control pipeline for interception. To see FOSDL17_1 in action, you can look at Figure 17.4.

Figure 17.4 *A UI button*

Summary

As you can see, a user interface system is a non-trivial task to accomplish, but it can be done and done well if you put enough thought into what you are doing. Of course, that applies to anything you do in programming. Well, except for drinking soda, which you definitely do a lot of while programming (at least I do). You don't really have to put a lot of thought into drinking soda.

CHAPTER 18

The Road Ahead

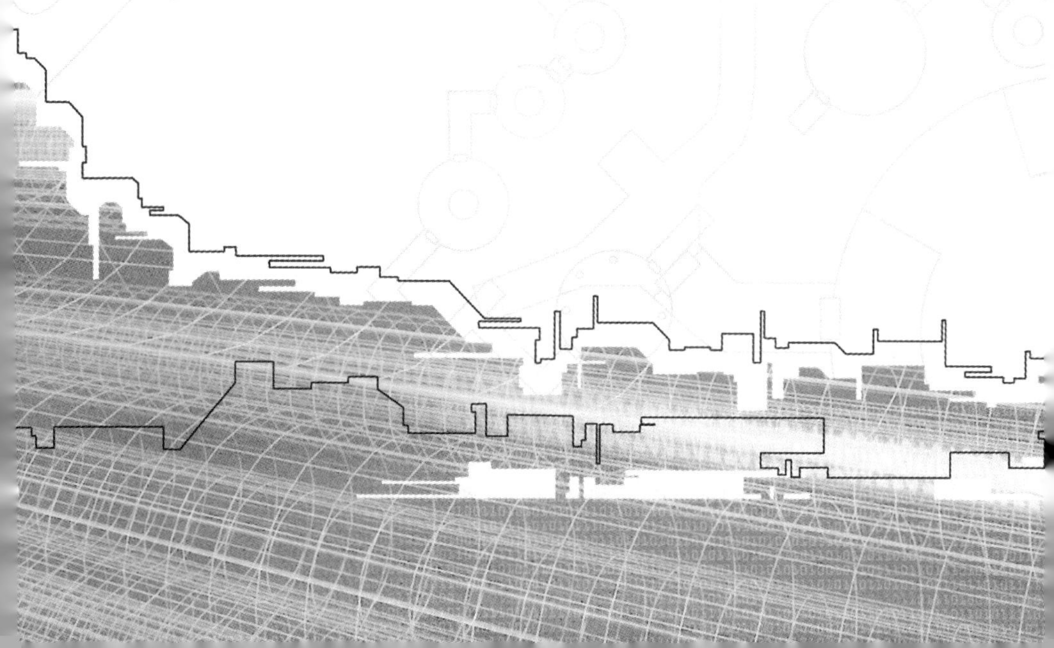

And so, inevitably, we reach this point—the end of the book. I know that I had a swell time writing it, and I hope you enjoyed reading it, maybe learned something, or at the very least found a use for it other than propping up a table leg that doesn't quite sit right.

Where You Have Been

Although this book is on the smaller side, as all of the books in the *Focus On* series are, you have come a long way since Chapter 1. You have seen the ins and outs of all of the SDL subsystems, from video to audio to threads and timers to event handling. This gives you a solid foundation in SDL that, even on its own, is enough for you to start developing SDL applications.

Of course, you couldn't stop there. The add-on libraries of SDL_mixer, SDL_ttf, and SDL_image are just too darn helpful not to use, and they are just as easy to work with as SDL itself. In fact, sometimes they're even easier—such as using SDL_mixer's powerful capabilities instead of merely the audio subsystem of SDL (which I still say is way too primitive to be of much use without some sort of add-on library).

Finally, you saw an SDL-based application framework built from nothing. The particularly spiffy thing about the framework is that it will compile on any platform that SDL supports, provided you have a C++ compiler. Just compiling works most of the time; to really try it out and tweak things still takes a bit of time, but that's not nearly as big of a deal.

Where You Can Go from Here

Well, for one thing, you could create some SDL-based games. Also, SDL and its add-on libraries are always being expanded and there are plenty of add-on libraries that I did not cover, so you might want to check them out.

Also, if you like SDL but would prefer to use a 3D API, you know that SDL can integrate rather well with OpenGL. There are several resources that you can use to go in that direction. I suggest *OpenGL Game Programming* (Premier Press, 2001) by Dave Astle and Kevin Hawkins. Sure, there is a bunch of stuff that is WIN32-specific, but you can skip those parts. Besides, those guys are friends of mine, so I am morally obligated to plug their book.

As many have done before you, you might spot a piece of SDL that needs enhancement. This is how most of the add-on SDL libraries came to be. That's one of the beautiful things about SDL—it is a living body of work to which many people contributed over time. Sure, some add-on libraries aren't the greatest, but not everything that is gold glitters.

Summary

So hey, have a good time programming in SDL. It's a lot of fun, generally very easy, and you can make things look just as professional as the multimillion-dollar houses out there. If you choose to write games for yourself and your friends, if you are going the shareware route (it can and does work for many people), or if you are working your way into the industry, the best of luck to you.

Index

D

E

F

K

L

M

License Agreement/Notice of Limited Warranty

By opening the sealed disc container in this book, you agree to the following terms and conditions. If, upon reading the following license agreement and notice of limited warranty, you cannot agree to the terms and conditions set forth, return the unused book with unopened disc to the place where you purchased it for a refund.

License:
The enclosed software is copyrighted by the copyright holder(s) indicated on the software disc. You are licensed to copy the software onto a single computer for use by a single user and to a backup disc. You may not reproduce, make copies, or distribute copies or rent or lease the software in whole or in part, except with written permission of the copyright holder(s). You may transfer the enclosed disc only together with this license, and only if you destroy all other copies of the software and the transferee agrees to the terms of the license. You may not decompile, reverse assemble, or reverse engineer the software.

Notice of Limited Warranty:
The enclosed disc is warranted by Premier Press, Inc. to be free of physical defects in materials and workmanship for a period of sixty (60) days from end user's purchase of the book/disc combination. During the sixty-day term of the limited warranty, Premier Press will provide a replacement disc upon the return of a defective disc.

Limited Liability:
THE SOLE REMEDY FOR BREACH OF THIS LIMITED WARRANTY SHALL CONSIST ENTIRELY OF REPLACEMENT OF THE DEFECTIVE DISC. IN NO EVENT SHALL PREMIER PRESS OR THE AUTHORS BE LIABLE FOR ANY OTHER DAMAGES, INCLUDING LOSS OR CORRUPTION OF DATA, CHANGES IN THE FUNCTIONAL CHARACTERISTICS OF THE HARDWARE OR OPERATING SYSTEM, DELETERIOUS INTERACTION WITH OTHER SOFTWARE, OR ANY OTHER SPECIAL, INCIDENTAL, OR CONSEQUENTIAL DAMAGES THAT MAY ARISE, EVEN IF PREMIER AND/OR THE AUTHORS HAVE PREVIOUSLY BEEN NOTIFIED THAT THE POSSIBILITY OF SUCH DAMAGES EXISTS.

Disclaimer of Warranties:
PREMIER AND THE AUTHORS SPECIFICALLY DISCLAIM ANY AND ALL OTHER WARRANTIES, EITHER EXPRESS OR IMPLIED, INCLUDING WARRANTIES OF MERCHANTABILITY, SUITABILITY TO A PARTICULAR TASK OR PURPOSE, OR FREEDOM FROM ERRORS. SOME STATES DO NOT ALLOW FOR EXCLUSION OF IMPLIED WARRANTIES OR LIMITATION OF INCIDENTAL OR CONSEQUENTIAL DAMAGES, SO THESE LIMITATIONS MIGHT NOT APPLY TO YOU.

Other:
This Agreement is governed by the laws of the State of Indiana without regard to choice of law principles. The United Convention of Contracts for the International Sale of Goods is specifically disclaimed. This Agreement constitutes the entire agreement between you and Premier Press regarding use of the software.